Nginx

From Beginner to Pro

■ ■ ■

Rahul Soni

Apress®

Nginx: From Beginner to Pro

Rahul Soni
Kolkata, West Bengal
India

ISBN-13 (pbk): 978-1-4842-1657-6   ISBN-13 (electronic): 978-1-4842-1656-9
DOI 10.1007/978-1-4842-1656-9

Library of Congress Control Number: 2016951451

Managing Director: Welmoed Spahr
Acquisitions Editor: Louise Corrigan
Development Editor: Corbin Collins
Technical Reviewer: Eduardo Balsa
Editorial Board: Steve Anglin, Pramila Balen, Laura Berendson, Aaron Black, Louise Corrigan, James DeWolf, Jonathan Gennick, Todd Green, Robert Hutchinson, Celestin Suresh John, Nikhil Karkal, James Markham, Susan McDermott, Matthew Moodie, Natalie Pao, Gwenan Spearing
Coordinating Editor: Nancy Chen
Copy Editor: Karen Jameson
Compositor: SPi Global
Indexer: SPi Global

Distributed to the book trade worldwide by Springer Science+Business Media New York, 233 Spring Street, 6th Floor, New York, NY 10013. Phone 1-800-SPRINGER, fax (201) 348-4505, e-mail orders-ny@springer-sbm.com, or visit www.springer.com. Apress Media, LLC is a California LLC and the sole member (owner) is Springer Science + Business Media Finance Inc (SSBM Finance Inc). SSBM Finance Inc is a Delaware corporation.

For information on translations, please e-mail rights@apress.com, or visit www.apress.com.

Apress and friends of ED books may be purchased in bulk for academic, corporate, or promotional use. eBook versions and licenses are also available for most titles. For more information, reference our Special Bulk Sales–eBook Licensing web page at www.apress.com/bulk-sales.

Any source code or other supplementary materials referenced by the author in this text is available to readers at www.apress.com. For detailed information about how to locate your book's source code, go to www.apress.com/source-code/.

Printed on acid-free paper

*This book is dedicated to the open source community
at large who keep pushing the limits of what software can achieve!*

Contents at a Glance

Contents

About the Author

Rahul Soni worked at Microsoft for a decade (2004–2014) before becoming completely fascinated and then pulled into open source technologies. He consulted on IIS, .NET, and SharePoint during his Microsoft tenure.

There was no looking back when he realized how much could be achieved using the open source stack. Nginx and the MEAN stack floored him completely, and he founded Attosol Technologies (http://www.attosol.com) to pursue his passion. This book is an honest attempt from a guy who has always been into a proprietary stack, but ultimately found that the open source community is exciting enough to leave the corporate world.

Rahul is a man of simple taste and loves reading, listening to music, and traveling. When not working, he can be found hanging around with his wife Neha and their two kids Anika and Aarav.

About the Technical Reviewer

Eduardo Balsa has worked in system administration for the last 13 years, focusing on server scaling and security. His work on the Fintech and web marketing sector has led him to push web server software to its limits and to gather an extensive knowledge of the ins and outs of their deployment, configuration, and day-to-day maintenance.

Eduardo is adept at system-wide automation and of the K.I.S.S. principle and passionate about tinkering and photography.

You can find him online at https://ebalsa.org.

Acknowledgments

There are many people who I would like to acknowledge since they have directly or indirectly played a huge role in getting this book released.

Igor Sysoev - The creator of Nginx who solved a problem that pushed web delivery to the next level.

The open source community at large, which has helped Nginx along its way.

Apress, for their support in releasing this book.

All the editors at Apress, who reviewed the book and helped me express myself better.

Nancy Chen, the coordinating editor, for being flexible and supportive throughout!

Microsoft, where I learned a lot about IIS and other web technologies.

And my family, who understood and supported me more than I ever imagined possible when I took up this project!

CHAPTER 1

■ ■ ■

Introduction to Nginx Web Server

When you type http://www.xyz.com in your browser, you probably don't even notice the HTTP (or HTTPS) that almost every URL is prefixed with. Browsing the Internet is fun, but what lurks underneath is nothing short of magical. It starts with a request; leaves your home WiFi router or network; hops through multiple network locations across the globe; and eventually reaches its destination, which is just another server whose job is to deliver what you are looking for. This final server is what you typically refer to as a *web server*.

That is, of course, an oversimplification of what a web server and HTTP is. But as we go along, you will learn the nitty-gritty around how this communication takes place, and where Nginx fits.

Nginx (pronounced engine-x) is the brainchild of Igor Sysoev. Its development started around 2002, and it was publicly released in 2004. It is available at www.nginx.org and is described by the Nginx team as "a free, open-source, high-performance HTTP server and reverse proxy, as well as an IMAP/POP3 proxy server." Nginx is known for its high performance, stability, rich feature set, simple configuration, and low resource consumption.

HTTP Basics

HTTP stands for HyperText Transfer Protocol. Since the dawn of the Internet, HTTP has been playing a key role in delivering the content worldwide. In simple terms, you can consider HTTP as a set of rules for transferring files. If you notice carefully while browsing a website, you will find that there are files (like images, text, video, etc.) that display in your browser directly, while others (like zip, rar, etc.) get downloaded.

Think about it for a second: why does one file get downloaded, while others get rendered or played in the browser directly? The answer is simply because of how the web server and web client (typically your web browser) are interacting behind the scenes. You can think of HTTP as a language in which the web server and a web client communicates. As a website user, you are simply consuming the visual elements that the website creators planned for you. Hence, unless you are curious, you will hardly notice the underlying communication.

It is almost like using a refrigerator. You just need to know that it is used to preserve your food by keeping it cold and what goes in normal comes out chilled. You would hardly ever bother about how it actually works.

As an IT pro or a web developer, it is imperative that you understand how communication is taking place behind the scenes. Your knowledge of HTTP is extremely important in the context of this book. This knowledge will help you configure your web server in such a way that you get the best performance out of your web servers and ensure happy visitors on your website.

Can you "see" what HTTP looks like? Of course you can! There are multiple tools at your disposal, but for now let us seek help from your favorite browser's built-in developer tools. For brevity, we have chosen to use Google Chrome for the examples in this book. The steps will be quite similar if you use Mozilla Firefox or Internet Explorer.

© Rahul Soni 2016
R. Soni, *Nginx*, DOI 10.1007/978-1-4842-1656-9_1

- Start Chrome.

- Open Developer Tools using the menu. (Command + Alt + I or CTRL + Shift + I)

- Switch to Network tab.

- Browse to `www.amazon.com` and wait until the page loads.

- Sort it by the Name column (click on the tab header) and examine a few packets.

- In Figure 1-1, a specific CSS that starts with AmazonUI-xxxxxxxxx has been selected.

- We won't be sharing details of all the headers at this point because the idea is to give you a little overview about how HTTP communication happens between your browser and the web server.

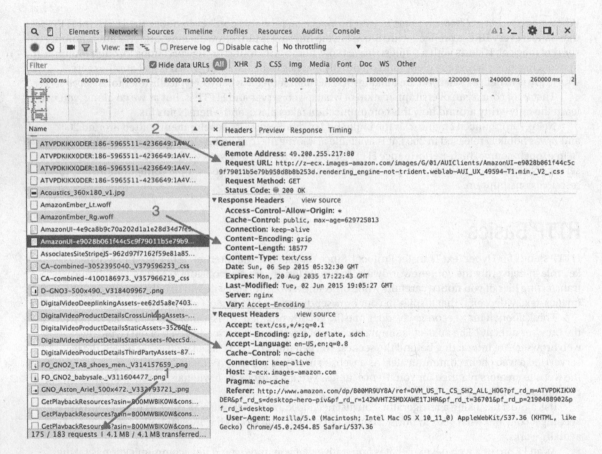

Figure 1-1. *View the inner details of an HTTP request*

There are many things that should be noted in Figure 1-1. It has been annotated so that you can easily check the details:

1. The browser made 183 requests to render just 1 page!

2. In the Headers section, you can see the HTTP communication in action.

    a.   Request URL: The request made by the browser for a specific asset.

    b.   Remote Address: The IP address of the resource along with port information. The port defaults to 80 for an HTTP request.

    c.   Request Method: The method tells the server and you can consider it as a verb. In this example, it is telling the server that it is only interested in receiving data and not POSTing it. Status Code = 200 means that the server said "All okay!"

3.   Response Headers: Similar to the request headers, there are response headers. It is telling a lot of things that is in plain English, but the key is to understand that it is not talking to you. In fact, it is talking to the browser. For example, when it says Content-Encoding is gzip, it simply means that all the data is compressed at the server side using the gzip algorithm and the browser is supposed to decompress that data. You can clearly see how important this discussion between the server and the browser is. All of these put together make your browsing experience a joy.

4.   The question now is this: how and why did it send the data in a compressed format? What if the browser had no clue about compression? Well, that part is taken care of by the *request headers*. The browser sent a header called Accept-Encoding with a value of gzip, deflate, sdch. It was an HTTP way of telling the server, "You know what, let's save on bandwidth! I can decompress the data using gzip, deflate & sdch. I would prefer if you send it using gzip though (since gzip is the first option)!" Essentially, what happened was that the request header went all the way to the server, and the server obliged, as you saw in the previous point, by sending the data that was compressed using gzip.

Interesting, right? All this and more for just one request! Thanks to HTTP, as an end user, you will never have to bother about such gory details.

By the way, did you notice the server header in Figure 1-1 (labeled no. 3)? It says the web server is Nginx! It is not a coincidence. You will find that the adoption of Nginx has increased rapidly in recent times. It has, in fact, become the number one web server for the top 10,000 busiest sites in the world. Among the top 1,000 websites of the world today, almost 40 percent use Nginx!

Extremely busy websites including Netflix, Dropbox, Pinterest, Airbnb, WordPress, Box, Instagram, GitHub, SoundCloud, Zappos, and Yandex use Nginx as part of their infrastructure, and for good reasons.

What Is a Web Server?

In simple words, a web server is a server that hosts an application that listens to the HTTP requests. It is the web server's responsibility to hear (i.e., to understand HTTP) what the browser is saying, and respond appropriately. Sometimes, it could be as simple as fetching a file from the file system and delivering it to the web browser. At other times, it delegates the request to a handler that performs complicated logic and returns the processed response to the web server, which in turn transfers it back to the client! Typically, the server that hosts web server software is termed a web server or *a* web front-end server.

If you are new to the web server's world, don't worry. By the time you are done reading this book, you will have a good grasp on the subject.

Although there are quite a few web servers around, three dominate: Apache, Microsoft Internet Information Services (IIS), and Nginx combined have captured around 85 percent of the market. Each web server has its space and its user base. When you are making a choice, you should evaluate wisely based on your workload. It becomes extremely crucial to make a diligent effort *while* you are setting up your web server, since migration from one web server to another is typically a painful exercise. Sometimes, it is just not possible and you have to rewrite a lot of code.

Historically, the fight for market share used to be between Apache and IIS, until Nginx showed up. Since then, Nginx received its fifth consecutive "Web Server of the Year Award" from W3Techs in 2015. It is also a testament to the power of Nginx, and why Nginx should not be ignored for your web hosting needs.

Seven Reasons Why You Should Be Using Nginx

Making a decision about which server to choose is often a debatable subject. Even more, the IT pros typically get used to working with specific software. Nginx acts as a complementary solution to most web servers. The idea is not to replace your existing infrastructure completely, but to augment it with Nginx in ways that you get the best of both worlds. In the upcoming section you will learn about the reasons why you should seriously consider adding Nginx servers to your web farm.

It's Fast

The online users today have very low threshold of tolerance for slow websites. With smartphones and tablets available at your fingertips and so much of social data to consume, everybody seems to be in a rush. Innovation hence will not cut it alone. The website has to have equally good performance. As if this was not enough, Google now incorporates page load time into its search rankings. In essence, poorly performing websites will find it increasingly difficult to succeed.

Fast page load times builds trust in your site and leads to more returning visitors. If your site is slow, you are most certainly going to lose your visitors to your competition. Recent surveys reveal that users expect the page to load in less than 2 seconds, and 40 percent of them will abandon your website if it takes more than 3 seconds!

Nginx has solved the performance problem and that is one of the biggest reasons for all the praise and awards it bags. It is extremely fast, and shines even under high load.

It Can Accelerate Your Application

Not only Nginx is extremely fast, but it can also act as an acceleration toolkit for your existing application. The idea is to drop Nginx in front of an existing set of web servers and let it take care of routing traffic to the back end intelligently. This way, you can offload a lot of tasks to Nginx and let your back-end server handle more data intensive tasks. In effect, you will find that the users have been served the content while your back end was churning out the data.

It Has a Straightforward Load Balancer

Setting up a hardware load balancer is quite costly and resource intensive. It requires a lot of expertise to handle and also takes a considerable amount of time to set up. After a physical installation of the devices, you can definitely reap the rewards from your hardware load balancer, but you are locked in with the solution and hardware that may require servicing at times. In any case, you add one more layer of complexity in your infrastructure by using a hardware load balancer.

With Nginx you can set up a pretty straightforward and fast software load balancer. It can immediately help you out by sharing load across your front-end web servers.

It Scales Well

With Apache and IIS, it is a common pain: The more connections, the more issues. These servers solved a big problem around bringing dynamic content to the web server instead of static files, but scalability has always been a challenge. Keep in mind that scalability and performance are not the same problem.

Let's say you have server that can handle 1000 concurrent connections. As long as the requests are short and the server is able to handle 1000 connections/second, you are good. But the moment a request starts taking 10 seconds to execute, the server simply starts crawling and you see the domino effect where one thing fails after another. If you have large files available for download, your server will most likely choke with a high number of concurrent connections. Apache and IIS servers are not suitable for this kind of load, simply because of the way they have been architected. They are also prone to denial of service attacks (DoS). Unfortunately, adding more resources like CPU and RAM doesn't help much. For example, if you double the RAM or CPU, that doesn't mean the server will be able to handle 2000 concurrent connections. As you can see, the issue is not with performance, but with scale.

Nginx is one of the very few servers (along with Node.js) that is capable of addressing this issue, which is often referred to as C10K problem (a term coined in 1999 by Dan Kegel for 10,000 concurrent connections).

You Can Upgrade It On the Fly

Nginx provides you an ability to reconfigure and upgrade Nginx instances on the fly without interrupting customer activity. It is an extremely important capability because every server and every service needs patching at times. With Nginx you can patch your production environment reliably without completely bringing down your services levels.

It's Affordable to Install and Maintain

Nginx performs pretty well even on servers with a very low hardware footprint. Even with default settings, you can get much more throughout from an Nginx server compared to Apache or IIS.

It's Easy to Use

Don't be intimidated by the lack of a user interface (UI). Nginx is easy if you understand how to use it. The configuration system is pretty well thought out and once you get up to speed, you will thoroughly enjoy it!

Main Features of Nginx

Nginx is a fantastic web server and a lot more. This section introduces some of its more important features.

More Than Just a Web Server

At its core, you can consider Nginx to be an *event-based reverse proxy server*. That may come as a surprise to many, because mostly Nginx is usually said to be a web server.

A *reverse proxy* is a type of proxy server that retrieves resources from the servers on behalf of a client. It can be helpful to offload the number of requests that the actual web server ends up handling. Figure 1-2 illustrates what a proxy server does.

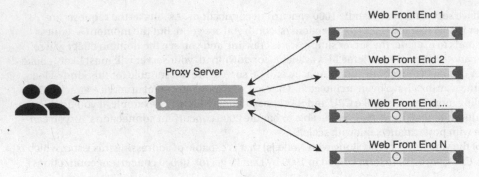

Figure 1-2. *A typical proxy server*

Modular Design

It has an extremely extensible architecture due to its support for plug-ins. Even basic things like SSL and compression are built as modules. The real power lies in the fact that you can rebuild Nginx from source and include or exclude the modules that you don't need. This gives you a very focused executable that does precisely what you need. This approach has a downside too, though. If you decide to incorporate another module at a later point, you will need to recompile with appropriate switches. The good angle to this is, Nginx has a fairly robust way of upgrading its live processes and it can be done without interrupting the service levels.

As of this writing, www.nginx.org hosts as many as 62 modules for very specific purposes. There are plenty of other third-party Nginx modules available as well to make your job easier. The ecosystem is thriving and helping Nginx to become even more powerful as time passes. You will learn more about modules in the coming chapters in detail.

Asynchronous Web Server

Nginx gains much of its performance due to its asynchronous and event-based architecture whereas Apache and IIS like to spin new threads per connection, which are blocking in nature. Both IIS and Apache handle the threads using multithreaded programming techniques. Nginx differs in the approach completely. It does not create a separate thread for each request. Instead it relies on events.

Reverse Proxy and Load Balancing Capability

Nginx analyzes the request based on its URI and decides how to proceed with the request. In other words, it is not looking at the file system to decide what it has to do with it. Instead, it makes that decision based on the URI. This differentiation enables Nginx to act as a very fast front end that acts as a reverse proxy and helps balance the load on the application servers. It's no exaggeration to say that Nginx is a reverse proxy first and a web server later.

Nginx can also fit very well in a hybrid setup. So, the front-end job is taken care of by Nginx, and everything else gets delegated to the back end (to Apache, for instance).

Low Resource Requirement and Consumption

Small things that go a long way, define Nginx. Where other web servers typically allow a simple plug-and-play architecture for plug-ins using configuration files, Nginx requires you to recompile the source with required modules. Every module that it requires is loaded directly inside of an Nginx process. Such tweaks along with smart architectural differences ensure that Nginx has a very small memory and CPU footprint on the server and yields a much better throughput than its competition. You will learn about the Nginx architecture with granular details in the coming chapters.

Unparalleled Performance

Nginx is probably the best server today when it comes to serving static files. There are situations where it cannot be considered the best (like dynamic files), but even then, the fact that it plays well as a reverse proxy ensures that you get the best of both worlds. If configured well, you can save a lot of cost that you typically incur on caching, SSL termination, hardware load balancing, zipping/unzipping on the fly, and completing many more web-related tasks.

Multiple Protocol Support: HTTP(S), WebSocket, IMAP, POP3, SMTP

As a proxy server, Nginx can handle not only HTTP and HTTPS requests, but also mail protocols with equal grace. There are modules available that you can use while compiling your build and Nginx will proxy your mail-related traffic too.

SSL Termination

Secure Sockets Layer is a necessity for any website that deals with sensitive data. And, just like any other necessity, there is a cost involved. When it comes to web traffic, SSL also induces an extra processing overhead on the server side where it has to decrypt the request every time. There lies a catch-22 situation: If you remove the SSL, you are opening yourself up for attacks and if you use SSL, you end up losing a little bit on speed (or additional cost due to scaling out)!

Since Nginx has the capability of acting as a load balancer, you can give it additional work as well. Essentially, the idea of an SSL termination (Figure 1-3) is that the request will come to the load balancer on a secure channel but will be sent to the other web servers without SSL. This way, your web server acts faster and eventually your requests go out to the clients in a secure manner as well.

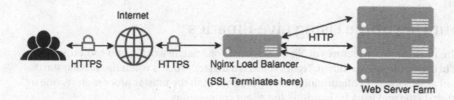

Figure 1-3. Nginx as a Load Balancer and SSL Terminator

HTTP Video Streaming Using MP4/FLV/HDS/HLS

You have already learned that the Input/Output (IO) in Nginx doesn't block if the client is slow. Video streaming is typically a very IO-intensive process, and Nginx does a great job here. It has multiple modules that help you provide streaming services. To give a little perspective as to what is special about video streaming, imagine watching YouTube. You can easily skip the video from one position to another and it almost immediately starts serving the content. The key here is to *not* download the entire file at one shot. The request, hence, should be created in such a way that it has certain markers in the query string, like this:

```
http://www.yoursite.com/yourfile.mp4?start=120.12
```

The preceding request is asking the server to send the content of yourfile.mp4 starting from (notice the start query string) 120.12 seconds. This allows random seeking of a file in a very efficient way.

Extended Monitoring and Logging

Failure to log and finding the problems in production farm is extremely crucial if you are to run a successful web service. Monitoring a web server, however, on a regular basis is a challenging and time-consuming task for any IT pro.

The more servers you have, and the more traffic you get, the harder it becomes. There are all sorts of nasty people out there who have ulterior motives to bring the website down and disrupt your web service. The best way to ensure safety, hence, is to be cautious and alert. Log as much as possible and ensure that you *react proactively*.

Nginx writes information about issues it encounters to a file called an error log. Windows users may consider it similar to an event log. You can configure it to log based on its levels. For example, if you tell Nginx to write anything above error severity, it will not log warning logs at all.

It also has an access log that is similar to W3C logs created by other web servers. You can change the fields that you would like to log, and even configure it to ignore common status codes like 2xx and 3xx. This is a pretty neat feature, since it ends up creating much smaller log files instead of huge ones that may get created if you are managing busy servers.

Graceful Restarting

The way Nginx is designed, you can easily upgrade Nginx. You can also update its configuration while the server is running, without losing client connections. This allows you to test your troubleshooting approach, and if something doesn't work as desired, you can simply revert the settings.

Nginx brings a very interesting way of controlling your processes. Instead of bringing the entire service down, you can send *signal* values to the master process by using an Nginx command with a switch. You will learn about it in detail in upcoming chapters, but for now you can imagine saying something like nginx -s reload, a command that will simply reload the configuration changes without recycling the worker processes. Simple, but effective!

Upgrades without Downtime Using Live Binaries

This is probably one of the most powerful features of Nginx. In the IIS or Apache worlds, you can't upgrade your web server without bringing the service down. Nginx spawns a master process when the service starts. Its main purpose is to read and evaluate configuration files. Apart from that, the master process starts one or more worker processes that do the real work by handling the client connections.

If you need to upgrade the binary, there are simple steps and commands that you need to issue in order to make the new worker processes run at tandem with the older ones. The new requests will be sent to the newer worker processes that have the latest configuration loaded in it. If by any chance, you find out that the upgrade is causing issues, you can simply issue another set of commands that will gracefully return the requests to the older process that already has the previous working configuration loaded in it. How neat is that?

Enterprise Features of Nginx Plus

Nginx has two versions. The basic version is free, and the paid option is called Nginx Plus. Nginx Plus has quite a few important features that are very helpful for managing busy sites. Choosing Nginx Plus helps you save a lot of time. It has features like load balancing, session persistence, cache control, and even health checks out of the box. You will be learning about the overall differences shortly in this chapter.

Support Available with Nginx Plus

Community support is free for Nginx, but e-mail and phone support are not. Nginx Plus comes packaged with support options. You can buy different kinds of support options based on your need and criticality of the business. Nginx Plus contains many additional benefits as you will see in the next section.

Advantages of Nginx Plus

Nginx is a reliable solution for any website or service that is looking for scalability, high performance, and reliable solutions. You can download it directly from the website and build the binaries yourself as discussed earlier. However, there are a few modules that are not available unless you licence Nginx Plus. The key difference here is that while Nginx is available in source form that you can compile according to your needs, Nginx Plus is available only in binary form.

The core features (HTTP server, core worker process architecture, SPDY, SSL termination, authentication, bandwidth management, reverse proxy options for HTTP, TCP, and Mail) are available in both Nginx and Nginx Plus.

Load balancing and application delivery is not available in the same capacity, though. Nginx Plus provides features, discussed in this section, which are not available in Nginx.

Advanced HTTP and TCP Load Balancing

Nginx Plus enhances the reverse proxy capabilities of Nginx. Imagine Nginx Plus as Nginx running on steroids. There are four methods of load balancing in Nginx that are common to both versions: Round-Robin, Least Connections, Generic Hash, and IP Hash.

Nginx Plus adds the least time method in its stack (more on these methods later). The load balancing methods in Nginx Plus are extended to support multicore servers in an optimized way. The worker processes share the load balancing state among each other so that traffic can be distributed more evenly.

Session Persistence

HTTP is a stateless protocol. You make a request, the server responds, and that's it. But you may argue that this is not what it feels like. For instance, you go to your mail server, log in, and check your mail. If you right-click a message and open it in a new window, it doesn't reauthenticate you. If the request was stateless, how would such a thing be possible?

The logging-in behavior makes it appear that the server knows you. To make this happen, plenty of things have to happen in the background. Cookies, sessions, and timeouts typically govern how the websites behave for logged-on users.

This implies that if your session or cookie is lost or tampered with, you will be logged out automatically. It also implies that there is "some" work done at the server side for every user. It would make a lot of sense, that if the request has gone to Server 1 for a User A, the subsequent requests from User A go to the same Server 1. If this doesn't happen, and the request ends up at Server 2, it would ask the user to reauthenticate. This behavior is referred to as *session persistence*. Nginx Plus load balancer identifies and pins all requests in a session to the same upstream server. It also provides a feature called *session draining*, which allows you to take a server down without interrupting established sessions.

Content Caching Enhanced Capabilities

Caching is an activity by the server to temporarily hold a static resource, so that it doesn't need to be retrieved from the back end every time a request is made for the same resource. It improves speed and reduces load on the back end servers.

Nginx Plus can cache content retrieved from the upstream HTTP servers and responses returned by FASTCgi, SCGI, and uwsgi services. The cached object is persisted in the local disk and served as if it is coming from the origin.

However, there is a caveat to caching. What if the content in the back end has changed? The server will keep sending older files to the client, which is not what you would like. To avoid such scenarios, Nginx Plus allows purging of cache. You will need to use one of the many tools available to purge the cache. You can purge selected subset of requests or everything if you need to.

Application Health Checks

Nobody likes to visit a site that is down. If your site suffers frequent outages, it is likely that people will lose trust soon. Health check is a way where you let Nginx handle failures gracefully. Who wouldn't like a self-healing and self-servicing robot? Health check is like a robot that goes to the service station automatically when it thinks it is not performing well.

Health checks continually test the upstream servers and instruct Nginx Plus to avoid servers that have failed. This simply implies that the servers will be "taken care of" by itself, and your end users won't see the error pages that they might have, in case there was no real person monitoring the servers.

If yours is a very busy site, this feature can be considered as one of the biggest reasons why you should go with Nginx Plus!

HTTP Live Streaming (HLS) and Video on Demand (VOD)

Before learning about HTTP live streaming, let us explain the differences between *streaming, progressive downloads, and adaptive streaming*. This will help you understand why Nginx plays a special role in this arena.

With increasing bandwidth every day and reduced costs, delivering rich content has never been easier. Technically, there is a media file that you have sent to the browser or mobile device, so that it just plays. The problem is that the size can be overwhelming to download. Clients want the content to play as soon as possible and there are multiple ways to do this.

Streaming

When you stream content, you typically mean that the viewer clicks on a button and video/audio starts playing after an initial amount of buffering. At the back end, you will need to use dedicated streaming software. This software will ensure that the data rate of the encoded file is less than that of the bandwidth. It ensures that the encoded file is small enough to be streamed through the limited bandwidth at disposal. Keep in mind that every streaming software has its own set of requirements of media files so that it can function as expected.

Progressive Download

In contrast to streaming, progressive download enables you to use simple HTTP web servers. The video that is delivered using this technique is typically stored at the client side and played directly from the hard drive. This is a big difference, since streaming media is not stored locally at all! From a user experience perspective, the software takes care of playing the file as soon as enough content is downloaded. Sites like YouTube, CNN, and many other video sites don't use streaming servers. They deliver it using progressive download. Since the data is stored locally before playing, the user experience is a lot better than streaming.

Adaptive Streaming

As the name suggests, this is streaming with a twist. It automatically adapts to the client's bandwidth. It uses streams in such a way, that when the connection is good the viewer gets a higher-quality content. As you can guess, if the connection quality deteriorates, a lower data rate is opted for. This also means that the video quality might get too blurry at times and the users will blame the service rather than their own network connection. You will need dedicated streaming software to do adaptive streaming.

That little detour should have given you a reasonably decent understanding of where Nginx fits. Nginx is widely used to deliver MP4 and FLV video content using progressive downloads. It is very efficient in delivering content due to its non-blocking I/O architecture and support for huge number of concurrent connections.

Nginx Plus takes it even further. It allows you to support adaptive streaming functionality for video-on-demand services. This way, the bitrate is automatically adjusted in real time. It also has bandwidth throttling capabilities so that the fast clients and download accelerators don't suck up your entire bandwidth.

Nginx Plus uses HLS/VOD module to provide even more flexibility and support for H.264/AAC. This helps a lot, since you don't have to repackage the MP4 content for adaptive streaming. It provides real-time transformations from mp4 to HLS/MPEG-TS. There are other modules that you can use together so that the intellectual property is not compromised.

HTTP Dynamic Streaming (HDS/VOD)

It is an alternative method for delivering adaptive streaming media to your clients. It uses different file formats that are prepared initially using Adobe's f4fpackager tool. This tool generates the files that are necessary for the clients. Nginx f4f handler simply delivers it to the clients.

Bandwidth Management for MP4 Media

With Nginx Plus, you have multiple directives that can be used to limit the rate of download. Essentially, it defines limits that activate after a specified time. It saves you from denial of service attacks because users who are putting more loads on the servers are automatically identified and throttled.

Another smart thing it does is to allow the content to stream without any limit for the first N seconds so that the data is buffered appropriately. After that the limit automatically applies. On one hand it helps clients with quicker play time, and on the other hand it discourages download accelerators.

Live Activity Monitoring

Nginx Plus comes with a real-time activity monitoring interface (Figure 1-4). It is quite friendly and easy to use. For a live view of a demo website to see how it looks, try http://demo.nginx.com/status.html.

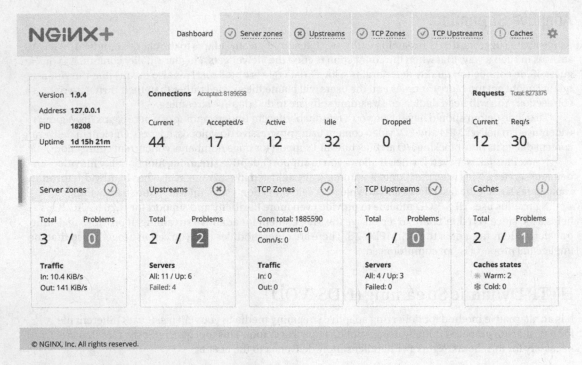

Figure 1-4. *Live activity monitoring using Nginx Plus*

As you can see in Figure 1-4, information about current connections, requests, and many other counters are listed here. Notice how clearly it shows that there are a couple of problems in the upstream servers. This interface is exposed through HTTP and it implies that you can access it using a browser without logging on your server.

Nginx Commercial Support

Sometimes, when you face a challenge in a production farm and your team is not able to resolve issues, you can rely on community support. However, there is no direct accountability and guarantee that your issue will be resolved.

At that point, having a commercial support option offered by Nginx Plus comes to rescue. You will have the experts from Nginx support team covering your back. Standard support covers you during the business hours (9 a.m. to 5 p.m.), whereas premium support covers you 24/7. With premium support you get phone support as well.

In case it is found that the issue is due to a bug in the software, premium support can help you get the bug fixed as soon as possible. In short, premium support is the best and fastest support you can get from Nginx Inc.

Differences between Apache and Nginx

Nginx and Apache are both versatile and powerful web servers. Together they serve more than 70 percent of the top million websites. At times they compete, but often they are found complementing each other. One important thing to point out here is that they are not entirely interchangeable. You will need to pick them up carefully according to your workload.

History

Apache Software Foundation (ASF) is the umbrella under which Apache is developed. Apache has been around since 1995 and developed under ASF since 1999. It is the clear winner today in terms of overall market share. Apache has widespread support, and you will find plenty of expertise to hire and solve your hosting needs. Nginx is the new kid in the block and seen widespread adoption since 2008. Between June 2008 and June 2015, it has grown from 2 percent to 21 percent among the top million sites. For the top 10,000 websites, the story is even better. It has grown mostly at the cost of Apache, which saw its market share drop from 66 percent to 49 percent in the same time period.

Performance

For Apache users, there is a choice of multiprocessing modules (MPM) that control the way the requests are handled. You can choose between mpm_prefork, mpm_worker, mpm_event. Basically mpm_prefork spawns processes for every request, mpm_worker spawns processes, which in turn spawn threads and manages the threads, mpm_event is further optimization of mpm_worker where Apache juggles the keep alive connections using dedicated threads. If you haven't already noted, these changes are all for the better and evolutionary.

Nginx was created to solve the concurrency problem and it did by using a new design altogether. It spawns multiple worker processes that can handle thousands of connections each! It is completely asynchronous, non-blocking, and event-driven. It consumes very little resources and helps in reducing cost of scaling out of a web server. The web server can be upgraded on the fly without losing the connected visitors and reduces downtime of your service.

Resource Requirements

Nginx needs fewer resources than Apache because of its new architecture. Fewer resources = Lower cost = More profit.

Availability

Apache is present more widely across operating systems whereas Nginx is not. Most of the famous Linux distros have Nginx, which can be downloaded using rpm, yum, or apt-get but it is almost always an extra step. Consider this, for installing Apache (on CentOS 7), you can run the following command and everything is all set (there is a dedicated chapter for that coming up with all the details).

```
yum install httpd
```

For Nginx, you will need to do something like the following:

1. vi /etc/yum.repos.d/nginx.repo

2. Add the following text:

```
[nginx]
name=nginx repo
baseurl=http://nginx.org/packages/centos/$releasever/$basearch/
gpgcheck=0
enabled=1
```

3. Use the following code:

```
yum install nginx
```

It is not that it is hard; it is just that it needs some extra little steps to make it work. With more popularity, it is possible that in the coming time it will become more generally available.

Proxy and Load Balancing Server

Nginx was designed as a reverse proxy that doubles up as a web server. This is quite different than Apache since it was designed as a general purpose web server. This feature gives an edge to Nginx since it is more effective in dealing with a high volume of requests. It also has good load balancing capability. Quite often, Nginx acts as a web accelerator by handling the request in the front end and passing the request to the back-end servers when required. So, Nginx in the front end and Apache in the back end gives you the best of both worlds. They are more complementing than competing from this perspective.

Static vs. Dynamic Content

As mentioned earlier, Nginx has a clear advantage when serving static content. The dynamic content story is quite different though. Apache has a clear, early mover advantage here. It has built-in support for PHP, Python, Perl, and many other languages. Nginx almost always requires extra effort to make it work with these languages. If you are a Python or Ruby developer, Apache might be a better choice since it will not need CGI to execute it. Even though PHP has good support on Nginx, you still need to dedicate a little time to get PHP-based solutions that work directly on Nginx. For example, installing WordPress on LAMP stack is super easy, and even though it can be easily done on a LEMP stack, you will still need to configure some nuts here, and some bolts there. You get the idea!

Configuration

Apache's basic configuration ideology is drastically different from Nginx. You can have a .htaccess file in every directory (if you like) using which you can provide additional directions to Apache about how to respond to the requests of that specific directory. Nginx on the other hand interprets the requests based on the URL, instead of a directory structure (more on this later). It doesn't even process the .htaccess file. It has both merits (better performance) and demerits (lesser configuration flexibility). Although for static files the requests are eventually mapped to the file, the core power of parsing the URI comes to play when you use it for scenarios like mail and proxy server roles.

If you come from an Apache background, you will need to unlearn a lot of concepts while migrating to Nginx. The differences are many from a configuration perspective, but most people who migrate from either side say that once you learn the nuances, you will find the Nginx configuration quite simple and straightforward!

Modules (or Plug-Ins)

Both Apache and Nginx have a robust set of modules that extend the platform. There is still a stark difference in the way these extensions are added and configured. In Apache, you can dynamically load/unload the modules using configuration, but in Nginx you are supposed to build the binaries using different switches (more on this in the next chapter). It may sound limiting and less flexible (and it is), but it has its own advantages. For example, the binaries won't have any unnecessary code inside it. It requires and forces you to have a prior understanding of what you need the specific web server to do.

It is also good in a way, because mostly it is seen that even though the modular software has modules, web administrators end up installing much more than what they need. Any unnecessary module that is loaded in the memory is extra CPU cycles getting wasted. Obviously, if you are wasting those cycles due to lack of planning, it all adds up eventually and you will get poorer performance from the same hardware!

Documentation

Due to the early mover advantage, Apache has a lot to offer when it comes to documentation. The web is full of solid advice, books, blogs, articles, trainings, tools, use cases, forum support, configuration suggestions, and pretty much everything you will need from an Apache web-administration perspective.

The documentation for Nginx has been evolving and getting better rapidly but is still way less compared to Apache. That doesn't mean it is bad, it just means that it is competing in this area; and most likely, it will become better as more and more people join in.

Support

The support system for Apache is very mature. There are a lot of tools available to help you maintain your web server well. There are plenty of third-party companies that support Apache by providing different support levels. There are IRC channels available as well, which makes community support easier.

Nginx does have support as mentioned earlier, but lacks the richness and maturity because of its late entry. The fact that it is straightforward, simple to configure, and robust helps Nginx to a great extent. In a way, simplicity is where Nginx wins and with time and adoption, it can only get better!

Summary

In this chapter, you have learned about the basics of a web server and where Nginx fits. You now know the most common reasons why Nginx is preferred over other web servers. It is extremely important that you use the right tool for the right kind of project, and we believe that this chapter has helped you in understanding the use cases more suitable for Nginx. You should also be comfortable with the differences of Nginx and Nginx Plus and if you have already deployed it in production, you would be more than happy to know that there are multiple support levels available with Nginx.

In the next chapter, you will learn about setting up an Nginx web server.

CHAPTER 2

■ ■ ■

Installing Nginx

You don't learn to walk by following rules. You learn by doing, and by falling over.

—Richard Branson

Based on your requirements, you can choose to download the precompiled packages or compiled binaries with their components from the Nginx website. If the basic and default set of binaries do not suit your needs, you can choose to download the packages from source and compile it yourself. Both the methods have its pros and cons, and in this chapter you will learn the details in a step-by-step manner. Quite often, you will need to use modules that are not a part of the default setup. In such cases, there is no other way than to compile the binaries accordingly.

Before you start your first deployment of Nginx, you will need to prepare your environment to perform the steps mentioned in this chapter. In today's world, there are a variety of choices when it comes to configuring your infrastructure. For ease of demonstration and cross-platform support, we have chosen to go with VirtualBox for virtualization, and two famous Linux distributions of the Fedora (CentOS) and Debian (Ubuntu) family. We will make sure to provide you the commands for each distros so you can practice on either of them.

Preparing Your Environment

Here is what is required:

- A spare physical machine or virtualization software like VirtualBox. You can download Oracle VirtualBox from https://www.virtualbox.org.

- Based on your choice, you can download either or both of the Linux distributions CentOS or Ubuntu Server.

- Download CentOS from https://www.centos.org/download or Ubuntu Server from http://www.ubuntu.com/download/server. You can also download the ready-to-use VirtualBox VM images from http://www.virtualboxes.org. The server versions used in this book are CentOS 7 and Ubuntu Server 14.04.

- For a detailed step-by-step direction to install and configure CentOS on VirtualBox, you can visit http://www.attosol.com/centos-setup-and-networking-using-virtual-box.

- Once your VMs are up and running, the first step is to update the packages that are installed on the server by default. You will require root access to update the packages. The steps to update the packages are the following:

© Rahul Soni 2016
R. Soni, *Nginx*, DOI 10.1007/978-1-4842-1656-9_2

- On CentOS:

```
# su -
# yum update
On Ubuntu:

# sudo apt-get update
# sudo apt-get upgrade
```

- You will also need some basic utilities on the servers to enable you to perform steps mentioned throughout this book. Again you will require root access to install these packages.

  On CentOS:

```
Install Lynx (a text based browser):
# yum install lynx

Install Nano (a text editor in case you are not comfortable using vi):
# yum install nano

Install wget (a text based downloader that will help download files):
# yum install wget

Install ssh (a secure shell to sllow remote login):
# ssh is installed by default on CentOS
```

■ **Tip** Since you will find many different configuration steps, it is better to save a snapshot of the server. This way, you can play around and revert back safely if anything goes wrong. Open VirtualBox, click the server name, change the tab by clicking the Snapshots button, and click the Camera button. For the purpose of this book, a snapshot is created called Basic.

On Ubuntu:

```
Install Lynx:
# sudo apt-get install lynx

Install Nano:
# nano is installed by default on Ubuntu

Install wget:
# wget is installed by default on Ubuntu

Install ssh:
# sudo apt-get install ssh
```

Installing Nginx Using Pre-Built Packages

Using Package Manager is the easiest way of installing, updating, upgrading, and removing software packages in Linux. You can download the package from the source by adding the Nginx repository configuration in the repository files on the server.

Nginx product releases are of two types: namely, *stable* (even version numbers) and *mainline or development* (odd version numbers). The "stable" versions are tried and tested versions. It consists of major bug fixes but no new features are added in the stable version. The "mainline" version includes new features and bug fixes and usually is good for testing future versions of the product. In our examples we will be using the stable version but the steps to implement and configure mainline version is the same.

Install Nginx Pre-Built Package

In this section, you will learn about installing Nginx on two different distros of Linux, namely, CentOS and Ubuntu. It is recommended that you follow along.

On CentOS

- Login as root, or open the terminal window and use su to change to root user.

- Add Nginx repository to the server repository list. There are two ways of performing this step:

  Method 1:

  - Create the Nginx repository file in the yum.repos.d directory and then add the repository configuration by editing the nginx.repo file.

    ```
    # nano /etc/yum.repos.d/nginx.repo
    ```

  - Add the below text in nginx.repo file.

    ```
    [nginx]
    name=nginx repo
    baseurl=http://nginx.org/packages/centos/7/$basearch/
    gpgcheck=0
    enabled=1
    ```

  - Save the file.

  Method 2:

  - Download the nginx-release package from Nginx servers.

    ```
    # wget http://nginx.org/packages/centos/7/noarch/RPMS/nginx-release-
    centos-7-0.el7.ngx.noarch.rpm
    ```

  - Now install the Package Manager repository.

    ```
    # rpm -Uvh nginx-release-centos-7-0.el7.ngx.noarch.rpm
    ```

- Now that the package repository is in place, you can install Nginx using this command:

  ```
  # yum install nginx
  ```

- You can verify the Nginx installed version using the -v command option:

  ```
  # nginx -v
  nginx version: nginx/1.8.0 (expected output)
  ```

On Ubuntu Server

Ubuntu PPA, which is maintained by volunteers, has Nginx in their package repository list and may include some additional modules, but it is not the latest version as what is found on http://nginx.org. To ensure that you have the latest version installed on your server, you will need to add the Nginx repository in the sources.list file.

1. Open terminal window and open the sources.list file using the command

   ```
   sudo nano /etc/apt/sources.list
   ```

2. You can add the Nginx repository links at the bottom of the file. Scroll down to the very bottom of the file and add the two lines below:

   ```
   deb http://nginx.org/packages/ubuntu/ trusty nginx
   deb-src http://nginx.org/packages/ubuntu/ trusty nginx
   ```

3. Save the file.

4. Now you can download the package lists from the repositories and update them with the information for the newest versions of the packages and their dependencies. You can do that by typing the following command:

   ```
   sudo apt-get update
   ```

5. You will get the following error regarding the missing signature key. It is happening because gpg is trying to sign the nginx release and check its signature. But the signing key is missing on the server and hence gpg is not able to validate the nginx package:

   ```
   Reading package lists... Done
   W: GPG error: http://nginx.org trusty Release: The following signatures couldn't
   be verified because the public key is not available: NO_PUBKEY ABF5BD827BD9BF62
   ```

6. Download and add the nginx signature key using the command below:

   ```
   # wget http://nginx.org/keys/nginx_signing.key
   # sudo apt-key add nginx_signing.key
   ```

7. Now try re-synchronizing the package index from the sources:

   ```
   #sudo apt-get update
   ```

8. Now that the package list is updated and indexed, you can install Nginx:

   ```
   # sudo apt-get install nginx
   ```

9. You can verify Nginx installed the version:

   ```
   # nginx -v
   ```

Nginx Folder Structure

It is important to understand how the Package Manager-based Nginx installation folder structure looks. It will help you to locate the configuration files if you want to make any configuration changes such as changing the user account under which Nginx process executes, enables, or disables mime types for your website; modify FastCGI execution parameters; identify the default document root and error logs directory; or understand where the error logs files and Nginx executable are.

- You can get the complete list of all Nginx configuration details and its version by using the –V command option with nginx. Here is a sample output of the command:

```
# nginx -V
nginx version: nginx/1.8.0
built by gcc 4.8.2 20140120 (Red Hat 4.8.2-16) (GCC)
built with OpenSSL 1.0.1e-fips 11 Feb 2013
TLS SNI support enabled
configure arguments:
 --prefix=/etc/nginx
 --sbin-path=/usr/sbin/nginx
 --conf-path=/etc/nginx/nginx.conf
 --error-log-path=/var/log/nginx/error.log
 --http-log-path=/var/log/nginx/access.log
 --pid-path=/var/run/nginx.pid
... output trimmed ...
```

The Package Manager-based installation installs Nginx under /etc/nginx directory. It installs all necessary configuration files like nginx.conf file, which has the web server configuration details. It has a mine.types and fastcgi_params file that contains all the mime types that are enabled on the web server and fastcgi configuration details. All these default configurations enable the Nginx server to start:

```
# ls -F /etc/nginx/
conf.d/          koi-utf  mime.types  scgi_params   win-utf
fastcgi_params   koi-win  nginx.conf  uwsgi_params
```

- The Nginx executable nginx is located in the system executable directory /usr/sbin/nginx. Since it is executing using the root user, you will need to be a root user or need to do su or sudo to start or stop the process:

```
# ls -l /usr/sbin/nginx
-rwxr-xr-x. 1 root root 890992 Apr 21 21:06 /usr/sbin/nginx
```

- By default, the document root directory is located at /usr/share/nginx/html/. It consists of a sample index.html and 50x.html file. You can deploy your application in the same document root directory and Nginx will serve the content:

```
# ls  /usr/share/nginx/html/
50x.html   index.html
```

- The default error files and HTTP logfiles are located at /var/log/nginx/. By default, there are two files: access.log and error.log. You will have to implement some sort of log file rotation mechanism such that your logfiles don't grow up too large. You will learn more about these files and its configuration details in chapter 10.

- Try Lynx to browse to the http://localhost and you should be presented with the default index page. (If you get an alert saying Unable to connect to remote host, simply start the Nginx server using systemctl start nginx):

```
# lynx http://localhost
```

■ **Tip**   You can edit the nginx.conf file to make any configuration changes. You have to be a root user or sudo the command to make the changes (i.e., sudo nano /etc/nginx/nginx.conf). You will need to restart nginx processes to ensure the configuration changes takes effect.

You now have a working version of Nginx on the server. In this section you understood the steps required to perform the Package Manager-based Nginx installation. You also learned what the default Nginx installation directory structure looks like and identified some of the configuration parameters that are available in an nginx.conf file. You will learn about all the configuration details in depth in chapter 5.

Uninstall Nginx

Before you continue with the next section of installing Nginx from source, you would want to remove Nginx that you just installed using Package Manager. The steps to uninstall Nginx are given in this section.

On CentOS

```
# yum remove nginx nginx-common
```

On Ubuntu

```
# sudo apt-get purge nginx nginx-common
```

The preceding command removes all the traces of Nginx installation. On CentOS, though, the log and cache directories are not deleted, which are located at `/var/log/nginx` and `/var/cache/nginx` respectively. You will have to manually remove them.

■ **Note**   Uninstalling Nginx using the commands just described does not remove the yum repository nginx. repo and source.lists entry for Nginx. You will have to remove it manually if you do not want Package Manager-based installation.

Downloading Nginx from Source

Installing Nginx is easy as you have seen. However, there are multiple scenarios where you may need extra functionality or drop an existing one. The way Nginx is architected, you cannot make configuration changes and pull in or plug out the modules (as you typically do in Apache or IIS). In these cases, you will need to rebuild Nginx from source.

Another reason why you may want to build from source is when you would like to have a fresh installation of Nginx with all the customization built in. This way, you won't have to configure Nginx on each of your servers separately.

To configure Nginx with third-party modules, this also requires you to build from source. Sometimes, you may hit a bug and would like to patch your Nginx source code with customization that serves your particular requirement. Overall, it is extremely important that you understand why you need to learn building Nginx from source.

Downloading Nginx

You can download the source code of Nginx by visiting the website www.nginx.org/en/download.html. The stable version available as of this writing is `nginx 1.8.0`. The package is in GNU zip format (i.e., tar.gz). You can download the package directly on the server using the wget command as shown:

```
# wget http://nginx.org/download/nginx-1.8.0.tar.gz
```

Extracting the Nginx Archive

After having downloaded the package you will need to extract the `nginx-1.8.0.tar.gz`. You can unpack the source code directly in your home directory. When you unpack the package, it will by default create the `nginx-1.8.0` folder. This is the directory from where you will be compiling and configuring Nginx. To extract the package, type this:

```
# tar xzf nginx-1.8.0.tar.gz
```

Understanding the Nginx Source Directory

After the package is extracted you will find some directories and files in the source directory. You will now see what is included in the source directory. Table 2-1 shows the structure of Nginx source code and here is the output of the source directory:

```
# ls -al
```

```
-rw-r--r--. 1     1001     1001 249124 Apr 21 19:42 CHANGES
-rw-r--r--. 1     1001     1001 379021 Apr 21 19:42 CHANGES.ru
-rw-r--r--. 1     1001     1001   1397 Apr 21 19:41 LICENSE
-rw-r--r--. 1     1001     1001     49 Apr 21 19:41 README
drwxr-xr-x. 6     1001     1001   4096 Sep 26 12:44 auto
drwxr-xr-x. 2     1001     1001   4096 Sep 26 12:44 conf
-rwxr-xr-x. 1     1001     1001   2478 Apr 21 19:41 configure
drwxr-xr-x. 4     1001     1001     68 Sep 26 12:44 contrib
drwxr-xr-x. 2     1001     1001     38 Sep 26 12:44 html
drwxr-xr-x. 2     1001     1001     20 Sep 26 12:44 man
drwxr-xr-x. 8     1001     1001     71 Sep 26 12:44 src
```

Table 2-1. *The different directories included in the Nginx source*

Directories/Files	What Is Included
Auto	Contains different configuration options, like modules file for modules those will be installed by default, options file that include different configuration options, etc.
confls	Contains Nginx configuration files like nginx.conf and fastcgi.conf.
configure	This file contains all the configuration details and parameters that are required to compile Nginx. The output of the configure file will create a Makefile.
contrib	Contains the geo2nginx module.
Html	Contains the default index.html and 50x.html file that will be configured on the root website location.
Src	Contains the source code of nginx, html, mail, etc.
Man	Contains all the manual pages for Nginx.

Installing Nginx Binaries

Now that you have Nginx downloaded and extracted, you will need compiling tools and dependent packages before you start compiling Nginx. To begin with, you will need to prepare the server with all the compilation tools. Compiling a package requires a GCC compiler. After compiling you will need a utility, make, that will build all the programs from the source and then finally install the build on the server.

■ **Note**   Most of these compilation tools are already available in the CentOS and Ubuntu repositories. When you use the compilers from the repository, it ensures all the dependent packages are installed along with the package. If you choose to go with a different version of GCC compiler, you will have to take care of lot of other dependent packages, which is out of the scope of this book.

Build Tools for Compilation

If you choose to build Nginx according to your requirements, you will need to follow the steps in this section based on your Linux distro.

On CentOS

CentOS with its yum-based package management enables you to install packages individually, like yum install nginx or use the group install option with yum to install a group of packages together.

- You can list the group of packages by using the group list command option with yum.

  ```
  # yum group list
  ```

  Sample output of yum group list:

  ```
  ... output trimmed ...
  Available Groups:
     Compatibility Libraries
     Console Internet Tools
     Development Tools
     Graphical Administration Tools
     Legacy UNIX Compatibility
  ... output trimmed ...
  ```

- You will need the Development Tools package group to install all the required compilation and build packages. You can check the list of packages that are available in a particular package by using the group info command.

  ```
  # yum group info "Development Tools"
  ```

- Sample output of the group info of Development Tools:

  ```
  Group: Development Tools
   Group-Id: development
   Description: A basic development environment.
   Mandatory Packages:
     +autoconf
     +automake
      binutils
     +bison
     +flex
     +gcc
     +gcc-c++
      gettext
     +libtool
      make
  ... output trimmed ...
  ```

- If you are curious to know about the different packages that are included in the "Development Tools" and their versions, you can use the following command:

  ```
  # yum group install "Development Tools" --assumeno
  ```

- You can use the command below to install Development Tools without prompting you for confirmation:

```
# yum group install "Development Tools" --assumeyes
```

- Once you are done installing the Development Tools, it is always a good idea to run the update command to update your system:

```
# yum update
```

- You can check GCC and Make versions by using the following command:

```
# gcc --version
gcc (GCC) 4.8.3 20140911 (Red Hat 4.8.3-9)

# make --version
GNU Make 3.82
Built for x86_64-redhat-linux-gnu
```

On Ubuntu

- To check for a list of packages that are available with Ubuntu, you will need to use this command:

```
# sudo apt-cache search all | more
```

"apt-cache search" command lists all available packages from the repositories added in the /etc/apt/sources.list file. It is different from the "yum group list" command we used in CentOS as "yum group list" lists all the available groups where as "apt-cache search" shows all the packages, not the groups.

- To install Development Tools in Ubuntu the command is this:

```
# sudo apt-get install build-essential
```

"build essential" package contain the list of packages that are essential for building packages on Ubuntu servers. When you install "build-essential" package it will check for all the dependent packages and will install them for you.

- You must also update the system after the packages are installed to ensure all components are up to date:

```
# sudo apt-get update
# sudo apt-get upgrade
```

- You can verify the GCC and Make version:

```
# gcc –version
gcc (Ubuntu 4.8.4-2ubuntu1~14.04) 4.8.4

# make –version
GNU Make 3.81
```

Install Dependent Packages

With the development components installed and available on the system, you can now start installing the dependent packages that will enable features in the Nginx web server.

PCRE Library

PCRE is an abbreviation of Perl Compatible Regular Expression. PCRE is used to implement regular expression pattern matching. You will need PCRE to enable using regular expressions when configuring different Nginx directives and the URL Rewrite or HTTP Rewrite module. CentOS and Ubuntu already have a PCRE-compiled version installed on the server. If your server is missing the compiled package, you will need to install both the compiled and development libraries. The command to install is given in the following sections.

On CentOS:

```
# yum install pcre
Package pcre-8.32-14.el7.x86_64 already installed and latest version
```

Install the development libraries for PCRE:

```
# yum install pcre-devel
Installed:
  pcre-devel.x86_64 0:8.32-14.el7
```

On Ubuntu:

```
# sudo apt-get install libpcre3
libpcre3 is already the newest version.
```

Install the development libraries for PCRE

```
# sudo apt-get install libpcre3-dev
```

OpenSSL

OpenSSL is used to establish a secure channel between the web server and the client over SSL or TLS. You will need OpenSSL libraries for Nginx SSL modules. OpenSSL is installed by default on most of the new build Linux servers. In case your server is missing the package, you can refer to the command below to install OpenSSL.

You can check the version of OpenSSL using the version command. To get detailed information about an OpenSSL configuration and certificate directory you can use –a command with openssl version command:

On CentOS

```
# yum install openssl
# openssl version -a
OpenSSL 1.0.1e-fips 11 Feb 2013
```

```
built on: Mon Jun 29 12:45:07 UTC 2015
platform: linux-x86_64
```

   ... output trimmed ...

```
OPENSSLDIR: "/etc/pki/tls"
engines:  rdrand dynamic
```

   Install OpenSSL development libraries:

```
# yum install openssl-devel
```

```
Installed:
  openssl-devel.x86_64 1:1.0.1e-42.el7.9
```

On Ubuntu

```
# sudo apt-get install openssl
# openssl version -a
OpenSSL 1.0.1f 6 Jan 2014
built on: Thu Jun 11 15:28:12 UTC 2015
platform: debian-amd64
... output trimmed ...
OPENSSLDIR: "/usr/lib/ssl"
```

   Install development libraries:

```
# sudo apt-get install libssl-dev
```

zlib Library

The zlib library is used for compression. Compression is implemented on the web servers to improve data transfer speed and lower bandwidth utilization. Nginx uses zlib libraries in gzip module for compression.

   zlib-devel is one of the dependencies of OpenSSL-devel. So, you will have it installed already. To install zlib-devel individually you can use the following command:

On CentOS

```
# yum install zlib
Package zlib-1.2.7-13.el7.x86_64 already installed and latest version
```

   Development libraries for zlib:

```
# yum install zlib-devel
Package zlib-devel-1.2.7-13.el7.x86_64 already installed and latest version
```

On Ubuntu

You can install both the compiled and development libraries using the command below. You can assign multiple packages together to install:

```
# sudo apt-get install zlib1g zlib1g-dev
```

Compiling Nginx

Great! You have the server prepared with all the compilation tools. The dependent development packages are installed and configured, too. Next you will be using these to compile Nginx.

Understanding the ./configure Script

The source directory has a configure file that is used to scan for all the dependent packages on the server for Nginx. The configure script for Nginx checks for machine architecture, defines the Nginx root directory (/usr/local/nginx by default), threads, modules, and various different configuration and temporary paths. It will then create a Makefile that contains various steps that need to be taken. To have a closer look at what are different configuration parameters available with the configure script for Nginx you will need to use --help option. If you have been following the instructions in this book, ensure that you are in the nginx-1.8.0 directory before you run this command. You can use pwd command to know where you are. Below is a sample output of the configure --help:

```
# ./configure --help

  --help                          print this message

  --prefix=PATH                   set installation prefix
  --sbin-path=PATH                set nginx binary pathname
  --conf-path=PATH                set nginx.conf pathname
  --error-log-path=PATH           set error log pathname
  --pid-path=PATH                 set nginx.pid pathname
  --lock-path=PATH                set nginx.lock pathname

  --user=USER                     set non-privileged user for
                                  worker processes
  --group=GROUP                   set non-privileged group for
                                  worker processes
... output trimmed ...
```

Compile-Time Options

In this section you will see the different compilation options available with ./configure script and their uses. This section offers a brief description of various options; the more detailed and compressive explanation with examples can be found in subsequent chapters.

Nginx Users and Groups

Using these parameters, you will ensure Nginx worker process executes under a particular user. It is necessary to create a non-privileged user with a strong password. This configuration parameter can be changed by editing the nginx.conf file. Table 2-2 shows you more information about the user and group parameters.

Table 2-2. *Illustrates the Nginx user and group parameter of nginx.conf*

Command Parameter	Description
--user=USER	Used to specify non-privileged user for Nginx worker processes. Default is empty and Package Manager-based installation will create a user named nginx or www.
--group=GROUP	Used to specify non-privileged group for Nginx worker processes. Default is empty and Package Manager-based installation will create a group named nginx or www.

Syntax example:

```
./configure --user=nginx --group=nginx
```

Nginx Configuration Paths Options

These configure command option contains all the various Nginx configuration paths details. You can always change any of these paths by editing the nginx.conf file. Various parameters are shown in Table 2-3.

Table 2-3. *Illustrates the Nginx configuration paths*

Command Parameter	Description
--prefix=PATH	Nginx server path, all files except configuration and libraries. Default path is /usr/local/nginx and Package Manager-based installation uses the /etc/nginx directory.
--sbin-path=PATH	Nginx executable path, this path hosts the nginx executable file. Default path is /usr/local/nginx/sbin/nginx and Package Manager-based installation uses the /usr/sbin/nginx directory.
--conf-path=PATH	Nginx configurations path, this path will host the nginx.conf, mime.type and various other configuration files. By default, the file is located at /usr/local/nginx/conf/ and the Package Manager installation hosts the file at /etc/nginx/.
--pid-path=PATH	Nginx process nginx.pid file, this file will store the process ID of the Nginx process. By default, the file is located at /usr/local/nginx/logs/ and the Package Manager uses the path /var/run/.
--lock-path=PATH	Nginx lock file nginx.lock file, this file contains the lock information of the resources already in use by a particular process. By default, the file is located at /usr/local/nginx/logs and the Package Manager uses the path /var/run/.

Syntax example:

```
./configure --prefix=/etc/nginx
```

Nginx Log Path Options

These parameters are used to configure log files locations for error files, HTTP access file, temporary paths for FastCGI, and other applications. Table 2-4 shows you the parameters that can be tweaked to change the path for various log files.

Table 2-4. *Illustrates the log file locations for Nginx log files and applications*

Command Parameter	Description
`--error-log-path=PATH`	Nginx server error log path, this file will contain the filename that will contain errors, warnings, and diagnostic error output.
`--http-log-path=PATH`	Nginx server access log path, this file will contain the HTTP request log details of Nginx hosted web site. By default, the HTTP access and error log file directory is `/usr/local/nginx/logs/` and the Package Manager installs log files at `/var/log/nginx/`.
`--http-client-body-temp-path=PATH`	Temporary file location for HTTP requests. It holds the client request bodies.
`--http-fastcgi-temp-path=PATH` `--http-uwsgi-temp-path=PATH` `--http-scgi-temp-path=PATH`	Temporary file location for HTTP FastCGI, uWSGI, SCGI applications. This location stores temporary files with data received from FastCGI, uWSGI, and SCGI servers. By default, the temporary path folders are created under the `/usr/local/nginx/logs/` and the Package Manager configures `/var/cache/nginx/` directory.

Syntax example:

```
./configure --error-log-path=/var/log/nginx/error.log --http-log-path=/var/log/nginx/access.log
```

Enabling Nginx Modules

Table 2-5 shows a list of all the http modules that can be enabled when installing Nginx. These modules are not enabled by default when configuring Nginx from source. These http modules can be enabled using `--with-http<module-name>` options. It is highly recommended to install these modules during a compile-time option. You should enable the module that you would be using and as per the role of your Nginx server. If you need to enable a particular module after Nginx is configured the only option left is to recompile Nginx. Though Nginx update and upgrade has zero impact on your website, it is recommended to take extra precautions when recompiling from source.

Table 2-5. *Illustrates different modules that can be enabled for Nginx*

Command Parameter	Description
`--with-http_ssl_module`	This module provides support for HTTPS websites; this module requires OpenSSL to be enabled.
`--with-http_realip_module`	This module is used to get the real IP address of the client that is specified in the HTTP header.
`--with-http_addition_module`	This module is a filter module that is used to add text before and after a response.
`--with-http_sub_module`	This module is a substitution filter, and it is used to replace one specified string by another.
`--with-http_dav_module`	This module is used to enable WebDAV feature for file management using PUT, DELETE, MKCOL, COPY, and MOVE methods.
`--with-http_flv_module`	This module enables pseudo-streaming functionality for flash video file.
`--with-http_mp4_module`	This module enables pseudo-streaming functionality for .mp4, .m4v, or .m4a files.
`--with-http_gunzip_module`	This module is used to decompress content for clients that do not a support gzip encoding method.
`--with-http_gzip_static_module`	This module allows sending precompressed files with the .gz filename extension.
`--with-http_random_index_module`	This module picks a random file in a directory to serve as an index file.
`--with-http_secure_link_module`	This module is used to authenticate the requested link using the hash to protect resource from unauthorized access.
`--with-http_stub_status_module`	This module provides access to basic status information.
`--with-http_auth_request_module`	This module implements client authorization based on response code.
`--with-http_spdy_module`	This module provides support for Googles SPDY protocol. This is now a deprecated and is replaced by the newer HTTP/2 module.
`--with-http_xslt_module`	This is a filter module that transforms XML responses using XSLT stylesheets.
`--with-http_image_filter_module`	This is a filter module that is used to process JPEG, GIF and PNG images.
`--with-http_geoip_module`	This module is used for geo-targeting, it looks for client IP and compares it with the precompiled MaxMind database.
`--with-http_degradation_module`	This module is used to serve a particular error message when the server faces a low memory issue.

Syntax example:

```
./configure --with-http_ssl_module --with-openssl=${BUILD_DIR}/openssl-1.0.1e --with-http_
stub_status_module
```

Disabling Nginx Modules

Table 2-6 shows a list of some of the common modules that are enabled by default. You may choose to disable them when you have a server with a specific role. For example: if you want your server to be a dedicated web server, you don't want a proxy or mail module on your server. These http modules that can be disabled using the --without-http<module-name> options.

Table 2-6. *Illustrates different modules that can be disabled for Nginx*

Command Parameter	Description
--without-http_charset_module	Disables re-encoding Charset to another.
--without-http_gzip_module	Disables gzip compression module.
--without-http_ssi_module	Disable Server Side Include module.
--without-http_userid_module	Disables cookie-based client identification.
--without-http_access_module	Disables client IP address based access filtering.
--without-http_auth_basic_module	Disables HTTP Basic Authentication module that is used to validate user access.
--without-http_autoindex_module	Disables directory listing of the website.
--without-http_geo_module	Disables geo-module allowing you to define variables with values depending on the client IP address.
--without-http_map_module	Disables map module that is used to define map blocks.
--without-http_split_clients_module	Disables split testing module.
--without-http_referer_module	Disables blocking access to sites for requests with invalid "Referer" header.
--without-http_rewrite_module	Disables HTTP rewrite module.
--without-http_proxy_module	Disables HTTP proxy module used to redirect to another server.
--without-http_fastcgi_module	Disables FastCGI module.
--without-http_uwsgi_module	Disables uWSGI module.
--without-http_scgi_module	Disables SCGI module.
--without-http_memcached_module	Disables memcached module that is used to obtain responses from memcached server.
--without-http_limit_conn_module	Disables connection limit set as per the defined key rule.
--without-http_limit_req_module	Disables request processing limit set as per the defined key.
--without-http_empty_gif_module	Disables transferring single pixel transparent gif.
--without-http_browser_module	Disables identifying User Agent from request header field.
--without-http_upstream_hash_module	Disables HTTP load balancing method for server group where the client-server mapping is based on the hashed key value.
--without-http_upstream_ip_hash_module	Disables HTTP load balancing where requests are distributed across group of servers based on client IP address.

(continued)

Table 2-6. (*continued*)

Command Parameter	Description
--without-http_upstream_least_conn_module	Disables HTTP load balancing where a request is passed to the server with the least number of active connections.
--without-http_upstream_keepalive_module	Disables cache for connections to upstream servers.
--without-mail_pop3_module	Disables POP3 module for mail server proxy.
--without-mail_imap_module	Disables IMAP module for mail server proxy.
--without-mail_smtp_module	Disabled SMTP module for mail server proxy.

Syntax example:

```
./configure --without-http_proxy_module --without-mail_pop3_module
```

Optimization Modules

This section discusses some of the optimization options that can be used during compilation such as using a specific C compiler or compiling Nginx for a specific CPU architecture. There, parameters are not required for default installation, but you can use them for optimizing your Nginx server build or to build Nginx for a particular CPU architecture. Table 2-7 lists the different optimization parameters available for Nginx.

Table 2-7. *Illustrates different optimization parameters for Nginx*

Command Parameter	Description
--with-cc=PATH	Used to specify alternate location for C compiler.
--with-cpp=PATH	Used to specify alternate location for C preprocessor.
--with-cc-opt=OPTIONS	Used to add parameters that will be added to the CFLAGS variable.
--with-ld-opt=OPTIONS	Used to define additional parameters that will be used during linking.
--with-cpu-opt=CPU	Used to specify different processor architecture.

Prerequisite Modules

This section covers some of the list of prerequisite modules that can be enabled or disabled on an as-needed basis. Table 2-8 lists the options available for the PCRE module.

PCRE Options

Table 2-8. *Illustrates different PCRE module options*

Command Parameter	Description
--without-pcre	Disables PCRE libraries that are used for regular expression-based Nginx directive configuration and rewrite modules.
--with-pcre	Force PCRE libraries usage.
--with-pcre=DIR	Specifies path of the PCRE libraries, used when using specific version of PCRE libraries.
--with-pcre-opt=OPTIONS	Used to specify additional build options for PCRE.
--with-pcre-jit	Used to build PCRE with JIT compilation support.

MD5 Options

Table 2-9 lists the various options available to configure the MD5 module.

Table 2-9. *Illustrates different MD5 module options*

Command Parameter	Description
--with-md5=DIR	Specifies the path to md5 library sources.
--with-md5-opt=OPTIONS	Used to specify additional build options for md5.
--with-md5-asm	Uses md5 assembler sources.

SHA1 Options

Just like the MD5 module, SHA1 module can also be tweaked using various parameters as can be seen in Table 2-10.

Table 2-10. *Illustrates different SHA1 module options*

Command Parameter	Description
--with-sha1=DIR	Specifies the path to sha1 library sources.
--with-sha1-opt=OPTIONS	Used to specify additional build options for sha1.
--with-sha1-asm	Uses sha1 assembler sources.

zlib Options

To tweak compression-related aspects of the web server, use the parameters listed in Table 2-11 to configure the zlib module.

Table 2-11. *Illustrates different zlib module options*

Command Parameter	Description
--with-zlib=DIR	Specifies path of the zlib libraries, used when using specific version of zlib libraries.
--with-zlib-opt=OPTIONS	Used to specify additional build options for zlib.
--with-zlib-asm=CPU	Uses zlib assembler sources that are optimized for Pentium or Pentiumpro CPU architecture.

OpenSSL Options

Table 2-12 highlights a couple of options used for OpenSSL.

Table 2-12. *Illustrates different OpenSSL module options*

Command Parameter	Description
--with-openssl=DIR	Specifies path of the OpenSSL libraries, used when using specific version of OpenSSL libraries.
--with-openssl-opt=OPTIONS	Used to specify additional build options for OpenSSL.

Libatomic Options

Table 2-13 shows you the different parameters available for libatomic module.

Table 2-13. *Illustrates different libatomic module options*

Command Parameter	Description
--with-libatomic	Forces libatomic libraries.
--with-libatomic=DIR	Specifies path of the libatomic libraries, used when using specific version of libatomic libraries.

Other Options

There are yet another set of common parameters that can be used as can be seen in Table 2-14.

Table 2-14. Illustrates other options

Command Parameter	Description
--without-http	Disables HTTP server.
--without-http-cache	Disables HTTP cache.
--with-threads	Enables thread pool support.
--with-file-aio	Enables support for asynchronous disk IO operations.
--with-ipv6	Enables ipv6 support.
--build=NAME	Sets the build name.
--builddir=DIR	Sets the build location.
--add-module=PATH	Used to add third-party modules during compiling Nginx. You will specify the path of the module in this parameter.
--with-debug	Enables debug logging.

Third-Party Modules

As you saw in chapter 1, one of the many features of Nginx is its modular nature. It has a very extensible architecture that enables support for plug-ins. The open source developer community has been very active and has been contributing in the development and enhancement of Nginx functionality.

- You can find a list of all the third-party modules currently available at https://www.nginx.com/resources/wiki/modules/.

- You will need to patch Nginx in case of some third-party modules

- You will need to configure Nginx using the ./configure command with the --add-module command. Like the example shown below (ensure that you have downloaded the module):

```
# ./configure --add-module=../ngx_http_healthcheck_module
# make
# make install
```

Yes, it is that simple to enable any third-party module in Nginx.

Compiling and Installing Nginx

Before you start configuring Nginx, you will need to implement some mechanism to identify if the installed version of Nginx on your server is indeed the compiled version. The first method is by using the nginx -V command from the terminal, but that will give you the configuration settings of your Nginx server. Imagine a scenario where you would have to compile and install Nginx on tens of servers and you need to know if all those servers have the compiled version of Nginx serving the request. An easy way to get this done is by having some sort of customization done in the source itself such that it can be accessed from a browser from external machines. For example, you can edit the default index.html page, which is available in the Nginx source folder under the path nginx-1.8.0/html.

After having looked at all the different configuration options, you are now armed to create your own binary as it fits your requirement. Since you are looking for installing a web server, your Nginx configuration would like something like the one below. You have complete freedom to add or remove any module you wish. The command discussed next is identical for both CentOS and Ubuntu.

■ **Tip** Change the user to root using su on CentOS. In Ubuntu you will have to sudo every command.

Prerequisites

There are a few prerequisites tasks that you need to do, before you can manually configure Nginx.

- Create a group named 'nginx':

  ```
  # groupadd -r nginx
  ```

- Create a user name 'nginx':

  ```
  # useradd -r nginx -g nginx
  ```

Manual Configuration

Here are the commands that you will have to run separately in the terminal window:

```
# ./configure --prefix=/etc/nginx \
 --user=nginx \
 --group=nginx \
 --sbin-path=/usr/sbin/nginx \
 --conf-path=/etc/nginx/nginx.conf \
 --pid-path=/var/run/nginx.pid \
 --lock-path=/var/run/nginx.lock \
 --error-log-path=/var/log/nginx/error.log \
 --http-log-path=/var/log/nginx/access.log \
 --with-http_gzip_static_module \
 --with-http_stub_status_module \
 --with-http_ssl_module \
 --with-pcre \
 --with-file-aio \
 --with-http_realip_module \
 --without-http_scgi_module \
 --without-http_uwsgi_module \
 --without-http_proxy_module \
```

Below is the sample output of the above command. Here you can see that a Makefile was created in objs directory in the source folder. You can also see that configure was able to identify the PCRE, OpenSSL, and zlib libraries that we installed. You can also see that Nginx is showing you the exact location and log path directory as we mentioned.

```
... output trimmed ...
creating objs/Makefile
```

```
Configuration summary
  + using system PCRE library
  + using system OpenSSL library
  + md5: using OpenSSL library
  + sha1: using OpenSSL library
  + using system zlib library

  nginx path prefix: "/etc/nginx"
  nginx binary file: "/usr/sbin/nginx"
  nginx configuration prefix: "/etc/nginx"
  nginx configuration file: "/etc/nginx/nginx.conf"
  nginx pid file: "/var/run/nginx.pid"
  nginx error log file: "/var/log/nginx/error.log"
  nginx http access log file: "/var/log/nginx/access.log"
  nginx http client request body temporary files: "client_body_temp"
  nginx http fastcgi temporary files: "fastcgi_temp"
```

Now, you will need to execute the make command, which will compile all the code of the libraries to create a binary executable. Use the following command:

```
# make
```

Once the make command is executed successfully, the command ends with the following output:

```
... output trimmed ...
make[1]: Leaving directory `/home/nginx-1.8.0'
make -f objs/Makefile manpage
make[1]: Entering directory `/home/nginx-1.8.0'
sed -e "s|%%PREFIX%%|/etc/nginx|" \
    -e "s|%%PID_PATH%%|/var/run/nginx.pid|" \
    -e "s|%%CONF_PATH%%|/etc/nginx/nginx.conf|" \
    -e "s|%%ERROR_LOG_PATH%%|/var/log/nginx/error.log|" \
    < man/nginx.8 > objs/nginx.8
```

Now that the compilation is successful and the executable created, you can install Nginx using the command as shown:

```
# sudo make install
```

The make install command executes the install part of the Makefile. The command essentially makes directories that do not exist and copies the configuration files and binaries to the specific folder. The output clearly shows the steps followed.

Scripted Configuration

Alternately, you can create a configuration script that you can use across multiple servers without having to worry about any human error while commanding input. Below is a sample script file that contains everything that you have used earlier with individual commands. Here the assumption is that you are creating the file under the source nginx directory that is under nginx-1.8.0.

```
# nano scripted
```

Add the script in the file:

```
export BUILD_DIR=/{path of the source directory}
export NGINX_DIR=/etc/nginx
export SBIN_DIR=/usr/sbin
export PID_DIR=/var/run
export LOCK_DIR=/var/run
export LOG_DIR=/var/log/nginx
export RUN_DIR=/var/run
export CACHE_DIR=/var/cache

cd ${BUILD_DIR}
./configure \
                --prefix=${NGINX_DIR} \
                --sbin-path=${SBIN_DIR}/nginx \
        --conf-path=${NGINX_DIR}/nginx.conf \
                --pid-path=${PID_DIR}/nginx.pid \
        --lock-path=${LOCK_DIR}/nginx.lock \
        --error-log-path=${LOG_DIR}/error.log \
        --http-log-path=${LOG_DIR}/access.log \
        --http-client-body-temp-path=${CACHE_DIR}/client_body_temp \
        --http-fastcgi-temp-path=${CACHE_DIR}/fastcgi_temp \
        --with-http_gzip_static_module \
        --with-http_stub_status_module \
        --with-http_ssl_module \
        --with-pcre \
        --with-file-aio \
        --with-http_realip_module \
        --without-http_scgi_module \
        --without-http_uwsgi_module \
        --without-http_proxy_module \
        --user=nginx \
        --group=nginx \
```

Convert the script into an executable using the following command:

```
# chmod u+x scripted
```

Now, you can configure Nginx using a single command and then complete the installation with make and make install commands:

```
# ./scripted
# make
# make install
```

■ **Note**   Nginx does not start automatically when you do source-based installation. You will have to start the Nginx by manually running the nginx process like the case above /usr/sbin/nginx in the terminal window.

Enable Nginx Service on Reboot

Installing Nginx from source does not create the init script that will autostart the Nginx process after server reboot. Instead of reinventing the wheel, you can use the script that's available online. Visit https://goo.gl/3XufgG to access the script.

- You can download the script directly on the server as /etc/init.d/nginx file:

  ```
  # sudo wget -O /etc/init.d/nginx https://gist.githubusercontent.com/
  sairam/5892520/raw/b8195a71e944d46271c8a49f2717f70bcd04bf1a/etc-init.d-nginx
  ```

- Once the script is downloaded you will need to make it as an executable:

  ```
  # sudo chmod +x /etc/init.d/nginx
  ```

- You can now set the service to start automatically when the server reboots.

  On CentOS:

  ```
  # chkconfig --add nginx
  # chkconfig --level 345 nginx on
  ```

  On Ubuntu:

  ```
  # sudo update-rc.d nginx defaults
  ```

- You can verify if you are able to start Nginx using a basic service <process> start command:

  ```
  # service nginx start
  ```

Troubleshooting Service Start

It happens that once you have followed the steps as mentioned, there is a possibility of facing an issue of not being able to start the service. You may come across an issue like the following:

```
# journalctl -xn
-- Logs begin at Sun 2015-09-27 20:16:54 IST, end at Sun 2015-09-27 21:00:50 IST. --
Sep 27 20:57:37 ncentos.local systemd[1]: Unit nginx.service entered failed state.
Sep 27 21:00:44 ncentos.local systemd[1]: Reloading.
Sep 27 21:00:44 ncentos.local systemd[1]: [/usr/lib/systemd/system/dm-event.socket:10]
Unknown lvalue 'RemoveOnStop' in section 'So
Sep 27 21:00:44 ncentos.local systemd[1]: [/usr/lib/systemd/system/lvm2-lvmetad.socket:9]
Unknown lvalue 'RemoveOnStop' in section
Sep 27 21:00:50 ncentos.local systemd[1]: Starting SYSV: Nginx is an HTTP(S) server, HTTP(S)
reverse proxy and IMAP/POP3 proxy server
-- Subject: Unit nginx.service has begun with start-up
-- Defined-By: system
-- Support: http://lists.freedesktop.org/mailman/listinfo/systemd-devel
--
```

```
-- Unit nginx.service has begun starting up.
Sep 27 21:00:50 ncentos.local nginx[4971]: Starting nginx: nginx: [emerg] getpwnam("nginx")
failed
Sep 27 21:00:50 ncentos.local nginx[4971]: [FAILED]
Sep 27 21:00:50 ncentos.local systemd[1]: nginx.service: control process exited, code=exited
status=1
Sep 27 21:00:50 ncentos.local systemd[1]: Failed to start SYSV: Nginx is an HTTP(S) server,
HTTP(S) reverse proxy and IMAP/POP3 pro
-- Subject: Unit nginx.service has failed
-- Defined-By: system
-- Support: http://lists.freedesktop.org/mailman/listinfo/systemd-devel
--
-- Unit nginx.service has failed.
--
-- The result is failed.
Sep 27 21:00:50 ncentos.local systemd[1]: Unit nginx.service entered failed state.
```

That error clearly shows that an Nginx user does not exist. You will need the Nginx user account to execute the Nginx process as that is what our configuration step contains. You can add the user using the command shown below to resolve the above error:

```
# groupadd -r nginx
# useradd -r nginx -g nginx
        |              |
     User         Group
```

You now have a working version Nginx running on the server. The next and final step for this chapter is to verify whether the website is working.

Verifying Web Server Installation

The simplest way to verify if Nginx is working on the server is to check it locally. We already have lynx installed on the server, so we will use the same to verify the Nginx website.

```
# lynx http://localhost
```

Figure 2-1 shows that request has been served by the compiled version of Nginx.

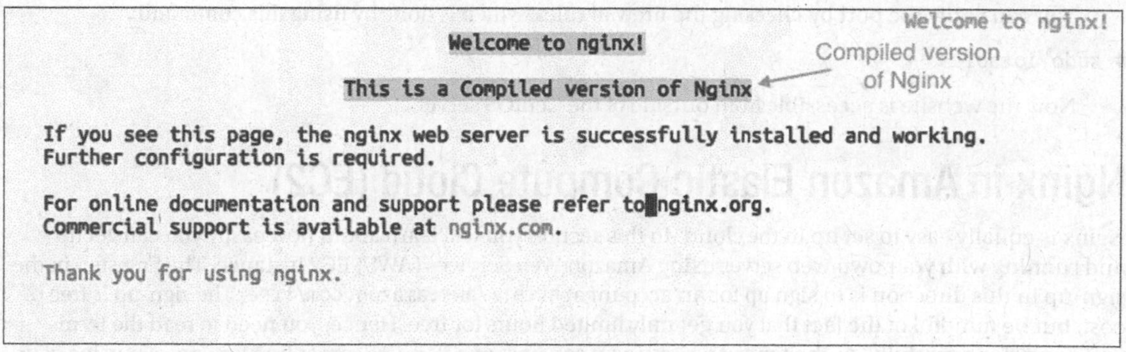

```
            Welcome to nginx!                     Welcome to nginx!
                                               Compiled version
       This is a Compiled version of Nginx ←      of Nginx

If you see this page, the nginx web server is successfully installed and working.
Further configuration is required.

For online documentation and support please refer to nginx.org.
Commercial support is available at nginx.com.

Thank you for using nginx.
```

Figure 2-1. *Compiled version of Nginx seen using Lynx*

You can check the Nginx process that is executing on the server using the following command:

```
# ps aux | grep nginx
```

The output is as follows:

```
root      5034  0.0  0.1  47156  1072 ?        Ss   21:05   0:00 nginx: master process /usr/
sbin/nginx -c /etc/nginx/nginx.conf
nginx     5036  0.0  0.2  47612  2088 ?        S    21:05   0:00 nginx: worker process
root      5075  0.0  0.0 112612   740 pts/0    S+   21:26   0:00 grep --color=auto nginx
```

Firewall Configuration

You will need to open port 80 on the server such that you can access the website from outside of the local server. You will need to configure the firewall for the same, as CentOS has port 80 blocked by default on the server.

On CentOS

The command to add port 80 in the firewall rules, you will need to execute the command below:

```
# firewall-cmd --permanent --add-port=80/tcp
Success
# firewall-cmd --reload
success
```

On Ubuntu

To open port 80 on Ubuntu, the command is iptables.

```
# sudo iptables -A INPUT -p tcp --dport 80 -j ACCEPT
```

You can verify the port by checking the firewall rules, which is done by using this command:

```
# sudo iptables -L
```

Now the website is accessible from outside of the CentOS server.

Nginx in Amazon Elastic Compute Cloud (EC2)

Nginx is equally easy to set up in the cloud. In this section you will learn about how easily you can get up and running with your own web server using Amazon Web Services (AWS) EC2 instance. The first step in the sign-up in this direction is to sign up for an account at http://aws.amazon.com/free. The sign-up is free of cost, but be mindful of the fact that you get only limited hours for free. Hence, you need to read the terms and conditions carefully. At the time of writing, you can host one *t2.micro* server free for one year using your credit card.

Creating an Amazon EC2 instance with Nginx installed is fairly simple and straightforward:

- Sign in using your user name at http://aws.amazon.com

- In the Compute section, click EC2.

- Click the Launch Instance button and you will be redirected to a UI with a wizard. You can use any Linux version. Choosing a 64-bit server is generally a better idea since it can address a wider memory address space. Figure 2-2 shows how the launch wizard looks like at the time of writing this book. For the purpose of this book, the first instance (Amazon Linux AMI) will be used.

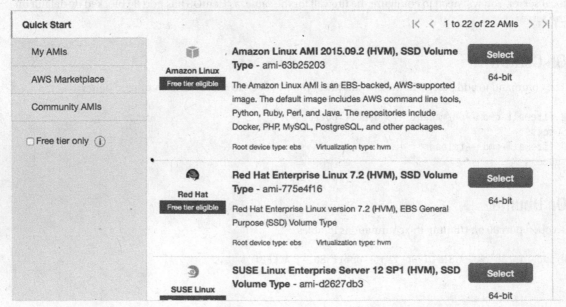

Figure 2-2. Amazon AWS EC2 Wizard - Step 1

- In step 2 of the wizard (see Figure 2-3), select t2.micro and click the Next:Configure Instance Details button.

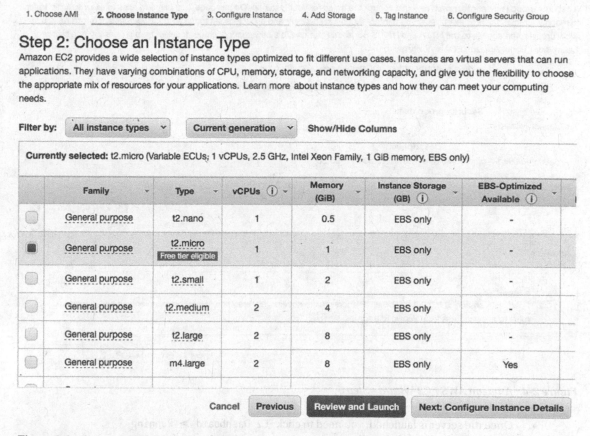

Figure 2-3. *Amazon AWS EC2 Wizard - Step 2*

- You can leave the defaults in steps 3 through 5 of the wizard. There are plenty of options to choose from, a discussion of which is beyond the scope of this book. However, they are quite simple to understand, and I urge you to read the documentation while you follow along with the steps.

- Step 6 is very crucial, since this is where you make your web server public. Click Add Rule and make the changes so that it looks similar to Figure 2-4. Basically, you will be adding one more rule to the firewall and allowing this server to be accessible on port 80 from anywhere.

Figure 2-4. *Amazon AWS EC2 Wizard - Step 6*

- Once the server is launched, you need to click `EC2 Dashboard ➤ Running Instances ➤ Your Server Name.`

- You can now click on the connect button and the pop-up will tell you how to connect to your server using SSH. For the demo server we set up, it asked to use the following command:

  ```
  ssh -i "mykey.pem" ec2-user@ec2-xx-xx-xx-xx.us-west-2.compute.amazonaws.com
  ```

- Once logged on the server, the steps were exactly how it has been explained earlier in this chapter. It took just two commands to get Nginx up and running. Point your browser to the IP address and you will find your web server running smoothly.

  ```
  sudo yum install nginx
  sudu service nginx start
  ```

Summary

In this chapter, you learned about various ways of installing Nginx in different Linux distros. You should now be comfortable with making a decision regarding installation using pre-built packages or building your own set of binaries. Both of these methods are useful in different scenarios, and it is important that you are comfortable with either option. While picking an option you should be mindful about the maintenance aspects of Nginx as well. You have also learned about some troubleshooting basics and automating tasks such as restarting Nginx whenever the server is rebooted. In the upcoming chapters, you will learn that Nginx can be reconfigured just as easily.

CHAPTER 3

Nginx Core Directives

By now, your Nginx server should be up and running. It is time to go ahead and take control over it! You can consider the directives as the nuts and bolts of your web server, using which ones you tweak by the way your web server performs. Nginx has a lot of directives and it is important that you know the basic semantics, so that you can fine-tune your server according to your requirements. You will learn about directives in detail in this chapter.

Location of Configuration Files

The Nginx configuration file is named `nginx.conf`. Depending on how you have installed Nginx, you can find the configuration in `/etc/nginx`, `/usr/local/etc/nginx`, or `/usr/local/nginx/conf`. You can run the following command to get the configuration path currently in use by Nginx:

```
ps -ax | grep nginx
```

For more concise output, use the following:

```
ps -ax -o command | grep nginx
```

The output will be something like this:

```
nginx: master process /usr/sbin/nginx -c /etc/nginx/nginx.conf
nginx: worker process
```

The -c switch above tells you the active configuration that is loaded in the process `/usr/sbin/nginx`

What Are Directives?

"Directive" is defined as an instruction or to direct. Directives define how Nginx runs on your server. As you already know from chapter 1, Nginx is modular. You can compile Nginx with the modules that you need in your environment and configure the modules using directives. Directives are of two types: simple directives and block directives.

- *Simple directive* - A simple directive can be as straightforward as a set of names and parameters separated by spaces, and ending with a semicolon. For example, the directive for worker processes looks like this:

```
worker_processes    1;
```

This tells Nginx to spawn only one worker process. You will learn in the upcoming chapters about why you should make this value equal to the number of processors on your server. For now, the core idea is to understand that this *directive* is giving direction to the master process of Nginx about how to spawn worker processes.

- *Block directive* - As the name suggests, it looks like a block of text enclosed by curly braces { } and contains a set of simple directives.

A typical Nginx configuration file is comprised of blocks as you can see in Figure 3-1. You can refer to the blocks as contexts. The outermost context is called the main context and contains simple directives along with other contexts like Context A and Context B. The contexts, in turn, contain a set of related directives.

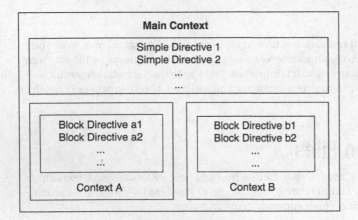

Figure 3-1. *Structure of Nginx Configuration file*

■ **Tip**   You can add comments in your configuration file by using a pound (#) sign.

Context Types

Every module in Nginx has a very discrete purpose and is controlled by the directives. The documentation clearly informs you about the context in which the directives can be used. Understanding this convention is helpful when configuring a specific module according to your needs.

There are quite a few different contexts available in Nginx: for example, main, events, HTTP, server, location, upstream, if, stream, mail, etc. Out of these, HTTP, events, server, and location are most commonly used. The contexts could be nested as well. This is what the basic overall structure of the configuration looks like:

```
# main block is not explicitly called as main, it is implied
main {
     simple_directives parameters;
     ...
     events{
        event_directives parameters;
        ...
     }
     http{
```

```
        http_directives parameters;
        ...
    server{
        server_directives parameters;
        ...
        location{
            location_directives parameters;
            ...
        }
      }
    }
}
```

Let's configure the server so that you can see the directives and contexts in action.

Understanding the Default Configuration

The default configuration of Nginx looks similar to the following:

```
user nginx;
worker_processes  1;
error_log  /var/log/nginx/error.log warn;
pid        /var/run/nginx.pid;

events {
    worker_connections  1024;
}

http {
    include       /etc/nginx/mime.types;
    default_type  application/octet-stream;
    log_format  main  '$remote_addr - $remote_user [$time_local] "$request" '
                      '$status $body_bytes_sent "$http_referer" '
                      '"$http_user_agent" "$http_x_forwarded_for"';
    access_log  /var/log/nginx/access.log  main;
    sendfile        on;
    #tcp_nopush     on;
    keepalive_timeout  65;
    #gzip  on;
    include /etc/nginx/conf.d/*.conf;
}
```

Simple Directives

The whole body could be referred to as the *main* context. There are a few simple directives defined in the main block:

- user directive has a default value of nobody. You can add user directive to define the account under which Nginx worker process will be executed on the server. The syntax for user directive is like user <user_name> <group_name>. The user should exist on the server before Nginx starts or else there will be an error while starting Nginx services.

■ **Tip**   Nginx should be executed under a least-privileged account.

- worker_process directive has a default value of 1 and it implies the number of worker processes that will be spawned by Nginx. Setting the value to *auto* is also permitted and in that case Nginx tries to autodetect the number of cores.

- error_log directive can be applied in multiple contexts like main, http, mail, stream, server, and location. Here, you see it applied in the main context. The first parameter /var/log/nginx/error.log tells you the the name of the file where the log file will be created, whereas the second parameter warn informs you that anything above the warning level will be logged.

  The logging levels are defined in increasing order as you can see from the list below and it is important to note that if you set the level to error, then the logs of type warning, notice, and info will be ignored. Keeping it to info is not recommended in production since the logs may become massive if your website is hit very frequently. The logs should be periodically analyzed to verify if it contains anything alarming.

  - info - Information

  - notice - Notice

  - warn - Warnings

  - error - Error

  - crit - Critical

  - alert - High Alert

  - emerg - Emergency

■ **Tip**   You should always set the log level to either warn or error.

- pid directive has a parameter that defines the file name that stores the process ID of the master process /var/run/nginx.pid. You may be thinking why does nginx log the PID to a file? Glad you asked! Imagine a scenario where you are supposed to check the uptime of a process. Running a command like ps -ax | grep nginx will help you get the current status and process id (PID), but you cannot really tell how long the process has been alive. To get this duration you may use a couple of commands like the following:

```
# ps -ax | grep nginx
30212 ?        Ss     0:00 nginx: master process /usr/sbin/nginx -c /etc/nginx/nginx.conf
30213 ?        S      0:00 nginx: worker process
```

- The first column contains the PID. In this case, 30212 is the PID of the master process.

```
# ps -p 30212 -o etime=
      15:00 <<< Process uptime
```

- You can now write a script or command to get the result like the following:

```
# ps -p `cat /var/run/nginx.pid` -o etime=
    15:40 <<< Process uptime
```

- This one liner is enough to get you the uptime and as you can guess, it can come in handy when you have to automate the monitoring of processes.

Events Context

After the simple directives in the default configuration, you will find a context called events. The events context can be declared only in the main context and there can be only a single events context defined within the Nginx configuration. With the use of directives in the event context, you can fine-tune the way Nginx behaves. There are just six different event directives.

- worker_connections directive allows a maximum of 1024 concurrent worker connections. The defaults in Nginx usually suffice. The number of concurrent connections you may get on a web server can be calculated roughly using the following (N = average number of connections per request):

```
(worker_processes x worker_connections x N) / Average Request Time
```

- use directive does not need to be applied explicitly since Nginx tries to use the most efficient method automatically. Basically, the use directive allows Nginx to support a variety of connection methods depending on the platform.

  - use select is the worst performing and is used when more efficient methods are not available on a platform. If you run Nginx in a Windows environment, this is what will get used. This reason alone should be a big deterrent for you to use Nginx on a Windows platform.

  - The other modes are poll (standard method), kqueue (efficient method on FreeBSD, OpenBSD, NetBSD and Max OSX), epoll (Linux), /dev/poll (Solaris, IRIX) and eventport (efficient method on Solaris 10).

- multi_accept is set to off by default. It means that a worker process will accept only one new connection at a time by default. It is a generally a good idea to enable multi_accept so that Nginx can accept as many connections as possible.

- accept_mutex is set to on by default, and it is generally left untouched. Basically, it means that the worker processes will get the requests one by one. This implies that the worker processes will not jump up for every request and go back to sleep if the number of requests is low.

- accept_mutex_delay comes into effect only when accept_mutex is enabled. As the name implies it is the maximum time to wait for the existing worker process to accept the new connection before initiating a new process to execute the request.

HTTP Context

The HTTP context (or block) can be considered the heart of the configuration system for an Nginx web server. In the default configuration you will notice the following directives:

- `include /etc/nginx/mine.types` - The include directive keeps the core configuration file clean. You can use this directive to keep related configurations in a separate file. Nginx will ensure that the file is loaded in-place when loading the configuration. At the same time, it will keep the main configuration readable and manageable.

  If you view `/etc/nginx/mime.types` you will find a block of text that is nothing but another directive called `types`. It maps file name extension to MIME types of responses. The extensions are case insensitive and there can be many extensions mapped to one type. The following snippet shows the structure of this file. Notice how `html htm shtml` extensions are all mapped to `text/html` MIME type.

```
types {
    text/html                       html htm shtml;
    text/css                        css;
    text/xml                        xml;
    image/gif                       gif;
    image/jpeg                      jpeg jpg;
    application/javascript          js;
...
...
    audio/midi                      mid midi kar;
    audio/mpeg                      mp3;
...
...
    video/x-flv                     flv;
    video/x-m4v                     m4v;
}
```

■ **Tip** MIME types describe the media type of content and guides the browser so that it renders the content appropriately in the browser instead of downloading the file. Assume you want to serve a file called `myfile.data`. If you simply create a file called `myfile.data` in your root folder (`/etc/nginx/html`), you might think that the browser will be able to render it when you type `http://localhost/myfile.data`. However, you will notice that the browser simply downloads the file since it doesn't know what kind of data it contains! MIME type completes this story. If you know that your file is a text file, you can simply modify the MIME type for text/plain so that it reads as the following:

```
text/plain       txt data;
```

By doing this, Nginx guides the browser that the extension of this file is `data`, but the `content` is plain text and could be displayed inside the browser. The browser obliges and renders the content right away, instead of downloading it!

MIME types can be helpful in other scenarios where you create a custom content with a new MIME type altogether. You can then create a client that understands the specific extension. Example: `application/pdf` is a MIME type that helps the clients like Adobe or Foxit Reader to read the PDF content directly from the web server.

- `default_type` directive has a value of `application/octet-stream`. It specifies the default MIME type if Nginx fails to find a specific one in the `/etc/nginx/mine.types`. It is this MIME type that guides the browser that it has to download the file directly.

- `log_format` directive configures the `ngx_http_log_module`. It writes the log in a specified format. The first parameter is the name of the format, in this case `main`. The second parameter is a series of variables (you will learn about it in detail soon) that will contain a different value for every request. Once you have named a `log_format`, you will need to use it.

```
log_format  main  '$remote_addr - $remote_user [$time_local] "$request" '
                  '$status $body_bytes_sent "$http_referer" '
                  '"$http_user_agent" "$http_x_forwarded_for"';
```

- `access_log` directive requires a path (`/var/log/nginx/access.log`) and name of a format (`main`). There is much more to `access_log` that you will learn in the upcoming chapters, but for now you can simply understand that every request you make from the server can be logged to a file so that you can analyze it later. A good web administrator takes very good care of these logs, and analyzes it periodically to find out issues that sometimes go unnoticed. These logs also prove to be helpful during troubleshooting scenarios.

- The default value for `sendfile` directive is `off` if the directive is not present. Nginx default configuration hence, turns it on. It is generally a good idea to enable it, since it ensures that the function is called with `SF_NODISKIO`. In simple words, it means that the call will not block on disk I/O. The data is loaded in chunks and sent appropriately to the client. As you can guess, it has a huge advantage and enables Nginx to scale very well, especially while serving large files.

- `tcp_nopush` directive is commented by default and the default value is off. This comes into effect only when you are using sendfile and basically directs the Nginx server to send the packets in full. Typically, you can leave it disabled.

- `keepalive_timeout` directive has a value of 65. Normally, when a connection is made to the server, you need not disconnect the connection straightaway. That is because a web page normally comprises of a lot of assets. It will not be very effective to create a new connection for every asset that is sent to the client.

  Hence, the first few connections are made to the server and then, they are *kept alive*. The idea is to deliver the rest of the assets on the same set of connections one after the other. Now, let's say there were 125 assets (css, js, html, images, etc.) in a page. When the client accesses the URL, it might create 2 connections or more (modern browsers open a lot more connections!). Assuming 5 connections were made, those assets will be delivered one by one to the client in parallel over 5 different connections! What do you think will happen to the open connections if the page is delivered in just 3 seconds? Well, they will continue to live and, as you can guess, will waste resources on the server. This is the reason why this directive exists. It allows the server to close the connection in 65 seconds automatically if the client doesn't return and the connection is idle. On a busy server, you may choose to reduce this timeout.

- `gzip` directive compresses the output so that lesser bandwidth is consumed per request. By default it is turned off, and it is recommended to turn it on.

- The last line in the configuration is yet another include and it is an interesting one! You can see that it accepts wild cards (`include /etc/nginx/conf.d/*.conf;`) and it implies that it will load all the configuration file sat once from the folder /etc/nginx/conf.d. In the next section you will see what is included in the `conf.d folder`.

The conf.d Folder

The /etc/nginx/conf.d folder contains two files, `default.conf` and `example_ssl.conf`. The example_ssl.conf file is fully commented out and not used until you have a requirement to host SSL. You will learn about SSL in chapter 13. In this section you will learn about the directives in `default.conf`.

The default configuration file looks like the following:

```
server {
    listen       80;
    server_name  localhost;

    #charset koi8-r;
    #access_log  /var/log/nginx/log/host.access.log  main;

    location / {
        root   /etc/nginx/html;
        index  index.html index.htm;
    }

    #error_page  404              /404.html;

    # redirect server error pages to the static page /50x.html
    #
    error_page   500 502 503 504  /50x.html;
    location = /50x.html {
        root   /usr/share/nginx/html;
    }

    # proxy the PHP scripts to Apache listening on 127.0.0.1:80
    #
    #location ~ \.php$ {
    #    proxy_pass   http://127.0.0.1;
    #}

    # pass the PHP scripts to FastCGI server listening on 127.0.0.1:9000
    #
    #location ~ \.php$ {
```

```
#    root          html;
#    fastcgi_pass  127.0.0.1:9000;
#    fastcgi_index index.php;
#    fastcgi_param SCRIPT_FILENAME  /scripts$fastcgi_script_name;
#    include       fastcgi_params;
#}

# deny access to .htaccess files, if Apache's document root
# concurs with nginx's one
#
#location ~ /\.ht {
#    deny  all;
#}
}
```

Please keep in mind that even though you see this section starting with `server { }` block, it is nested inside `http`!

Server Context

The server block can be set in multiple contexts to configure various modules (you will learn about modules in chapter 4), as shown in Table 3-1.

Table 3-1. Server directive in different modules

Module Name	Context	Details
ngx_http_core_module	http	Sets the configuration for a virtual server using server_name directives.
ngx_http_upstream_module	upstream	Sets the address and other parameters of a server. Useful in reverse proxy and load balancing scenarios.
ngx_mail_core_module	mail	Sets the configuration for a mail server.
ngx_stream_core_module	stream	Sets the configuration for a streaming server.
ngx_stream_upstream_module	upstream	Similar to ngx_http_upstream_module.

As you can imagine, it wouldn't be effective to have just one application per server. This is where the concept of *virtual server* comes in to play. Nginx has a mechanism that allows it to select a specific server and location block based on the request. Every request gets handled based on the configuration in a single server context.

Another interesting thing about the server directive is that it allows for *multiple* declarations adjacent to each other. In the configuration mentioned earlier, you can see one server block being configured such that it `listens` to port *80* with the `server_name` as *localhost*. You can override the `access_log` directive here if you wish. By default, it is commented out along with a `charset` directive.

Setting up a virtual server and its location context is one of the most common tasks when using Nginx; hence it is strongly adviced to do the following exercise to get the feel of it and play around.

HOW TO SET UP A BASIC SERVER TO SERVE STATIC CONTENT

Start from a blank slate

You can leave the defaults at the global level (`/etc/nginx/nginx.conf`) untouched for the purpose of this exercise. Start with navigating to the *conf.d* directory. `cd /etc/nginx/conf.d`.

- Take a backup of the *default.conf* file (so that it doesn't get loaded due to the include directive in nginx.conf) `sudo mv default.conf default.backup`

- The idea is to keep the configuration as organized as possible. Create a file called *virtual_servers.conf* with the following content. The intention is to host 2 different applications that should be browsable using

```
http://app1.com or http://www.app1.com
 http://app2.com or http://www.app2.com

server {
      listen 80;
      server_name app1.com www.app1.com;
      location / {
              root /etc/nginx/html/app1;
      }
}

server {
      listen 80;
      server_name app2.com www.app2.com;
      location / {
              root /etc/nginx/html/app2;
      }
}
```

■ **Tip** It is important to keep the port as 80 for a public-facing website, or else the end user will have to type the port explicitly in the URL (ex. `http://app1.com:8080`), and it won't be a good idea!

- Notice that there are 2 server blocks and both of them are listening on port 80 using the listen directive.

- There are 2 different directories called */etc/nginx/html/app1* and */etc/nginx/html/app2*. Both are mapped inside the location block, using the root directive.

- Set up your applications by navigating to the web root folder by executing `cd /etc/nginx/html`.

- Create 2 directories by executing `mkdir app1 app2`.

- Create an *index.html* file in both folders with text "Index for App1," and "Index for App2." This will make it easy for you to identify if you are hitting the right file.

- Let Nginx know that the configuration has changed. You can either restart Nginx by using `systemctl restart nginx` or reload the configuration without killing the nginx service using `nginx -s reload`. (-s stands for *signal*. The upcoming chapters will explain the signals in detail.)

Routing Rule #1

- If you browse to *http://localhost* using `curl http://localhost` the output will be *Index for App1*. Why? Basically, Nginx tries to match the host name (localhost here) to the values in `server_name` directive for each server block. In this case, it was not able to match either *app1.com, app2.com,* `www.app1.com,` *or* `www.app2.com`. Since it failed, it defaulted to the *FIRST* server block it countered that was listening on default port (80).

- Change the port to 81 for the first server block and execute `nginx -s reload`. Try `curl http://locahost` now, and you will see the output as *Index for App2*. This is because the default port is 80, and as per the previous point, the fallback happens to the first server block listening on port 80. Change the port back to 80.

Routing Rule #2

- Now, you have two blocks with the same port. How can you explicitly tell Nginx that the second server block is the default server block? To do this, you will have to add a directive called default_server to the listen directive. Change the listen directive of the second server block so that it reads `listen 80 default_server;`

- Try `curl http://localhost` again, and you will find the output as *Index for App2*.

■ **Note**   The `default_server` property is set on the listen port and not on the server name as you might guess!

Routing Rule #3

- You have a hawkeye if you found a problem with `default_server` already! What if you wouldn't want the first block or any server block to be the default block? In other words, you may want to NOT serve the request if the host header field is empty.

- Add the following text at the start of the *virtual_servers.conf* file and reload nginx configuration.

```
server {
    listen 80;
    server_name "" localhost 127.0.0.1;
    return 444;
}
```

- If you try *curl http://localhost* or *curl http://127.0.0.1* you should get a non-standard output like this:

```
Empty reply from server
```

Routing Rule #4

- If Nginx is listening on different IPs, Nginx first reads the IP address and port, and *then* tests the host header fields. This means that if you have a structure like the following, and a request is received for *app3.com* on 10.0.0.1, you will see the output from *app1. com* instead! This happens because Nginx couldn't find app3.com on 10.0.0.1 and hence defaulted to the first server block.

```
server{
    listen 10.0.0.1:80;
    server_name app1.com www.app1.com;
    ...
}

server{
    listen     10.0.0.1:80;
    server_name app2.com www.app2.com;
    ...
}

server{
    listen     10.0.0.2:80;
    server_name app3.com www.app3.com;
    ...}
```

Routing Rule #5

- You can use `default_server` on multiple ports. But on *one* IP and port, you cannot have two default servers. If you try doing that, you will get an emergency error message similar to the following:

```
nginx: [emerg] a duplicate default server for 0.0.0.0:80 in /etc/nginx/conf.d/
virtual_servers.conf:15
```

Visualizing Routing Rules

You can visualize the request flow in Nginx as shown in Figure 3-2.

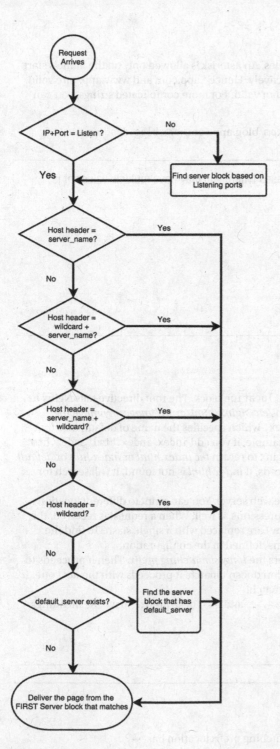

Figure 3-2. *Request flow in Nginx*

Wildcards Names

Wildcards are allowed in Nginx configuration with few rules. An asterisk is allowed only on the name's start and end and has to be suffixed or prefixed by a dot respectively. Hence *.app.com and www.app.* are valid. On the contrary, www.*.app.com and www.app.*.org are not valid. For more complicated strings, you can use valid (Perl) regular expressions, if required.

The good thing is that *.app.com matches `www.app.com`, blog.app.com, `www.blog.app.com`, etc.!

■ **Tip**   Try to keep your configuration file organized. In cases where you may have multiple values, it is generally a good idea to split the line like this:

```
server{
    listen    80;
    server_name app.com

                        www.app.com
                        *.app.com;

    ...
}
```

Location Context

You have already seen the usage of `root` directive inside a `location` block. The root directive tells Nginx to return */image/myimage.jpg* instead of fully qualified path */etc/nginx/html/app1/image/myimage.jpg*.

Another important directive in location block is `index`, which specifies the name of default files that is sent to the client if the file name is not specified. For example, if you add `index index.html index.htm default.htm;` inside location directive, you are telling Nginx to return *the index.html* or *index.htm* or *default. htm* if the URI is simply `http://www.app.com`. In other words, if *index.html* is not found, it will search for *index.htm*, and so on.

Location directive points to the actual content on the web server. You can point to different locations using different location directives and include regular expressions as well. When a request is received, the text in the URI is decoded and the adjacents slashes (if any) are replaced with a single slash. To find the appropriate location, Nginx then goes through its locations defined in the configuration.

Based on the requested URI, it selects and remembers the *longest matching prefix*. Then it proceeds to match regular expressions (if any). If one regular expression doesn't match, it proceeds with the next one. It stops processing the next regular expressions at the first match!

The location directive has four different modifiers: =, ~, ~*, and ^~. These prefixes have the meanings given in Table 3-2.

Table 3-2. *Location Modifiers*

Modifier	Meaning
~*	Case insensitive search. Ideal for most cases.
~	Case sensitive search.
^~	Do not check any regular expressions if the matching prefix location has ^~
=	Directs Nginx to do an exact match of URI and location. It is a good idea to provide exact matches for every URL that is frequently used so that Nginx doesn't need to do a search.

It is very crucial that you follow along in this section. The more you play with the configuration the better you will be able to handle it. Location directive happens to be one of the most important configurations in Nginx and it is extremely important that you master it.

LOCATION CONFIGURATION

Prepare Server with some files

In your */etc/nginx/html* create a folder called *common* and a file called *common/index.html.* Before you proceed, please ensure that you have the following structure. If there is a file missing, simply create that and key in some text so that you can identify the file. For the png files, you can download a couple of png files from the Internet and save it inside the common folder.

```
html
|-- 50x.html
|-- app1
|   `-- index.html
|-- app2
|   |-- home.html
|   `-- index.html
|-- common
|   |-- app.js
|   |-- index.html
|   |-- nginx.png
|   `-- nginx.PNG
`-- index.html
```

■ **Tip**   You can use `wget http://image_url` command to download any image from the Internet using a command line.

Load different configuration based on location directive

- Replace the content of the file you created earlier */etc/nginx/conf.d/virtual_server.conf* with the following:

```
server {
        listen 80;
        server_name 127.0.0.1 localhost;

        location /app1/ {
                root /etc/nginx/html;
                index index.html;
        }

        location /app2/ {
                root /etc/nginx/html;
                index home.html;
        }
}
```

- Execute `nginx -s reload` and try accessing the pages:

  - lynx http://localhost/app1 > Should work and you will see index.html

  - `lynx http://localhost/app2` > Should work and you will see home.html

- As you can see, different sections and configurations can be loaded based on your configuration. You will also notice that there are certain elements that are repeated and have the same value, like `root` attribute. Since the `root` directory is allowed in server context, you can restructure your configuration like the following:

```
server {
        listen 80;
        server_name 127.0.0.1 localhost;
        root /etc/nginx/html;

        location /app1/ {
                index index.html;
        }

        location /app2/ {
                index home.html;
        }
}
```

Handling Common Files using pattern matching

- Assume that the common folder contains a lot of assets that are common to both applications. Also assume that the files don't need to be changed often. In that case, you may decide to change the configuration for this section such that the file is cached at the client side for a much longer duration using certain directives.

- Modify your configuration file so that you have two additional location tags as follows. Notice the subtle prefixes. The first location block contains ~ prefix and matches the URIs that have png, jpg, or jpeg. If it matches, it adds an expires directive. In the second location block, the expires directive is set to 10 days. The expires directive adds some special headers to the files so that the browser caches it and serves it from the local cache. Expires max will set the value to Thu, 31 Dec 2037 23:55:55 GMT.

```
server {
      listen 80;
      server_name 127.0.0.1 localhost;
      root /etc/nginx/html;

      location ~ \.(png|jpg|jpeg)$ {
            expires max;
      }

      location ~* \.(png|jpg|jpeg)$ {
            expires 10d;
      }
}
```

- Once you have reloaded the configuration access the files: `http://localhost/common/nginx.png` & `http://localhost/common/nginx.PNG`

- Look at Figures 3-3 and 3-4 and notice how the headers got added.

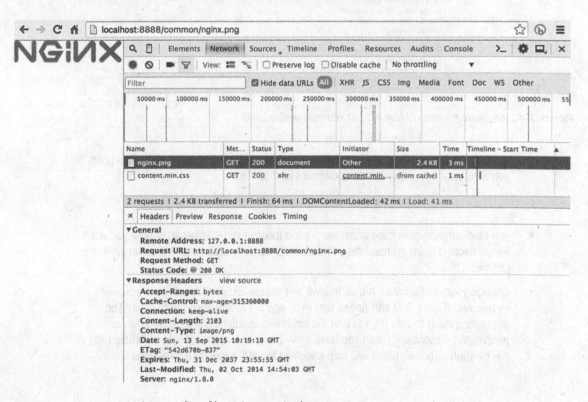

Figure 3-3. *Response for http://localhost/common/nginx.png*

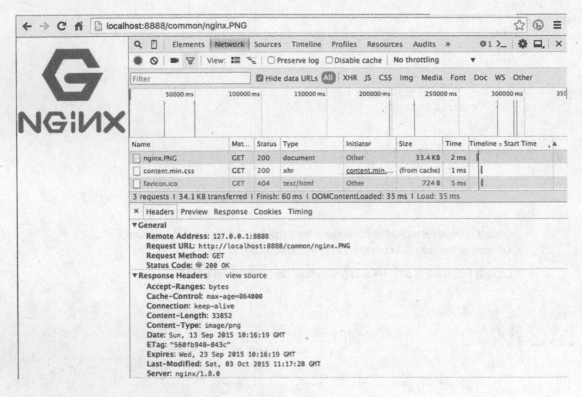

Figure 3-4. Response for http://localhost/common/nginx.PNG

- Notice how the headers have been added based on different location URIs. This gives you a very robust way of handling different kind of files.

Avoid Regular Expression Matching

- You have already seen case sensitive (~) and insensitive (~*) search. What if you would like to avoid regular expressions completely for some unique cases? You can prefix the URI with (^~).

- Change your configuration file as follows and access http://localhost/common/ nginx.PNG (Figure 3-5) and notice that max-age = 172800 seconds (2 days). The interesting thing to note here is that the other two locations still exist and they are unchanged. Essentially, when you have a ^~ prefix before the longest matching URIs in the location directive, Nginx will skip checking the other regular expressions.

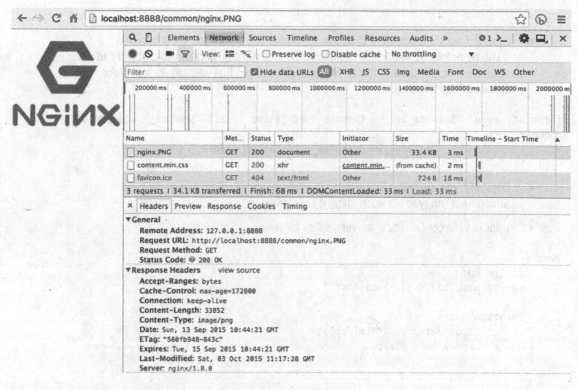

Figure 3-5. Response for `http://localhost/common/nginx.PNG`

```
server {
        listen 80;
        server_name 127.0.0.1 localhost;
        root /etc/nginx/html;

        location ^~ /common/nginx.PNG {
                expires 2d;
        }

        location ~ \.(png|jpg|jpeg)$ {
                expires max;
        }

        location ~* \.(png|jpg|jpeg)$ {
                expires 10d;
        }
}
```

Exact modifier

- Last, but not the least, there is an Exact modifier (=). Before you see it in action, it will be helpful to take a little detour and change the configuration so that you can visualize it easily. Update your */etc/nginx/nginx.conf* so that your log_format looks similar to the following:

```
log_format  main  '$remote_addr - $remote_user [$time_local] "$document_root$document_uri"
"$request"'
                  '$status $body_bytes_sent "$http_referer"';
```

- Basically, you are telling Nginx to log the information like $document_root and $document_uri (you will learn about it in detail later).

- Update your conf.d/virtual_server.conf as follows:

```
server {
        listen 80;
        server_name 127.0.0.1 localhost;

        location = / {
                root /etc/nginx/html/app2;
                index home.html;
        }
}
```

- Reload your configuration using `nginx -s reload`.

- In this block you are telling Nginx that *http://localhost* implies that it should consider */etc/nginx/html/app2* as the root path and *home.html* as its default page.

- Try executing *curl http://localhost* and you will be surprised to find a 404! Why?

- Take a look at the access log using `tail /var/log/nginx/access.log`

```
"/etc/nginx/html/home.html" "GET / HTTP/1.1"404 168 "-"
```

- Notice that it is not pointing to /etc/nginx/html/app2/home.html. Instead! Does it mean that Nginx didn't catch the location directive? Of course not, it did catch it, but it did an internal redirect to the / page and since there was no location defined, it failed with a 404. To fix this, change the configuration as follows and retry:

```
server {
        listen 80;
        server_name 127.0.0.1 localhost;

        location = / {
                root /etc/nginx/html/app2;
                index home.html;
        }
```

```
    location / {
            root /etc/nginx/html/app2;
    }
}
```

- In other words, the exact modifier will speed up your processing even more, since Nginx will not need to parse other regular expressions. It will terminate its search as soon as it finds an exact match and does an internal redirect to the page that you are looking for!

Location Context Special Cases

You have already seen an interesting internal redirection case using index directive. As discussed earlier, there are two location blocks in play at tandem, and that is what makes it interesting and confusing at times. There are other directives as well that cause some special redirections.

try_files

This directive checks if the file exists in a specified order. If it finds a file among a predefined list, it is processed and the files next in the list are ignored. If you would like to check a directory, you need to suffix a slash (/) at the end of the name. If none of the files are found, an internal redirect happens as per the last parameter in the list. try_files directive allows you to get rid of if directive since you no longer have to check if the file exists or not. if directive is extremely inefficient since it is evaluated every time for every request. A good rule of thumb is to avoid if directive completely (you will learn more about if directive in coming chapters).

An example should clarify this. Take a look at the configuration and notice that the root is set to */etc/nginx/html*. The two location blocks are pretty similar to each other. Both of them are applying similar rules to jpg, jpeg, and png files. The only difference is that the second location block has a try_files block while the first one doesn't. The try_files directive is set such that it will look for the file ($uri), and if it doesn't find the file, it looks for the folder called ($uri/). If it doesn't find the folder either, it returns */nginx.png* from the root that is defined in this location context (*/etc/nginx/html/common*).

```
server {
        listen 80;
        server_name 127.0.0.1 localhost;
        root /etc/nginx/html;

        location ~* \.(jpg|jpeg)$ {
                root /etc/nginx/html/common;
        }

        location ~* \.(png)$ {
                root /etc/nginx/html/common;
                try_files $uri $uri/ /nginx.png;
        }
}
```

This implies that if you browse:

http://localhost/common/nginx.png > It will work.

http://localhost/common/file.png > Returns *nginx.png* since file.png doesn't exist.

http://localhost/nginx.PNG > It will work and return the actual nginx.PNG file since it exists.

http://localhost/nginx.png > It will work too!

http://localhost/non_existent.png > It will return the fallback image file /*nginx.png*.

http://localhost/non_existent.jpg > ERROR! 404, since there are no files to try!

http://localhost/existingfile.jpg > Works if you have the file in the defined root folder.

If you replace the line below,

```
try_files $uri $uri/ /nginx.png;
```

with

```
try_files $uri $uri/ /nginx.png =404;
```

it will mean that if the fallback file (/nginx.png) doesn't exist, Nginx will return a 404 code.

There is yet another interesting thing you can do with try_files! You can give it a named location and have it handled in a different location block altogether.

```
location ~* \.(png)$ {
        root /etc/nginx/html/common;
        try_files $uri $uri/ /nginx.png @mylocation;
}

location @mylocation{
        ...
        #do something here
        ...
}
```

rewrite

rewrite directive is another very flexible directive. It takes regex as an input and redirects (or terminates if needed) the requests. It supports four flag parameters:

- last - Stops the current processing and starts a search for a new location matching the changed URI.

- break -Stops processing using break directive.

- redirect - A temporary redirection using status code 302.

- permanent - A permanent redirection using status code 301.

The bigger question is this: why would you redirect your traffic?

A small but clichéd answer is this: change is the only constant. Sometimes, even after a lot of planning the content location changes due to myriad reasons like change in framework, reorganization of assets, back-end change, etc. In these cases, the rewrite directive comes in really handy. Imagine that the folder structure you have been working with has changed, and *common* is now called *vendor_assets*.

```
server {
      listen 80;
      server_name 127.0.0.1 localhost;
      root /etc/nginx/html;

      location /common/ {
              rewrite ^(/common/)(.*) /vendor_assets/$2 last;
      }
}
```

Writing good Perl regular expressions is beyond the scope of this book, but basically what is happening in the rewrite directive above is no rocket science. Parenthesis implies groups and it gets extracted in variables like $1, $2, and so on. In the group, the expression says to extract everything that starts with / common/ into a group ($1) and everything after that (.*) in another variable $2. This regular expression is now replaced with a constructed string, /vendor_assets/$2 (where $2 implies the rest of the URI originally sent to the server). The attribute last, as discussed earlier, tells Nginx to stop processing the current request and start a new search for this new location.

In short, it tells Nginx to redirect the current URL *http://localhost/common/nginx.png* to a new url *http://localhost/vendor_assets/nginx.png*.

error_page

error_page directive is a another straightforward directive that helps Nginx to return a specific error page using internal redirect. You can customize your error pages to your liking and make it more meaningful for the end users. It can be used inside http, server, location, and if blocks.

```
error_page 404        /404_not_found.html;        #Applies to status code 404.
error_page 500 502 503 504 /50x_server_error.html; #Applies to status code 500, 502, 503 & 504.
error_page 404        =200    /funnypic.png;        #Instead of sending 404, it will send a png
with status code 200.
```

An error_page block like the following can be used to handle the errors in an elegant way. As you can see, an exact modifier is used for 50x.html so that no other location expressions are evaluated in case of errors.

```
error_page   500 502 503 504   /50x.html;
    location = /50x.html {
        root   /usr/share/nginx/html;
    }
```

Verify the Correctness of Configuration

When you make changes to the configuration file, it is a good idea to check if the configuration file has any issues. You can execute the following command to check it. The -t switch tells Nginx to test the configuration without loading it and -c is the path of the configuration that has to be checked.

A success looks like this:

```
nginx -t -c /etc/nginx/nginx.conf
nginx: the configuration file /etc/nginx/nginx.conf syntax is ok
nginx: configuration file /etc/nginx/nginx.conf test is successful
```

In case of failure, it points you to the precise line where there is an issue:

```
[root@wsfe1 ~]# nginx -t -c /etc/nginx/nginx.conf
nginx: [emerg] unknown directive "xx_junk_directive" in
/etc/nginx/conf.d/virtual_server.conf:8
nginx: configuration file /etc/nginx/nginx.conf
```

Allow Directory Listing

Athough it is not considered a good idea to allow listing of a directory, at times it is required to enable directory listing of specific areas of your website. Nginx has directory listing disabled by default, and to enable it you will need to use autoindex directive. This is how you can use it:

```
server {
        listen 80;
        server_name 127.0.0.1 localhost;
        root /etc/nginx/html;

        location /common/ {
                root /etc/nginx/html;
                index NON_EXISTENT_FILE;
                autoindex on;
        }
}
```

If you recall, the directory structure for *common* has *index.html* file existing already. If you access *http://localhost/common* now, it will show you the index file instead. To enure that you see a directory listing, set the index directive so that the file that doesn't exist. If Nginx finds there are no index files, and autoindex is turned on, it will automatically generate a page for you showing the directory listing as can be seen in Figure 3-6.

```
←  →  C  ⌂  [ ] localhost:8888/common/                           ☆  ⓑ  ≡
```

Index of /common/

```
../
app.js                              13-Sep-2015 04:42              22
index.html                          13-Sep-2015 04:30              18
nginx.PNG                           03-Oct-2015 11:17           33852
nginx.png                           02-Oct-2014 14:54            2103
```

Figure 3-6. Directory listing of a folder in Nginx

Deny Access to Any Specific Location

A common request for a web server is to block access to specific folders for authorization or stopping the configuration file from being downloaded, etc. As you can guess, this is fairly easy to do as well.

```
server {
        listen 80;
        server_name 127.0.0.1 localhost;
        root /etc/nginx/html;

        location /vendor_assets/ {
                deny all;
        }
}
```

If you try to accees *http://localhost/vendor_assets/* now, you will get a 403 forbidden message from Nginx.

Proxy the Requests to Apache

You will learn about proxying in detail in the coming chapters. For now, you can simply take a quick look at the configuration file (conf.d/default.conf) that has been renamed earlier to conf.d/default.backup.

Assume that you want to use Apache for listening to PHP requests, you can use the following block for location so that the requests for *.php will get proxied to Apache:

```
# proxy the PHP scripts to Apache listening on 127.0.0.1:80
#
location ~ \.php$ {
    proxy_pass    http://127.0.0.1;
}
```

Proxy the Requests to FastCGI

For the reasons similar to the previous section, you can choose to redirect the traffic using the following to FastCGI listening on a different port.

```
# pass the PHP scripts to FastCGI server listening on 127.0.0.1:9000
```

```
#
location ~ \.php$ {
    root           html;
    fastcgi_pass   127.0.0.1:9000;
    fastcgi_index  index.php;
    fastcgi_param  SCRIPT_FILENAME  /scripts$fastcgi_script_name;
    include        fastcgi_params;
}
```

Nginx Variables

Nginx has a concept of variables that comes in quite handy at times. You have already seen a few predefined variables like $document_root and $document_uri in action.

Even though they look very convenient, it should be used sparingly. The reason is that they get evaluated at runtime. In other words, every request where you encounter a variable will be evaluated at runtime taking extra CPU cycles! As you can guess, if you are using too many variables, it can toll on the server. Don't use variables as template macros. Think about using an include directive instead whereever you can. With that little bit of caution, lets take a look at a practical situation where variables can help you.

- Open your */etc/nginx/nginx.conf* and change the log_format to a string like this:

```
log_format  main  '$remote_addr - $remote_user [$time_local] "$request" '
                  '$status $body_bytes_sent "$http_referer"';
```

- Reload your configuration, and make a request using curl http://localhost/
- Take a look at your access.log using tail command.
- tail */var/log/nginx/access.log*

```
127.0.0.1 - - [14/Sep/2015:06:18:22 -0400] "GET / HTTP/1.1" 200 23 "-"
```

- The log is helpful, but can you tell where exactly it is serving the file from?
- While configuring the Nginx server, it makes sense to extend the logging so that it logs a little more information. This way, you can check your path and troubleshoot your location expressions quite easily.
- Open your nginx.conf again, and change the log_format so that it contains a couple of extra variables, like this:

```
log_format  main  '$remote_addr - $remote_user [$time_local] "$document_root$document_uri"'
                  '"$request" $status $body_bytes_sent "$http_referer"';
```

- Reload your configuration, make a new request, and check your acess logs using tail again. Notice the presense of the document path and file name. You can clearly see where the page is being served from!

```
127.0.0.1 - - [14/Sep/2015:06:25:48 -0400] "/home/nginx_new_home/index.html""GET / HTTP/1.1"
200 23 "-"
```

Make sure that you remove these variables once your troubleshooting is done. There is more to variables than what you have seen just now and we will cover that in appropriate chapters.

A Quick Note about Nginx Official Documentation

Nginx is pretty well documented, and there are a couple of links you should keep handy. We have made conscious efforts of not replicating what can be easily found online in the official documentation. The book is written in a conversational tone with practical situations in mind. Here are the links that we just talked about:

- Nginx official documentation page - http://nginx.org/en/docs/

- Alphabetical index of directives - http://nginx.org/en/docs/dirindex.html

- Alphabetical index of variables - http://nginx.org/en/docs/varindex.html

If you go the index of directives, you will see every directive listed there. Take a look at the documentation of gzip, for example, in Figure 3-7.

Syntax: `gzip` on | off;
Default: gzip off;
Context: http, server, location, if in location

Enables or disables gzipping of responses.

Figure 3-7. *Gzip documentation on the official site*

Notice that the first line talks about syntax followed with the default value, and ends with Context where it tells you that you can use gzip in http, server, location, and if blocks! Once you understand the meaning of directives, context, and Nginx configuration structure, it gets really easy to read through the documentation and find out more about the directives and different variables.

Summary

This chapter has introduced you to configuring Nginx primarily as a web server. You have learned about the modular nature of the configuration files. By now, you should be pretty comfortable with the way the default configuration files have been created for you during installation time. Try reading the */etc/nginx/conf.d/default.backup (or default.conf* if you haven't already renamed it) file and you should be able to grasp everything that's going on there. The core focus of this chapter was to configure Nginx in order to serve static files and give you a decent idea of the jargon used in Nginx.

You have also learned about the routing principles used in Nginx, and how to use different directives in appropriate contexts. You can now configure Nginx for common tasks like serving static files, allowing directory listing, denying access to files/folders, and handling or rewriting requests using location directive.

If you take a look at Nginx documentation now, you should feel right at home since you will be able to decipher the different terminology commonly used in Nginx esoteric circles.

In the next chapter, you will learn about Nginx modules.

CHAPTER 4

■ ■ ■

Nginx Modules

Modules are those little pieces of code that give a specific feature or functionality in Nginx. It is because of these modules that you can identify if Nginx is behaving as a web server, reverse proxy server, or a load balancing server. Hence, it is important to understand what modules are and how they formulate the Nginx HTTP request processing structure.

What Are Modules?

The Oxford dictionary defines a module as "any of a number of distinct but interrelated units from which a program may be built up or into which a complex activity may be analyzed." In simpler words, you can say a module is an independent piece of code that has its own functionality, its own requirement, and its own unique identity that works in conjunction with other pieces of code to build a wholistic structure.

As mentioned earlier, Nginx is modular. It is so much so that right from the initial request, the pieces of code that are executed are all defined in modules. For example, when Nginx is serving you a static index. html file, or when you are requesting for an HTTPS page, or even when your request is proxied to another server, every function is carried out through various modules. These modules are independent packages or software that are included within the "nginx" binary when you compile Nginx. It is a significant difference between Nginx and Apache, since you cannot dynamically add modules in Nginx. You will need to recompile Nginx to load or unload a particular module.

■ **Note** Apache uses the Dynamic Shared Objects (DSO) concept in which you can load or unload modules at runtime after Apache has been compiled. Using DSO, modules are not included in the main Apache (httpd) process; and hence it allows you to dynamically load or unload modules.

Module Installation

After installing Nginx you can verify which modules are installed on your server using the `Nginx -V` command. Below you can see the default installation of different modules on CentOS and Ubuntu Server.

Default Installation

The steps for default installation of Nginx are mentioned in chapter 2's section "Install Nginx Pre-Built Package." The next section covers a list of modules that are included during default installation of Nginx.

© Rahul Soni 2016
R. Soni, *Nginx*, DOI 10.1007/978-1-4842-1656-9_4

On CentOS Server

On CentOS you can see that the installation is a clean installation and there are no third-party modules included by default.

```
$ nginx -V
nginx version: nginx/1.8.0
built by gcc 4.8.2 20140120 (Red Hat 4.8.2-16) (GCC)
built with OpenSSL 1.0.1e-fips 11 Feb 2013
TLS SNI support enabled
configure arguments: --prefix=/etc/nginx --sbin-path=/usr/sbin/nginx
--conf-path=/etc/nginx/nginx.conf --error-log-path=/var/log/nginx/error.log
--http-log-path=/var/log/nginx/access.log --pid-path=/var/run/nginx.pid
--lock-path=/var/run/nginx.lock --http-client-body-temp-path=/var/cache/nginx/client_temp
--http-proxy-temp-path=/var/cache/nginx/proxy_temp
--http-fastcgi-temp-path=/var/cache/nginx/fastcgi_temp
--http-uwsgi-temp-path=/var/cache/nginx/uwsgi_temp
--http-scgi-temp-path=/var/cache/nginx/scgi_temp --user=nginx --group=nginx
--with-http_ssl_module --with-http_realip_module --with-http_addition_module
--with-http_sub_module --with-http_dav_module --with-http_flv_module
--with-http_mp4_module --with-http_gunzip_module --with-http_gzip_static_module
--with-http_random_index_module --with-http_secure_link_module
--with-http_stub_status_module --with-http_auth_request_module --with-mail
--with-mail_ssl_module --with-file-aio --with-ipv6 --with-http_spdy_module
--with-cc-opt='-O2 -g -pipe -Wp,-D_FORTIFY_SOURCE=2 -fexceptions -fstack-protector
--param=ssp-buffer-size=4 -m64 -mtune=generic'
```

On Ubuntu Server

Ubuntu Server includes few third-party modules in the default installation of Nginx:

```
$ nginx -V
nginx version: nginx/1.8.0
built with OpenSSL 1.0.1f 6 Jan 2014
TLS SNI support enabled
configure arguments: --with-cc-opt='-g -O2 -fPIE -fstack-protector
--param=ssp-buffer-size=4 -Wformat -Werror=format-security -D_FORTIFY_SOURCE=2'
--with-ld-opt='-Wl,-Bsymbolic-functions -fPIE -pie -Wl,-z,relro -Wl,-z,now'
--prefix=/usr/share/nginx --conf-path=/etc/nginx/nginx.conf
--http-log-path=/var/log/nginx/access.log --error-log-path=/var/log/nginx/error.log
--lock-path=/var/lock/nginx.lock --pid-path=/run/nginx.pid
--http-client-body-temp-path=/var/lib/nginx/body
--http-fastcgi-temp-path=/var/lib/nginx/fastcgi
--http-proxy-temp-path=/var/lib/nginx/proxy --http-scgi-temp-path=/var/lib/nginx/scgi
--http-uwsgi-temp-path=/var/lib/nginx/uwsgi --with-debug --with-pcre-jit --with-ipv6
--with-http_ssl_module --with-http_stub_status_module --with-http_realip_module
--with-http_auth_request_module --with-http_addition_module --with-http_dav_module
--with-http_geoip_module --with-http_gunzip_module --with-http_gzip_static_module
--with-http_image_filter_module --with-http_spdy_module --with-http_sub_module
--with-http_xslt_module --with-mail --with-mail_ssl_module
--add-module=/build/buildd/nginx-1.8.0/debian/modules/nginx-auth-pam
```

```
--add-module=/build/buildd/nginx-1.8.0/debian/modules/nginx-dav-ext-module
--add-module=/build/buildd/nginx-1.8.0/debian/modules/nginx-echo
--add-module=/build/buildd/nginx-1.8.0/debian/modules/nginx-upstream-fair
--add-module=/build/buildd/nginx-1.8.0/debian/modules/ngx_http_substitutions_filter_module
```

Module Categories

Nginx modules can be split into five different catagories based on their functionality. When you build Nginx binary, the Core and Event modules are included by default. The HTTP, Mail, and Stream modules enable Web Server, Mail Proxy, and Reverse Proxy or Load Balancer functionality repectively into Nginx.

Out-of-Box Modules

Nginx source has some modules that are included by default and they can be enabled or disabled during compile time using --with or --without options. The core modules cannot be disabled; they are the required components of Nginx. You can modify the rest of the modules depending on your requirement and functionality expected. There are some OOB modules that have dependencies on third-party components like PCRE, OpenSSL that can be included during compile time. Table 4-1 lists all the different categories of modules and the key modules included in the Nginx source.

Table 4-1. *Nginx module types*

Module Types	Module Name	Description
Core	ngx_core_module ngx_error_log_module ngx_conf_module	This includes modules that enable network and application protocols. It includes modules that handle logging, encryption, etc. It includes CPU architecture-specific Nginx configuration, it takes care of CPU affinity, thread pool allocation, memory management api, file and sockets IO, etc.
Event	ngx_events_module ngx_events_core_module	This includes connection processing methods that are event driven. Example connection pooling, etc.
HTTP	ngx_http_module ngx_http_core_module ngx_http_log_module ngx_http_upstream_module	This includes websServer functionality in Nginx and takes care of all HTTP requests.
Mail	ngx_mail_module ngx_mail_core_module	This includes mail proxy modules.
Stream	ngx_stream_module ngx_stream_core_module ngx_stream_proxy_module ngx_stream_upstream_module	This includes modules that enable proxy, load balance functionality in Nginx.

Third-Party Modules

Third-party or external modules extend Nginx functionality. Nginx has over 100 different third-party modules and the list is growing fast. Nginx has a huge and active community that keeps contributing in extending Nginx. You will look at some of the most popular and highly recommended third-party modules later in the chapter.

79

How Does a Module Work?

When you run the ./configure script when compiling Nginx, a list of pointers to the Nginx modules are made available. This list of all modules can be found in the *ngx_modules.c* file in objs directory. It defines the order in which modules are registered: that is, the order in which various handlers are called.

Module Structure

In the simplest form, modules consist of module information, module configuration, handlers, filters, and load balancer functions (refer to Figure 4-1). The module information contains details about the handlers that are provided by the module. The module configuration contains the structure of the module and different commands or directives that are exposed by the module. Handlers consist of the functions that do that actual work on the input and provide the output. Filters contain functions that do different manipulations that are possible on the output of the handler. Load balancer function comes into the picture when different upstream or downstream servers are defined.

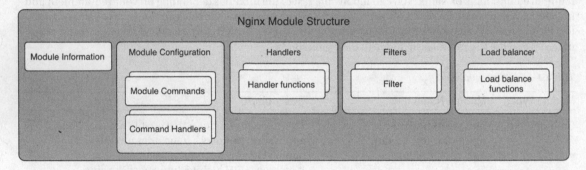

Figure 4-1. Nginx Module Structure

How Modules Fit in Nginx

Here are the steps in which a request is processed in Nginx (Figure 4-2 illustrates this graphically):

1. Start Nginx web server.

2. Nginx *master process* gets initiated.

3. Read *nginx.conf*.

4. Creates *worker process(es), memory allocation,* and other architectural specific configuration as per the CPU architecture.

5. Based on the context like HTTP, MAIL, and STREAM, it creates a list of module handlers and maps them as per their location in the *nginx.conf*.

6. If a request is http://abc.com, the request is processed in http context.

7. It will check for the content module handler need to process the request and the respective handler grabs the request and starts working on it.

8. Once the request is processed, the output is handed over to the filters like gzip, headers, rewrite, etc. The filters will manipulate the output further depending on their order of execution.

9. If there is any load balancer or proxy module, the respective module will further handle the output.

10. Finally, the response is sent over to the client.

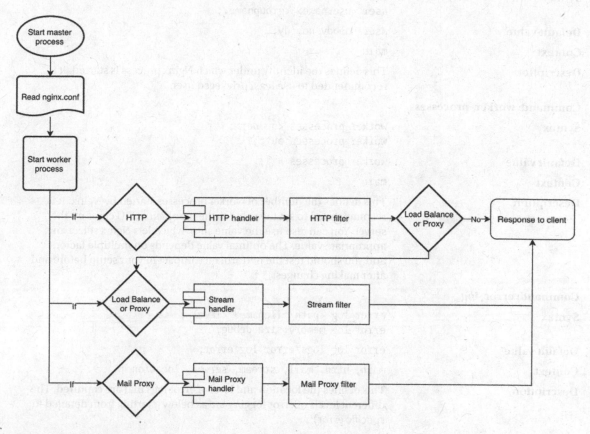

Figure 4-2. *Nginx module process*

Configuring Default Modules for Optimal Performance

Now that you know a bit about the internal working of Nginx, it is important to configure modules such that you get optimum performance from your server. You will see some configuration that helps reduce performance overhead on the web server. You will see some of the core, event, and HTTP modules that are configured on the web servers. Modules are implemented in nginx.conf file in the form of directives or module commands. Some of the directives can be implemented at multiple context and you will find them mentioned along with the commands below.

Core Module

Table 4-2 lists some of the frequently used commands in the core modules. The list describes different directives and its configuration parameter. The list of core modules lies in the main context ahead of event, HTTP, mail, stream, and other context.

Table 4-2. ngx_core_module directives

Command: user	
Syntax	`user <username>;` `user <username> <groupname>;`
Default value	`user nobody nobody;`
Context	`main`
Description	This defines the identify under which Nginx process is started. It is recommended to use least privileged user.

Command: worker_processes	
Syntax	`worker_processes <number>;` `worker_processes auto;`
Default value	`worker_processes = 1;`
Context	`main`
Description	This defines the number of worker processes started by Nginx. It is recommended to set the value to the number of CPU cores on the server. You can also use the value auto, which lets Nginx select an appropriate value. The optimal value depends on multiple factors and you should test the performance impact in your setup before and after making changes.

Command: error_log	
Syntax	`error_log <path/filename> <level>;` `error_log memory:size debug;`
Default value	`error_log logs/error.log error;`
Context	`main, http, mail, stream, server, location`
Description	This defines the location and level of error logs that are captured. The different levels of error logging are as below (starting from detailed to specific error): `debug`: detailed information; used for debugging. `info`: information message, lot of details; not very useful. `notice`: only notices will be logged; not very useful. `warn`: warning messages; indicates some kind of problem. `error`: error logs; errors while serving pages. `crit`: only critical problem that needs attention. `alert`: alert messages of important issues. `emerg`: emergency messages when the system is unstable.

(continued)

Table 4-2. (*continued*)

Command: pid	
Syntax	`pid <path/filename>;`
Default value	`pid logs/nginx.pid;`
Context	`main`
Description	This stores the process ID of the master process. You may think, why save a value of a process identifier in a file?
	It serves multiple purposes, especially signaling that the process has at least started successfully. It is also a cheaper way to poll a file in contrast to getting the output of the `ps -ax	grep` command. However, please be mindful that this approach is not fail-safe. It is possible that the process is dead for long, and the PID file contains stale information.
	In general, the PID files are created by daemons that should only be run once on a system. When the process starts, it also creates the lock file. As long as the lock file exists, it won't start another process. If the lock file exists, but the process id mentioned in the PID file is not running, the daemon can be considered as dead. It may also imply a crash or improper shutdown of the daemon, in which case it might initiate a special startup or restart scenario.
Command: worker_rlimit_nofile	
Syntax	`worker_rlimit_nofile <number>;`
Default value	`none`
Context	`main`
Description	This defines the maximum number of open files for the worker processes. You can increase the limit without restarting the main process.

Events Module

Commands in events context (shown in Table 4-3) determine how Nginx handles connections at a general level. Many times you may not need to configure most of the commands as they are configured by default by Nginx. But you may want to configure a couple of directives for better performance.

Table 4-3. *Event module directives*

Command: worker_connections	
Syntax	worker_connections <number>;
Default value	worker_connections 512;
Context	events
Description	This defines the maximum number of simultaneous connections that can be treated by the worker process. Keep in mind that worker_connections cannot exceed worker_rlimit_nofile if configured.
Command: debug_connections	
Syntax	debug_connections <address>; debug_connections <CIDR>;
Default value	none
Context	events
Description	This defines debug logging for selected client connection. You can specify IPv4 or IPv6 address of a client.

HTTP Module

This context holds configuration parameters for web server that define how Nginx handles HTTP and HTTPS connections (see Table 4-4). This context also includes server context that can occur multiple times as it defines a specific virtual server.

Table 4-4. *HTTP module directives*

Command: include	
Syntax	include <username>; include <mask>;
Default value	none
Context	any
Description	This defines including syntactically correct files or mask. Instead of making a long and cluttered nginx.conf file, you can define a virtual server in a specific configuration file and include them directly in the nginx.conf file. Example: include conf/mime.types; include /etc/nginx/proxy.conf; include vhost/abc.com.conf; include /etc/nginx/vhosts/*.conf;

(continued)

Table 4-4. (*continued*)

Command: default_type

Syntax	`default_type <mime.types>;`
Default value	`default_type text/plain;`
Context	`http, server, location`

Description	This defines the default mime type of a response.
	Example:
	
	`default_type text/plain;`
	`default_type application/octet-stream;`

Command: log_format

Syntax	`log_format <name>;`
Default value	`log_format combined '$body_bytes_sent "$http_referer" "$http_user_agent" $remote_addr $remote_user "$request" $time_local $status';`
Context	`http`

Description	This defines the log format that defines variables that are used only at the time of writing the log. Some of the variables that can be used are as follows:
	
	`$body_bytes_sent`: number of bytes sent to a client as the response body, this does not include response header.
	`$http_referer`: identifies the URL of the page that is requested.
	`$http_user_agent`: identifies the agent or browser that requested the resource.
	`$remote_addr`: IP address of the client making the request.
	`$remote_user`: Username specified if basic authentication is used.
	`$request`: raw HTTP request URL.
	`$time_local`: local server time that served the request.
	`$status`: A numeric value of the HTTP Statuc Code during the response.
	Example:
	
	`log_format combined '$remote_addr - $remote_user [$time_local]`
	`"$request" $status $bytes_sent "$http_referer" "$http_user_agent"`
	`"$gzip_ratio"';`

Command: access_log

Syntax	`access_log <path/filename> [format];` `access_log off;`
Default value	`access_log logs/access.log combined;`
Context	`http, server, location`
Description	This defines the path where logs are captured for the requests that are served by the server. When set to off, no logs are captured. The name combined implies the format of the log to be used while logging. In the log_format section previously mentioned you have seen how the log_format is named as combined with appropriate fields.

(*continued*)

Table 4-4. (*continued*)

Command: sendfile	
Syntax	`sendfile on	off;`
Default value	`sendfile off;`
Context	`http, server, location`
Description	This defines enabling Nginx to send static content directly from the kernel instead of looking for the resource on disk again. This prevents context switching and enabling a speedy delivery of resources. If you are serving static content, enabling this is essential where as if you are using the server as a reverse proxy this setting does not make any sense.
Command: tcp_nopush	
Syntax	`tcp_nopush on	off;`
Default value	`tcp_nopush off;`
Context	`http, server, location`
Description	This enables sending response header and the full file in one packet rather then sending it in chunks. This parameter should be enabled with the `sendfile` option.
Command: tcp_nodelay	
Syntax	`tcp_nodelay on	off;`
Default value	`tcp_nodelay on;`
Context	`http, server, location`
Description	This enables Nginx to send data in chunks, hence avoiding network conjunction. This option is uses `keepalive` option that allows you to send data without initiating a new connection. This option is the exact opposite of `tcp_nopush` option you saw earlier.
Command: keepalive_timeout	
Syntax	`keepalive_timeout <number>;`
Default value	`keepalive_timeout 75s;`
Context	`http, server, location`
Description	This option sets a timeout value for a connection to stay alive. If you set `keepalive_timeout` to `zero` it will disable `keep_alive`.

(*continued*)

Table 4-4. (*continued*)

Command: listen	
Syntax	`listen <address>;` `listen <ip_address>:<port>;`
Default value	`listen *:80;`
Context	`server`

Description	This option sets address, IP address, or port on which the server will accept the request. You can use both IP address and port or port or address (i.e., URL or hostname). If you set a `default_server` with an IP address or address, it will become the default server for the specified address or port.
	Example:
	
	`listen www.abc.com;`
	`listen 127.0.0.1:8080;`
	`listen localhost default_server;`

Command: server_name	

Syntax	`server_name <address>;`
	`server_name *.<address>;`
	`server_name _;`

Default value	`server_name "";`
Context	`server`

Description	This option allows you to set the address using either an exact name or wildcard or a hash table to the listen port. Setting up a hash table enables quick processing of static data like server name, MIME types, request header strings, etc. Hash table uses the ngx_http_map module. Using a wildcard enables having multiple URL's using the same domain name. The catch-all server parameter "_" is used when no valid domain name exists.
	Example:
	
	`server_name www.abc.com one.abc.com;`
	`server_name *.abc.com;`
	`server_name _;`

Command: root	
Syntax	`root <path>;`
Default value	`root html;`
Context	`http, server, location`
Description	This option specifies the root location of the web content.

(*continued*)

Table 4-4. (*continued*)

Command: error_page

Syntax	`error_page code uri;`
Default value	`none`
Context	`http, server, location`
Description	This option allows you to set the URI for a specific error. Example:

```
error_page 403 www.abc.com/forbidden.html;
error_page 500 501 502 /50x.html;
```

Command: try_files

Syntax	`try_files file uri;`
Default value	`none`
Context	`server, location`
Description	This option tries to look for the existence of the file specified order or looks at the literal path you specified in the root directive and sets the internal file pointer. In the below example, when a request is made a `try_files` directive will look for index.html, index.php in the /website/root_directory. If it fails to find it, it will look into the `$document_root` directory specified at the root directive and serve the request. Example:

```
try_files /website/root_directory/ $uri;
```

Enabling Optional Modules

There are number of other modules that can be enabled and they have their own directives. You will see in this section how to enable gzip, FastCGI, and Basic Auth directives. These are optional and need not exist on all servers.

Gzip Module

The gzip modules help in compressing the responses. Table 4-5 lists the directives.

Table 4-5. *Gzip directives*

Command: gzip

Syntax	`gzip on	off;`
Default value	`gzip off;`
Context	HTTP, server, location
Description	This defines if Nginx will compress the responses.

(*continued*)

Table 4-5. (*continued*)

Command: gzip_comp_level	
Syntax	gzip_comp_level <level>;
Default value	gzip_comp_level 1;
Context	HTTP, server, location
Description	This defines how compressed the response should be on a scale of 1 to 9 where 9 is the most compressed. The higher the compression level the longer it takes to compress and decompress the data. Setting a higher compression level can actually result in slow performance on a website with high volume.
Command: gzip_types	
Syntax	gzip_types <mime.type>;
Default value	gzip_types text/html;
Context	HTTP, server, location
Description	This option enables compressing content with the specified mime type. It is very helpful to filter down the type of files that should be compressed. For example, it makes a lot of sense to compress files that are of type text (like JavaScript, CSS, html, etc.), but it doesn't usually help compressing a JPG or MPEG file. On the contrary, trying to compress an already compressed file ends up wasting CPU cycles, and often results in poor performance of a web server.

FastCGI Module

This module allows passing the requests to a FastCGI server for further processing. Table 4-6 shows the basic semantics of this directive.

Table 4-6. *FastCGI directives*

Command: fastcgi_pass	
Syntax	`fastcgi_pass <address>;`
Default value	`none`
Context	`location`
Description	This option enables address of FastCGI server. The address can be a URI or Unix socket. Nginx is not capable of handling CGI requests itself, so it hands it over to components that are better suited for the job. Typically, a web application like WordPress that uses PHP is configured using fastcgi. Example: `fastcgi_pass http://localhost:9000;` `fastcgi_pass unix:/fastcgi.socket;`

(*continued*)

Table 4-6. (*continued*)

Command: fastcgi_index	
Syntax	`fastcgi_index <name>;`
Default value	none
Context	`http, server, location`
Description	This option sets a file name that will be appended after a URI.
	Example:
	`fastcgi_index index.php;`

Command: fastcgi_split_path_info	
Syntax	`fastcgi_split_path_info <regex>;`
Default value	none
Context	`location`
Description	This option defines a regular expression that captures a value of the FastCGI path.
	Example:
	`fastcgi_split_path_info ^(.+\.php)(/.+)$;`

Command: fastcgi_param	
Syntax	`fastcgi_param <parameter> <value>;`
Default value	none
Context	`location`
Description	This option sets a parameter that should be passed to the FastCGI server. The value can contain text, variables, and other combinations.
	Example:
	`fastcgi_param SCRIPT_FILENAME $document_root$fastcgi_script_name;`

Basic Authentication

This directive enables authentication by the web server using the basic authentication technique, which is a cleartext (Base 64 encoded) way of authenticating a client. Table 4-7 shows the details.

Table 4-7. *Basic Authentication directives*

Command: auth_basic	
Syntax	`auth_basic <string>	off;`
Default value	`auth_basic off;`
Context	`http, server, location`
Description	This enables validation of users' credentials using basic authentication protocol. When set to off, your website will be accessible to everyone without any authentication taking place.

Command: auth_basic_user_file	
Syntax	`auth_basic_user_file <file>;`
Default value	none
Context	`http, server, location`
Description	This option uses a file that will keep username and password of the users that will be allowed access to website with basic auth enabled.
	The file should be in the following format:
	`username1:password1`
	`username2:password2:comment`
	`username3:password3`

Enabling Third-Party Modules

There are various sources on the Internet from where you can to get third-party Nginx modules. You can look for modules at the official Nginx website `https://www.nginx.com/resources/wiki/modules/`. Extending your server purely depends on the kind of services you are expecting off your Nginx server. There is no recommended or standard process you need to follow to install modules and use them. You will find most of the modules include README file that will guide you on the steps required to install the module.

Before you extend Nginx with any third-party module, you need to know about its dependencies. You will see an example of installing and implementing PAM Authentication Module on the server. The idea here is to show how you can identify and address dependencies of a module.

PAM Authentication

Let's assume that `Basic Authentication` module doesn't suit your requirement as well as you would have liked, and you want something more robust.

In such scenarios, it would be a pain to develop a module of your own. Thankfully, there is a module that is a great alternative for implementing a flexible authentication mechanism on your website. PAM is used for implementing various authentication methods like User, LDAP, SQL, and SSO-based authentication. You will see how to implement PAM Auth for non-root users on the server.

Compiling the Module with Nginx

Here are the steps you need to follow:

1. Begin by downloading the module from the author's Github repository. Download the latest version of the module; as of this writing the module version is 1.4.

```
# wget https://github.com/stogh/ngx_http_auth_pam_module/archive/v1.4.tar.gz
```

2. Extract the files:

```
# tar xzvf v1.4.tar.gz
ngx_http_auth_pam_module-1.4/
ngx_http_auth_pam_module-1.4/ChangeLog
ngx_http_auth_pam_module-1.4/LICENSE
ngx_http_auth_pam_module-1.4/README.md
ngx_http_auth_pam_module-1.4/config
ngx_http_auth_pam_module-1.4/ngx_http_auth_pam_module.c
```

As you can see, the module contains a README.md file that contains all the instruction for installing and configuring the module. The only file that is the core of the module is the C source file (ngx_http_auth_pam_module.c).

3. Open the scripted file that we used in chapter 2 and add the lines below at the bottom of the file.

```
--add-module=/home/username/ngx_http_auth_pam_module-1.4
```

4. Execute the file using ./scripted command.

5. The configure output will have an output like shown below:

```
...
configuring additional modules
adding module in /home/username/ngx_http_auth_pam_module-1.4
 + ngx_http_auth_pam_module was configured
...
```

6. Run the make command.

Below is an example of missing dependency while actual compiling the module. In this case, your server is missing the PAM development package on the server:

```
/home/username/ngx_http_auth_pam_module-1.4/ngx_http_auth_pam_module.c:13:31: fatal error:
security/pam_appl.h: No such file or directory
 #include <security/pam_appl.h>
                               ^
compilation terminated.
make[1]: *** [objs/addon/ngx_http_auth_pam_module-1.4/ngx_http_auth_pam_module.o] Error 1
make[1]: Leaving directory `/home/username/nginx-1.8.0'
make: *** [build] Error 2
```

7. To eliminate the error, you will need to install PAM module on Ubuntu Server; here is the command

```
sudo apt-get install libpam-dev (or yum install pam-devel on CentOS)
```

8. Run make command. This time the module is able to find the required component on the server and compilation is successful.

9. Run the sudo make install command.

10. Just to be sure, restart Nginx service and ensure the website is working as expected:

```
# service nginx start
```

Verifying Installation

Once you are done installing Nginx, you can verify the module installation. This shows you all the modules that are included during your scripted installation:

```
nginx version: nginx/1.8.0
built by gcc 4.8.4 (Ubuntu 4.8.4-2ubuntu1~14.04)
built with OpenSSL 1.0.1f 6 Jan 2014
TLS SNI support enabled
configure arguments: --prefix=/etc/nginx --sbin-path=/usr/sbin/nginx
--conf-path=/etc/nginx/nginx.conf --pid-path=/var/run/nginx.pid
--lock-path=/var/run/nginx.lock --error-log-path=/var/log/nginx/error.log
--http-log-path=/var/log/nginx/access.log
--http-client-body-temp-path=/var/cache/client_body_temp
--http-fastcgi-temp-path=/var/cache/fastcgi_temp
--with-http_gzip_static_module --with-http_stub_status_module --with-http_ssl_module
--with-pcre --with-file-aio --with-http_realip_module --without-http_scgi_module
--without-http_uwsgi_module --without-http_proxy_module --user=nginx --group=nginx
--add-module=/home/johndoe/ngx_http_auth_pam_module-1.4
```

Implementing the Module in Nginx

Now that the module is compiled in, follow these steps to configure it:

1. PAM includes two directives auth_pam and auth_pam_service_name. To implement PAM Auth with Nginx you will need to edit the nginx.conf file. You can insert the below two lines under the location directive as shown below:

```
location / {
    root    html;
    index   index.html index.htm;
    auth_pam        "Authentication Required...";
    auth_pam_service_name "nginx";
```

2. You will need to reload nginx configuration after the changes are saved:

```
sudo nginx -s reload
```

3. PAM uses `pam_unix.so` file for authentication and will be authenticating local users on the server. You need to ensure the Nginx worker process has read access to the `/etc/shadow` file. You can achieve this by adding the account to the "shadow" group, which is the default group for `/etc/shadow` file. The command to achieve the same is below:

```
sudo usermod -a -G shadow nginx
```

Validating the Module

You are almost set. To validate, do what follows:

1. You can now validate if the module is able to authenticate the user. You can use a Chrome extension called Postman.

2. Figure 4-3 shows request status without entering any credentials.

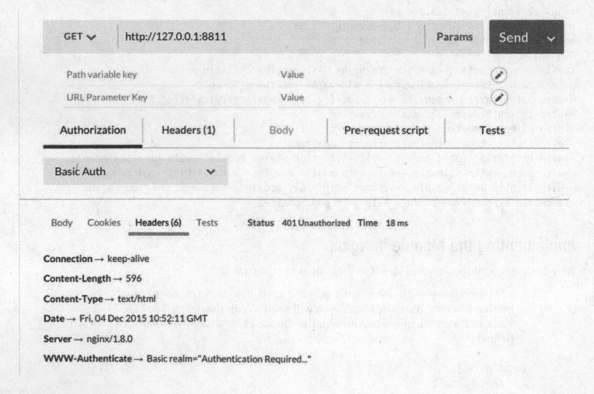

Figure 4-3. *Nginx requesting valid credentials*

3. Now, after you enter a valid username and credential, as shown in Figure 4-4, the request is processed successfully.

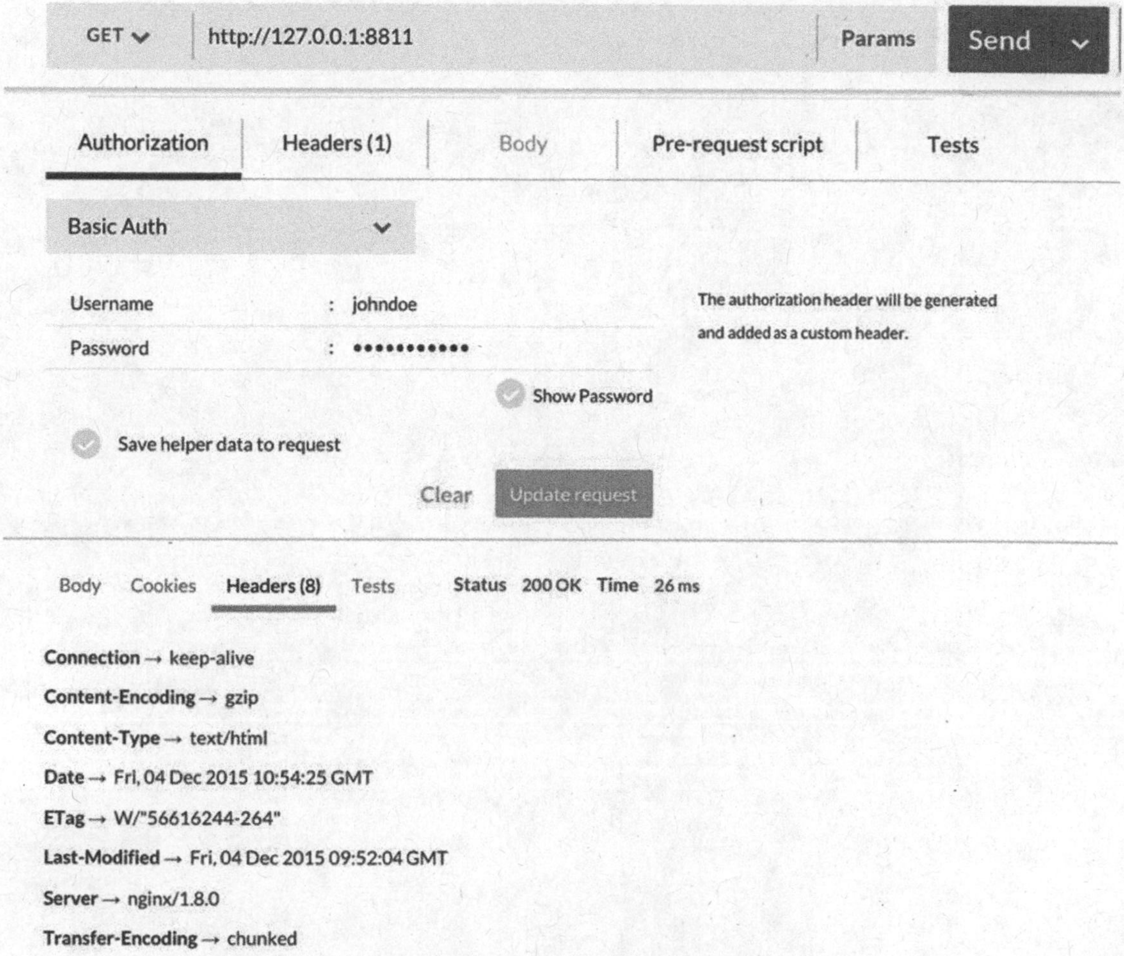

GET ⌄	http://127.0.0.1:8811		Params	Send ⌄

Authorization	Headers (1)	Body	Pre-request script	Tests

Basic Auth ⌄

Username   : johndoe

Password   : ••••••••••••

The authorization header will be generated
and added as a custom header.

✓ Show Password

✓ Save helper data to request

Clear   Update request

Body   Cookies   **Headers (8)**   Tests   Status **200 OK**   Time **26 ms**

Connection → keep-alive

Content-Encoding → gzip

Content-Type → text/html

Date → Fri, 04 Dec 2015 10:54:25 GMT

ETag → W/"56616244-264"

Last-Modified → Fri, 04 Dec 2015 09:52:04 GMT

Server → nginx/1.8.0

Transfer-Encoding → chunked

Figure 4-4. Nginx processes the request with valid credentials

---

■ **Note**   In CentOS 7 "**shadow**" group is missing and for security reasons /etc/shadow file does not have access to anybody except **root**. It is recommended that you do not fiddle around with "**shadow**" file. It is a very sensitive file and has passwords of local users, which are stored in encrypted format.

Summary

In this chapter you have learned about the modules in Nginx and how they define the core purpose of the web server. You should now be comfortable with setting up your server with custom modules based on your needs. You have also learned about the different categories of modules, and how it gets hooked in the request processing pipeline.

Nginx has good support for pluggable modules, and it is in your best interest to check them out regularly so that you don't end up reinventing the wheel by creating something that is is already present.

CHAPTER 5

∎∎∎

Nginx Core Architecture

Nginx was designed to get a very high throughput from your server, and the man behind the software was an exceptionally smart engineer, Igor Sysoev. Nginx solved a lot of performance problems in a very unique way because of the way it was architected. In this chapter, you will learn about the architecture in detail and how Nginx is able to work as well under the hood.

I will start with an analogy so that it is easier to understand and remember why things work the way they do, and how Nginx is different from other web servers.

A Quick Analogy

Question: What do powerful people want in general? *Answer*: More power!

Now, imagine yourself managing a very busy restaurant. You are famous and attract a huge number of guests. What will you want? If you said more guests, you are on the right track and your business will grow. However, relocating your restaurant is not an option, and your motto is to serve as many guests as possible without any deterioration in service.

Problem 1: Your restaurant has 100 seats and there is a gatekeeper that allows people to come and sit on a first-come first-serve basis. They order food and wait. Can it be handled better?

Problem 2: You have discovered that almost every guest who comes looks for water. Would you rather have one guy taking care of all water requirements (and also serve a welcome drink), or will you ask every waiter to take care of his own clients?

Problem 3: Your chef might be able to context switch in order to prepare different food for different people. But what if there was just one burner in your stove? As you can guess, he will now have to load/unload the utensils from the burner in order to get more done. And if he tries to cook way too many recipes at the same time, he will end up *throttling* and due to the lack of enough burner time, none of the dishes will cook properly.

Problem 4: What if you have a few waiters, but they don't talk to each other very much? Will it make sense that they don't do anything while the chef is actually cooking the dish? "I can't do much..." they say, since "I am *blocked* by the chef"!

Problem 5: What if the number of chefs or waiters you have is inadequate and they are getting burned out due to the never-ending series of requests?

Problem 6: If you have more than, say, 100 guests, the other guests remain outside in a queue and you may lose them to your competition.

Problem 7: Your staff is tired, not performing well, or it just might be an end of a shift. What happens to those customers who were being served by him? It won't be nice if they just pack up their bags when the clock hits 7 p.m. and go home. Right?

Problem 8: There are holidays ahead and you decide to renovate your restaurant. You know that it might take a few days. Will you close it down and lose revenue? What if the clients didn't like the new ambience; will you be willing to revert the renovation?

© Rahul Soni 2016
R. Soni, *Nginx*, DOI 10.1007/978-1-4842-1656-9_5

Managing a good restaurant is not an easy task. Since we don't have much expertise in it, we will not try to solve these problems for them either. Instead, the idea is to compare these problems from a web server perspective. The problems will be fixed in a different order as we go along so that it makes more sense and you can grasp the concepts easily.

The Master Process

Think of the master process as the owner of the restaurant described in the preceding section. The master process of Nginx is the one who performs privileged operations like reading from the configuration files, binding to ports, and spawning child processes when required. The worker processes are almost analogous to waiters in the restaurant. They do the running around and manage the show. Notice that the guests at the restaurant don't come to visit the owner. They are there to have food that the chefs make in the kitchen. The guests don't need to know who does the hard work behind the scenes. The chefs work in a dedicated manner to make the dish, and play a role analogous to slow input/output (I/O) or long-running networking calls in this story.

The worker processes are spawned as soon as the service is restarted, and you can change the number of worker processes inside your configuration file /etc/nginx/nginx.conf by using the worker_processes directive. It defaults to 1. The basic rule of thumb suggests keeping this value equal to the number of cores you have on your server. You can also set this attribute to auto and Nginx will try to auto-detect it. Once it is set, you can save your configuration and reload the configuration using nginx -s reload.

If you execute the following ps command, you will be able to see all your worker processes along with the master process. Notice that the process id (PID) for the master process in the output is 30921. All the child processes have a different PID but the parent process for all of them is 30921.

```
ps -ef --forest | grep nginx
root       30930 13588  0 01:58 pts/1    00:00:00             \_ grep --color=auto nginx
root       30921     1  0 01:58 ?        00:00:00 nginx: master process /usr/sbin/nginx -c /
etc/nginx/nginx.conf
nginx      30922 30921  0 01:58 ?        00:00:00  \_ nginx: worker process
nginx      30923 30921  0 01:58 ?        00:00:00  \_ nginx: cache manager process
nginx      30924 30921  0 01:58 ?        00:00:00  \_ nginx: cache loader process
```

After updating the worker_processes directive to 4 (in nginx.conf file) and reloading the configuration, the output appears as follows. You will notice that the master process didn't recycle since the PID is still 30921. On the contrary, the child processes have been recycled by the master process and all of them now have different PIDs.

```
root       30940 13588  0 02:00 pts/1    00:00:00             \_ grep --color=auto nginx
root       30921     1  0 01:58 ?        00:00:00 nginx: master process /usr/sbin/nginx -c /
etc/nginx/nginx.conf
nginx      30934 30921  0 02:00 ?        00:00:00  \_ nginx: worker process
nginx      30935 30921  0 02:00 ?        00:00:00  \_ nginx: worker process
nginx      30936 30921  0 02:00 ?        00:00:00  \_ nginx: worker process
nginx      30937 30921  0 02:00 ?        00:00:00  \_ nginx: worker process
nginx      30938 30921  0 02:00 ?        00:00:00  \_ nginx: cache manager process
```

The way the master process orchestrates the child worker processes solves *Problem #5*. Just like you would need to hire more chefs to handle more requests simultaneously, you might need to *scale up* and increase the total number of CPUs on your server, and tweak the worker_processes directive appropriately. Another way would be to better the disk or network throughput. Every bit that you can do to make the I/O better will help the overall performance of the web server. I/O happens to be the roadblock mostly, and adding other resources like CPU might not help if the I/O or network itself is slow. Careful analysis of your hardware is paramount!

In Figure 5-1 you will find multiple worker processes running along with the cache manager and cache loader. (You will learn more about caching in coming chapters.) Master Process is a very effective manager. It manages the resources that, in turn, carry on the actual work of serving the client requests.

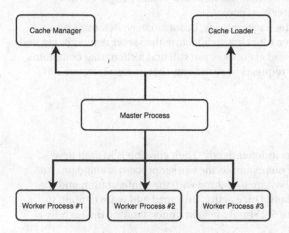

Figure 5-1. *Master Process with its child processes*

This effectively solves *Problem #2* so that dedicated processes execute their own jobs (just like you would ask a dedicated waiter to take care of the water needs in the restaurant!). The *cache loader* and *cache manager* are two dedicated resources that have been given a specific job of managing cache. The loader runs at the startup to load disk-based cache into memory and exits. It is smartly scheduled so that it doesn't consume unnecessary resources.

A cache manager, on the other hand, stays up if you have caching configured. It is in charge of cleaning up the cache files so that the cached files are pruned periodically, and it complies with the configured values. If you have carefully read the outputs mentioned earlier, you might have noticed the presence and absence of the following line in the two outputs. Essentially, the cache loader appeared in the first one, did its job and automatically exited:

```
nginx    30924 30921  0 01:58 ?        00:00:00  \_ nginx: cache loader process
```

Processes vs. Threads

Fundamentally, from the OS perspective, the work is done inside a process using one or many threads. The processes can be considered as a boundary created by the memory space. Threads reside inside a process. They are objects that load the instructions and are scheduled to run on a CPU core. Most server applications run multiple threads or processes in parallel so that they can use the CPU cores effectively. As you can guess, both processes and threads consume resources and having too many of either of them leads to *Problem #3* where the OS does a lot of context switching and starts throttling.

■ **Tip**   Simply bumping up the number of worker processes doesn't help much since you will be simply increasing the number of threads or process without increasing the CPU cores. If you increase the value of worker_processes directive to a large number, you will end up reducing the performance instead! When in doubt, keep the value of number of worker processes equal to the number of CPU cores on your web server.

Software like IIS and Apache use a multithreading approach to handle connections. In simple words, every thread takes care of a connection. As you can easily guess, there will always be a problem when you try to scale for thousands of simultaneous connections. This problem aggravates if the client has a slow connection speed. This situation is analogous to *Problem #1*, and the core issue is that people eat at a different pace and mostly it is slower than the rate a master chef cooks!

In a similar way, a typical web server often creates the pages quickly. Unfortunately, it doesn't have control on the clients' network speed. This means that in a blocking architecture the server resources get tied down because of slow clients. Bring a lot of slow clients, and eventually you will find a client that complains that the server is slow. What an irony! Nginx handles the requests in such a way that its resources are not blocked.

The Worker Process

Each worker process in Nginx is single threaded and runs independently. Their core job is to grab new connections and process them as quickly as possible (in our example, the worker process is analogous to the waiters)! When the worker processes are launched, they are initialized with the configuration and the master process tells them to listen to the configured sockets. Once active, they read and write content to disk, and communicate with the upstream servers. Figure 5-2 should help in understanding the high-level architecture.

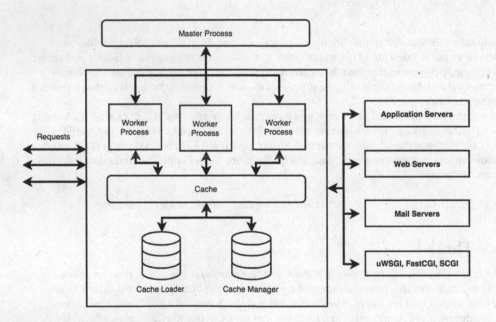

Figure 5-2. *Inside a worker process*

Since they are all forked from the master process, they can use the shared memory for cached data, session persistence data, and other shared resources.

■ **Note** In Windows, a thread is comparatively much lighter than a process. Luckily, this is not the case in Linux. On the contrary, synchronizing shared memory is expensive and Linux developers have managed to find a way to ensure that switching tasks is very fast and cheap. This is important, since in Nginx, they decided not to create multiple threads per process. You can use thread pools in special use cases where you can have multiple threads per process.

With the restaurant analogy, imagine that the waiters are not allowed to sit back and relax while the chefs are cooking the meal. Just like an effective manager would have liked, Nginx follows a callback system. Here the chefs call the waiters back to let them know that the meal is ready! So, basically the order is given to the chef, and the waiter is back in business. He takes orders from other customers, and if possible helps with the takeaway orders as well. This callback method works very well in serving a lot of customers and helps solve Problems #4 and #6.

With an effective worker processes non-blocking callback mechanism in place, the server is able to handle a lot more requests since the worker threads do not get blocked on slow I/O. They are neither waiting on the slow I/O from a back-end application server, nor they are waiting on a slow client!

Technically speaking, there is a run loop and it relies heavily on the idea of asynchronous task handling. It assumes that the tasks will be as non-blocking as possible. Figure 5-3 illustrates a typical run loop. These events can be about sockets being ready for read/write, or other system-related events that happen due to the way Nginx works with the files. Overall, the biggest issue with this approach is the assumption that the calls will be non-blocking, which is easier said than done!

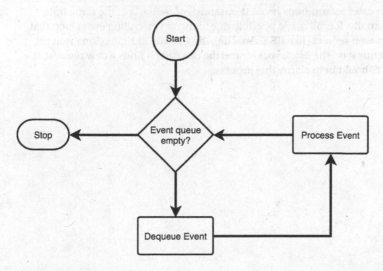

Figure 5-3. *A run loop*

If the call happens to be a blocking type, (for example, fetching a large file from a disk, a CPU-intensive process, or a synchronous database call from a back end, etc.), there is nothing much that the worker process can do during the meantime, except finish the job at hand, and attend to the system queue once done. This happens because of the fact that by default the Nginx worker process has only one thread to take care of the task. To take care of this issue, thread pools have been introduced in the later versions of Nginx (>1.7.11). Using thread pools, this issue is taken care of. For long-running blocking calls, a new thread is spun while the primary thread continues to serve other requests.

Remember that blocking calls are your biggest enemy from a web server administrator perspective. Try to remove the blocking wherever possible. Just because you have an option of thread pool shouldn't imply that you use it. There are places where it makes perfect sense, but careful analysis of the workload is paramount. Blocking has a tendency to degrade the performance in a BIG way!

State Machines

Nginx has different state machines. A state machine is nothing but a set of instructions that tell it how to handle a particular request. A HTTP state machine is the most commonly used, but you also have other state machines for processing streams (TCP traffic), mails (POP3, SMTP, IMAP), and so on.

When incoming requests hit the server, the kernel triggers the events. The worker processes wait for these events on the listen sockets and happily assigns it to an appropriate state machine.

Processing an HTTP request is a complicated process and every web server has a different way of handling its own state machines. With Nginx, the server might have to think whether it has to process the page locally, or send it to the upstream or authentication servers. Third-party modules go one step further by bending or extending these rules.

Primarily, one worker process can cater to hundreds (even thousands!) of requests at the same time even though it has just one thread internally. It is all made possible due to the never-ending event loop that is non-blocking in nature. Unlike other web servers (like IIS & Apache), the threads in Nginx don't wait till the end of the request. It accepts the request on the listen socket, and the moment it finds a new request, it creates a connection socket. Figure 5-4 should help clarify this process.

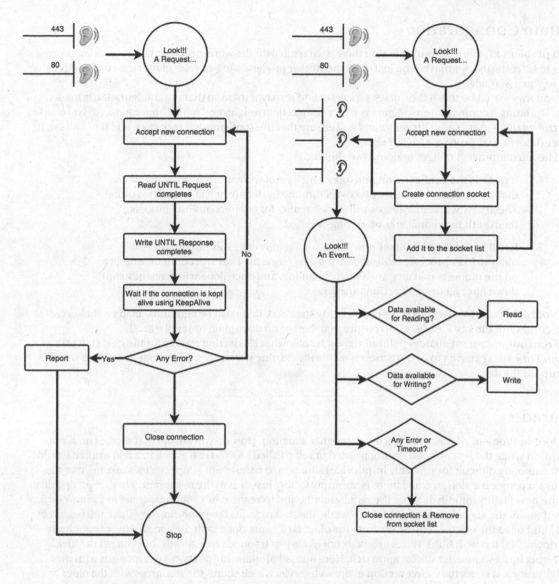

Figure 5-4. *Traditional web server request processing (left) and Nginx (right)*

Notice that in the traditional way (Figure 5-4, left), the threads or worker process is not freed up until the client consumes the data completely. If the connection is made to stay alive by using the keepalive setting, the resources allocated to this thread/process remains alive until the timeout of the connection.

Compare this to Nginx, and you will find that the newly created connection socket keeps listening for the events of the ongoing requests at its own pace. So, the kernel will let Nginx know that the partial data that is sent to the client has been received, and the server can send additional data. This non-blocking event mechanism helps to achieve high scalability on the web server. In the meantime, the listen sockets are free to serve additional requests!

Update Configuration

Recall problem #7. You just found out that there is an issue with the worker process and the worker process needs to be restarted. Or maybe you just want the worker processes to be aware of the new configuration change you just made.

One way would be to kill the worker processes and respawn them so that the configuration is loaded again. Updating a configuration in Nginx is a very simple, lightweight, and reliable operation. All you need to do is run `nginx -s reload`. This command will ensure that the configuration is correct, and if it is all set, it will send the master process a SIGHUP signal.

The master process obliges by doing two things:

1. It reloads the configuration and forks a new set of worker processes. This means, that if you have two worker processes running by default, it will spawn two more! These new worker processes will start listening for connections and process them with new configuration settings applied.

2. It will signal the old worker processes to gracefully exit. This implies that the older worker processes will stop taking new requests. They will continue working on the requests that they are already handling, and once done will gracefully shut down after all the connections are closed.

Notice that due to new worker processes being spawned, there will be additional load on the server for a few seconds, but the key idea here is to ensure that there is no disruption in service at all.

From our restaurant analogy point of view, it is somewhat like having waiters for the next shift take charge. They start catering to new customers, while the existing waiters complete their orders and simply pack up for the day.

Upgrade

Let's look at Problem #8 now. This is a much tougher situation. How do you ensure that there is no service disruption while the restaurant is getting painted or refurnished? As you can guess, in a real world it would be an extremely difficult (or probably impossible) situation to handle! For simplicity let's assume that the restaurant owner is a rich guy, and there is an empty facility just next to the restaurant. They might decide to rent the new facility, modify it as per the requirements, and have the new customers come to the new facility instead under the same brand name! All this while, the staff remains the same. So, they share the resources (staff) and once the existing customers from the older facility are done with their meals, the restaurant is shut down. Not too bad, huh? This is probably not as easy as it sounds realistically, but you get the idea.

Nginx has a somewhat similar approach. Here instead of spawning new worker processes with new configurations, it starts the newer version of the web server, which shares the resources with the older version. These keep running in parallel and their worker processes continue to handle traffic. If you find that your application is doing well with the newer version, you can send signals to kill the older version or vice versa!

This approach is amazingly efficient and is an ingenious solution to handle live upgrades of an entire web server. You will learn more about it with hands-on examples in chapter 9.

HTTP Request Processing in Nginx

Now that you know the overall architecture of Nginx, it will be easier to understand how a typical request is served end-to-end. Figure 5-5 should give you an overall idea about the request processing in Nginx. Consider that you have a website that requires a valid user to access the site and wants to compress every request that is served by the web server. You will see how different components of Nginx work together to serve a request.

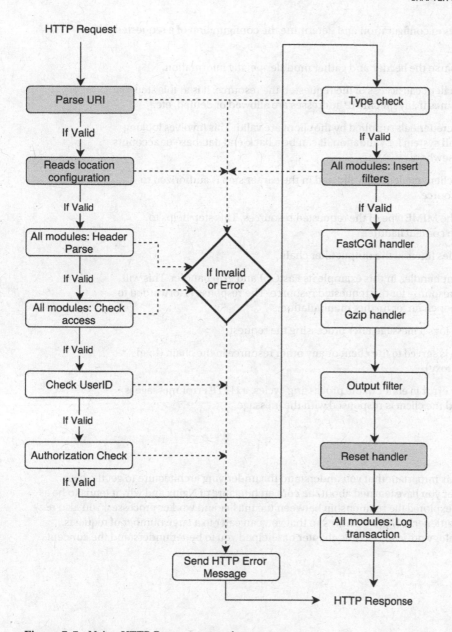

Figure 5-5. *Nginx HTTP Request processing*

The order in which modules are initiated can be found in the *modules* files under *auto* directory. The order is defined during when the `./configure` script is executed.

You can take a look at Figure 5-5 to understand the flow:

1. After reading the main context from the nginx.conf, the request is passed to http context.

2. The first step is to parse the Request URI to a filename.

3. Read the location configuration and determine the configuration of a requested resource.

4. All modules parse the header and gather module specific information.

5. Checks if the client can access of the requested the resource. It is at this step that Nginx determines if any specific IP addresses are allowed or denied, etc.

6. Checks if the credentials supplied by the client are valid. This involves looking at the back-end system for validation. It can be a back-end database or accounts configured elsewhere.

7. Checks if the client credentials validated in the earlier step is authorized to access the resource.

8. Determines the MIME type of the requested resources. This step helps to determine the content handler.

9. Inserts modules filters in the output filter chain.

10. Inserts content handler, in this example its FastCGI and gzip handler. This will generate the response for the requested resource. The response is forwarded to the output filter chain for further manipulation.

11. Each module logs a message after processing the request.

12. The response is served to the client or any other resource in the chain (load balancer or proxy).

13. If there is any error in either of the processing cycles, a HTTP error message is generated and the client is responsed with the message.

Summary

As a web administrator, it is important that you understand the underlying architecture to get the best throughput. In this chapter you have learned about the core architecture of Nginx and why it tends to be as efficient as it is. You have explored the relationship between the master and worker processes. You also now know about the kind of bottlenecks Nginx removes so that you can cater to a large number of requests.

We hope that the analogy presented in this chapter has helped you to better understand the concepts.

CHAPTER 6

■ ■ ■

Hosting Web Sites on Nginx

I started it as an experiment to boost the delivery of static content (my reference examples of that time were things like thttpd). But as soon as other people tried it in production, they immediately requested the proxy component, and the whole "web acceleration" direction had started. In short, NGINX evolved from a simple experiment with the idea of solving the C10k problem, to a complete solution for proxying, load balancing, SSL, static content acceleration, and a few unique capabilities.

—Igor Sysoev, http://bit.ly/nginx_interview

The above excerpt from an interview implies that Nginx never really started as a server for dynamic languages like PHP, etc. It evolved from being a static-only server to web accelerator, and so on. In short, Nginx is used for the goodness it provides from static files point of view, and uses its proxy capabilities to hand off the request to the back-end server or processes in order to handle dynamic requests. This gives you the best of both worlds. In this chapter, the focus is on serving the static content only. For brevity, only CentOS servers will be used on a virtual machine using VirtualBox.

Every website is different, not only from the content perspective, but also from the technology perspective. Primarily, you can categorize the applications as static or dynamic. It actually makes a lot of sense to host multiple websites on the same server if the server can handle it.

The static sites contain a lot of resources like images, stylesheets, JavaScript files, html, text, PDF, and so on. The basic nature of the content is that it is made once and served multiple times to the visitors. If you have to change the content, you will need to edit the file appropriately and update the server so that new content gets served to the audience.

The dynamic sites, on the other hand, have scripts and programming languages working at the back end emitting pages that your browser can understand and render directly. The key difference is that the page you view is never really saved on the server's disk. It also possible that what you are seeing on a page could be completely different from what others would see (for example, Facebook). These websites are very flexible in nature. However, keep in mind that even the most dynamic websites would still use a lot of resources that are static in nature. Nginx is not a programming language or framework that allows you to create dynamic pages. But it does help in front ending the dynamic applications with grace by serving static pages, scripts, style sheets, images, and other static content, while offloading the dynamic content generation to the back-end servers.

You don't always need to spin multiple servers in order to serve multiple websites. That would be a huge waste of server resources, especially if the websites are not attracting a lot of hits. It is often a good idea to host the website and scale up and scale out as needed.

© Rahul Soni 2016
R. Soni, *Nginx*, DOI 10.1007/978-1-4842-1656-9_6

SCALE UP VS. SCALE OUT

Scale Up: If you have a web server that attracts a lot of hits, it is possible that adding more CPU or RAM might help depending on the workload. An activity where you add more resources to the existing server is called scaling up the server.

Scale Out: Scaling up has its limitations, since you can only scale up as much as your hardware allows you to. Scaling out is the activity where you add more servers in order to keep up with the traffic. Most popular websites use scaled-out servers.

Server blocks in Nginx help you to map the website content and ensure that each domain points to the appropriate content only. You can host multiple websites on the same server and differentiate them using server blocks. If you are coming from an Apache background, the server directive is similar to a virtual host.

Web Server Setup

It is important that you practice as we go along. In this chapter, you will need to start afresh with two servers. You can use VirtualBox to create the CentOS servers. Before you create the servers, read through the article at http://attosol.com/centos-setup-and-networking-using-virtual-box. It will guide you in a step-by-step manner regarding the installation steps. Remember, you will need to set up the servers using different variables as discussed below.

We will call our servers WFE1 and WFE2. In chapter 8, you will learn about load balancing these servers. For now, creating two servers with hostname wfe1.localdomain and wfe2.localdomain should suffice.

Once your servers are provisioned, execute ip addr on both the servers and you will notice that the output is exactly the same (similar to Figure 6-1). In simple words, this implies that they are in their own isolated networks and will not be able to ping each other. Let's change this so that both the servers have different IPs.

```
                           wfe1 [Running]
[root@wfe1 ~]# ip addr
1: lo: <LOOPBACK,UP,LOWER_UP> mtu 65536 qdisc noqueue state UNKNOWN
    link/loopback 00:00:00:00:00:00 brd 00:00:00:00:00:00
    inet 127.0.0.1/8 scope host lo
       valid_lft forever preferred_lft forever
    inet6 ::1/128 scope host
       valid_lft forever preferred_lft forever
2: enp0s3: <BROADCAST,MULTICAST,UP,LOWER_UP> mtu 1500 qdisc pfifo_fast state UP
qlen 1000
    link/ether 08:00:27:90:7e:9a brd ff:ff:ff:ff:ff:ff
    inet 10.0.2.15/24 brd 10.0.2.255 scope global dynamic enp0s3
       valid_lft 85185sec preferred_lft 85185sec
    inet6 fe80::a00:27ff:fe90:7e9a/64 scope link
       valid_lft forever preferred_lft forever
[root@wfe1 ~]# _
```

Figure 6-1. Output of ip addr

VirtualBox creates the VMs in such a way that they are not interconnected by default due to security reasons. You can change this by changing the preferences for VirtualBox. The idea is to simply create a NAT network called CentOSFarm (see Figure 6-2).

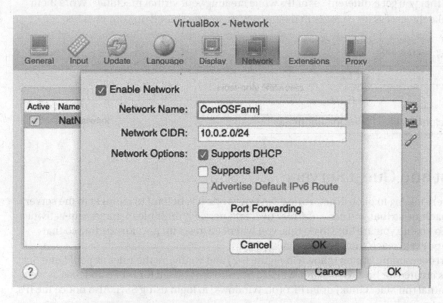

Figure 6-2. *Creating a NAT network*

Now that the NAT network is created, you need to change the server settings for both WFE1 and WFE2 as shown in Figure 6-3.

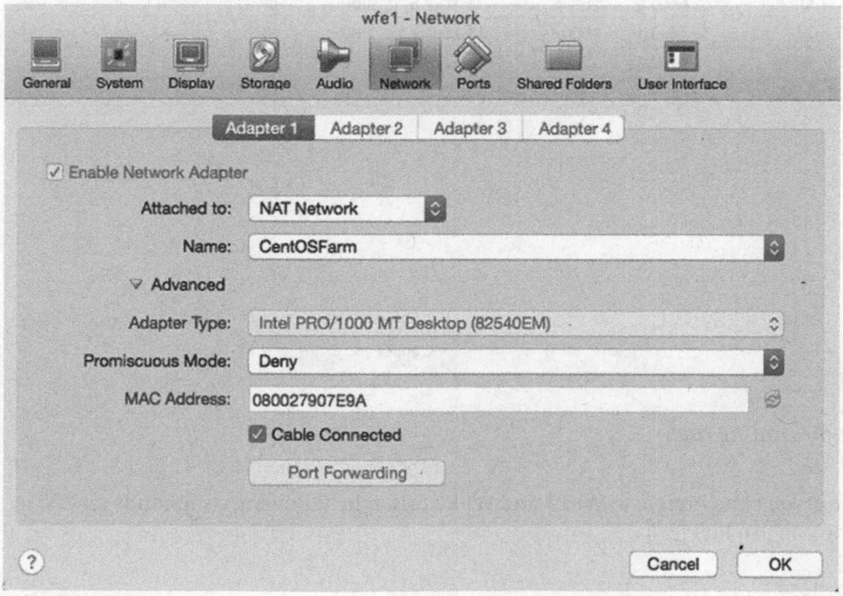

Figure 6-3. *Changing NAT network settings for WFE1 and WFE2*

Once you are done making these changes, you can run `ip addr` again on both terminals and you will find that they now have different IPs. If you try to use the ping command, you will find that both these servers are now connected and able to ping each other. Your lab setup, when complete, should have values as shown in Table 6-1. It is possible that you get a different set of IPs while creating your virtual machines. Write them down, so that you can make the necessary changes in the upcoming sections based on your own IPs.

Table 6-1. *Server Naming Convention*

Server Name	WFE1	WFE2
IP Address	10.0.2.6	10.0.2.7
HostName	wfe1.localdomain	wfe2.localdomain

Connecting Host and Guest Servers

So far you have your servers talking to each other using a NAT network. It is helpful to connect to the server's terminal from the host machine so that you can copy files over and perform multiple management activities directly from your host. To ensure you are able to do this, you will need to set up port forwarding so that VirtualBox allows your request to reach the guest servers.

You can click the port-forwarding button (shown in Figure 6-2) and configure the rules as per Figure 6-4. Notice that there are rules created for both WFE1 and WFE2. The rules are created for HTTP and SSH as well, so that you can use a terminal (on Mac/Linux) or PuTTY (on Windows) to login using SSH. Also notice the IPs, since they are the same as for Table 6-1.

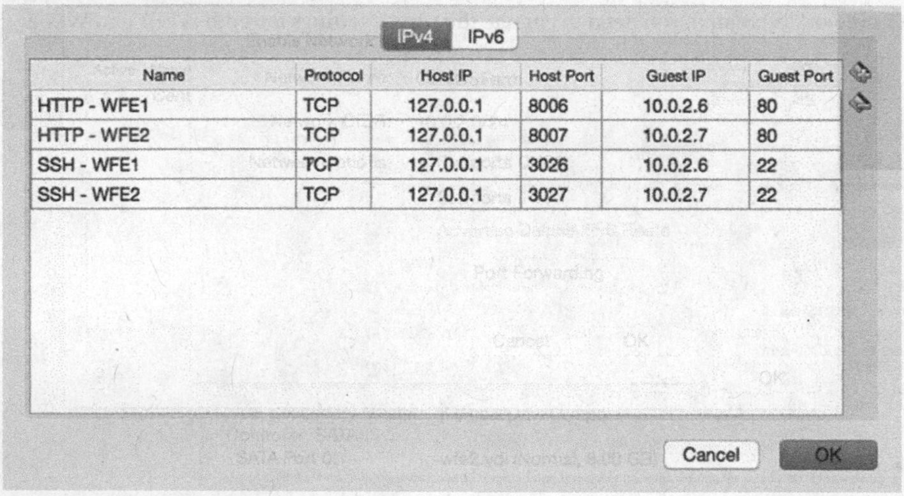

Name	Protocol	Host IP	Host Port	Guest IP	Guest Port
HTTP - WFE1	TCP	127.0.0.1	8006	10.0.2.6	80
HTTP - WFE2	TCP	127.0.0.1	8007	10.0.2.7	80
SSH - WFE1	TCP	127.0.0.1	3026	10.0.2.6	22
SSH - WFE2	TCP	127.0.0.1	3027	10.0.2.7	22

Figure 6-4. *Setting up port-forwarding rules*

Once the rules are set up, you can connect to WFE1 and WFE2 using the following commands on OSX and Linux (for Windows, you can use PuTTY):

```
#ssh -p 3026 root@127.0.0.1
#ssh -p 3027 root@127.0.0.1
```

Let's do a basic Nginx install now on both these servers. Execute the following commands on both servers sequentially (you have already learned what they do in chapter 2):

```
vi /etc/yum.repos.d/nginx.repo
```

Add the following text to the file:

```
[nginx]
name=nginx repo
baseurl=http://nginx.org/packages/centos/7/$basearch/
gpgcheck=0
enabled=1
```

Save and exit. Run the following command on both servers:

```
yum install -y nginx
nginx
```

At this point, if you try browsing from your host machine using the following URIs (the port-forwarding rules for HTTP were set in Figure 6-4), you should be able to view the pages hosted on your servers (Figure 6-5):

```
http://127.0.0.1:8006
http://127.0.0.1:8007
```

Welcome to nginx!

If you see this page, the nginx web server is successfully installed and working. Further configuration is required.

For online documentation and support please refer to nginx.org.
Commercial support is available at nginx.com.

Thank you for using nginx.

Figure 6-5. *Browsing an Nginx website using port forwarding from a host machine*

User Creation

So far, you have installed Nginx and connected the two servers using NAT network. You have also been able to use the secure shell (ssh) to connect to the servers using ssh -p 3026 root@127.0.0.1. However, there is a problem.

Connecting to the server using `root` account is not considered a secure web practice. Besides, in today's world where everything is going to the cloud, you often don't have a root access to begin with. If you are using AWS EC2 instance or Azure for hosting your virtual servers, an account will be provisioned for you automatically, and you would use that account to access your servers. Since you are working locally at the moment on your virtual machines hosted on VirtualBox, you have full liberty to play with all different accounts. You will be following good practices nevertheless.

Putting that small detour aside, let's start by creating normal users. Use the commands below (on both WFE1 and WFE2) to create a user and assign a password:

```
#useradd user1
#passwd user1
```

You can log out from the `root` prompt by using (`logout` command) and log back in using the following command:

```
ssh -p 3026 user1@127.0.0.1.
```

At the prompt, type `pwd` and you should see `/home/user1`.

Sample Applications

Now it's time to upload the website content to the web server. Instead of creating sample applications from scratch, you can visit https://github.com/attosol/nginx and download the zipped version of the repository. This repository is made only for the purpose of this book and contains various samples curated from the open source community.

Once downloaded, extract the zip file and navigate to the folder called `static`. It contains two subfolders called `site1` and `site2`. Both of them contain different website samples created using static content only. In this chapter, you will deal only with the static content.

Uploading Content

You can use copy command or an FTP client on your host server or desktop to make the data transfer easy. One of the popular tools is FileZilla; you can download it from https://filezilla-project.org/. It is open source and is extremely powerful. You can use Site Manager in FileZilla to set up your connection so that it is easy for you to upload content easily. Figure 6-6 will show you the details required to be filled in order to connect to the virtual server.

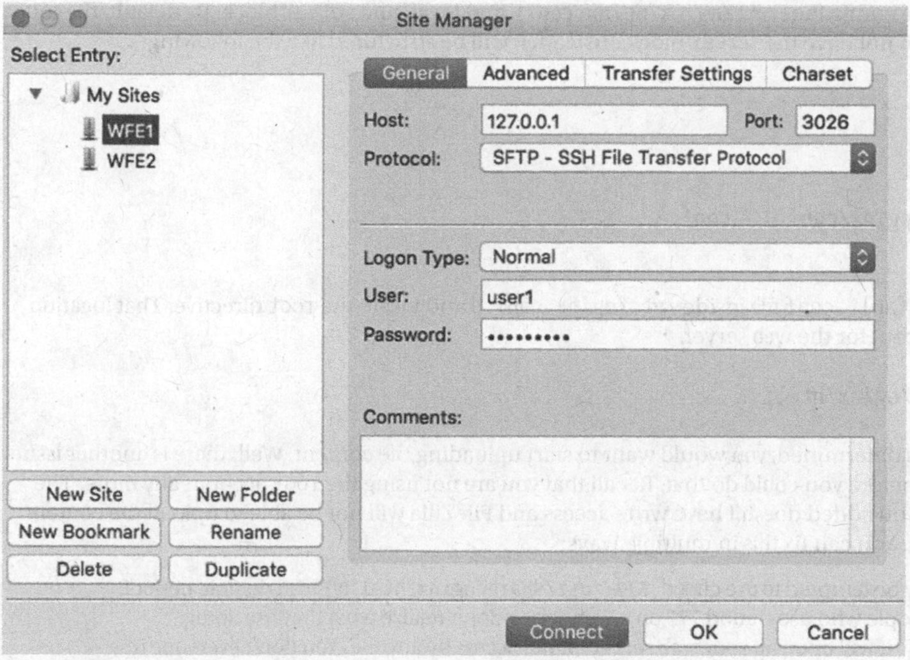

Figure 6-6. Using Site Manager to create connections for frequent use

Notice the use of port and protocol. Also notice that you can add multiple entries to store all your connections at once. Once you connect you will land inside /home/user1 by default.

Let's assume that you are working on some server that you have not provisioned yourself. It may be a bit tricky initially to figure out the default web path and configuration file location for your server. In the Linux world, there are a wide variety of distros available and the default location varies a lot. When stuck, you can use the following method to find the default configuration path of any Nginx server:

Step 1: Execute nginx -V and take a look at the --conf-path:

```
nginx version: nginx/1.8.1
built by gcc 4.8.3 20140911 (Red Hat 4.8.3-9) (GCC)
built with OpenSSL 1.0.1e-fips 11 Feb 2013
TLS SNI support enabled
configure arguments: --prefix=/etc/nginx --sbin-path=/usr/sbin/nginx --conf-path=/etc/
nginx/nginx.conf --error-log-path=/var/log/nginx/error.log --http-log-path=/var/log/nginx/
access.log --pid-path=/var/run/nginx.pid --lock-path=/var/run/nginx.lock --http-client-body-
temp-path=/var/cache/nginx/client_temp --http-proxy-temp-path=/var/cache/nginx/proxy_temp
--http-fastcgi-temp-path=/var/cache/nginx/fastcgi_temp --http-uwsgi-temp-path=/var/cache/
nginx/uwsgi_temp --http-scgi-temp-path=/var/cache/nginx/scgi_temp --user=nginx --group=nginx
--with-http_ssl_module --with-http_realip_module --with-http_addition_module --with-http_
sub_module --with-http_dav_module --with-http_flv_module --with-http_mp4_module --with-http_
gunzip_module --with-http_gzip_stati
```

Step 2: Open the config file (/etc/nginx/nginx.conf), and locate the `server` block. By default, the root configuration file will not have the `server` block. Instead, it will be structured like the following:

```
user  nginx;
...
http {
    ...
    include /etc/nginx/conf.d/*.conf;
}
```

Step 3: Open `default.conf` file inside /etc/nginx.conf.d and locate the `root` directive. That location will be your default root for the web server.

```
root   /usr/share/nginx/html;
```

Once the root is determined, you would want to start uploading the content. Well, there is another issue that you need to fix before you could do that. Recall that you are not using the `root` account any more. The `user1` account that you added doesn't have write access and FileZilla will not be able to upload the content directly to the server. You can fix this in multiple ways:

- You may be tempted to use `chmod 777 /usr/share/nginx/html`. NEVER do that, period! Most people who use chmod 777 on a web server don't realize what they are doing. Basically, it will open up your web server for full access by anyone. You don't everyone in the world to come over and mess around with your servers. If you have already done that by mistake, use `chmod 755 /usr/share/nginx/html` to fix the permissions.

- You can change the ownership of the root folder so that the allowed users can upload the file. Assuming `user1` is one of the allowed users, you can use the following command to allow access to `user1`:

```
chown user1 /usr/share/nginx/html.
```

- The previous approach doesn't scale well if you have multiple members uploading to the same directory (which is often the case). To fix that, you can create a group and add users to that group instead.

  - Create a new group called `www` by using this command:

```
groupadd www
```

  - Modify the `user1` information such that it belongs to this group `www`.

```
usermod -a -G www user1
```

  - Make this group an owner (similar to `chown` command that is used for a user) of the root path /usr/share/nginx/html. `-R` switch is used to ensure that all permissions are set recursively.

```
chgrp -R www /usr/share/nginx/html
```

  - Now, grant write permission to this group on the root directory.

```
chmod -R g+w /usr/share/nginx/html
```

114

Almost done! This group exercise may appear a bit cumbersome, but it will keep your web server in good shape from a security perspective. After all this exercise, you should be ready to upload the folder to the root path. Upload the content that you downloaded earlier so that the structure looks like Figure 6-7. Please note that none of the files or directory names have been modified.

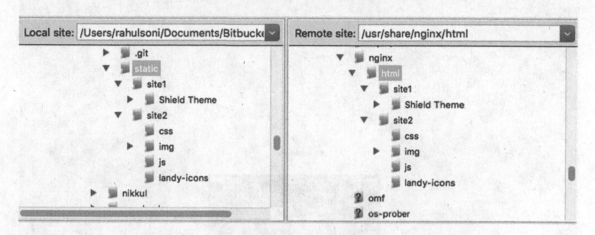

Figure 6-7. *Uploading files*

You can see the website named Shield Theme hosted inside a subdirectory under site1, whereas site2 contains another website called Landy along with its dependencies.

Hosting Websites

Your servers are now up and ready to host the websites. But there are still issues that you should be aware of. If you browse to http://localhost:8006/site2/index.html, you will find the website being rendered as Figure 6-8 depicts.

As you can see, the URI is still localhost and there is a path /site2/index.html that is being rendered in the browser. Even though the site is rendering, it is not an individual website. An isolated website should be such that when you type http://localhost:8006 as your URI, you should be able to see this page as in Figure 6-8. Not only that, but the content of the site2 should not be rendered from the root site at all. At the moment, the root site is the only website for Nginx, and the configuration needs to be fixed.

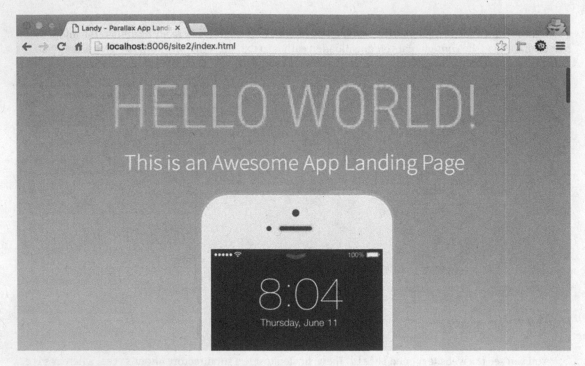

Figure 6-8. Website rendering as a relative path

As you have already learned, the default configuration file of Nginx (/etc/nginx/nginx.conf), contains an include directive (include /etc/nginx/conf.d/*.conf;) at the end of the configuration file, and it ensures that all the conf inside conf.d directory gets loaded as part of the Nginx configuration.

It is a good idea to rename the default.conf file as a template (say, default.template) and create other websites based on the default.template. The reason why this renaming is done is to ensure that this template doesn't get included from the nginx.conf due to the include directive. To rename, use the following command:

```
# mv /etc/nginx/conf.d/default.conf /etc/nginx/conf.d/default.template
```

Follow the renaming with a configuration reload (use nginx -s reload) and refresh your browser (http://localhost:8006/). The page wouldn't load, and this is fine.

From here on in this book, wherever you read *reload configuration*, it would mean executing the command nginx -s reload. Also, most commands here would work without sudo, but a few need sudo before that. If any of the commands do not work without sudo, try it again with sudo.

It is a good practice to keep the name of the configuration similar to your domain name. In this chapter, you will make two websites hosted at site1.com and site2.com. These websites should render if someone uses www.site1.com or www.site2.com as well. Start by making a copy of the template using the command that follows:

```
# cp /etc/nginx/conf.d/default.template /etc/nginx/conf.d/site1.conf
```

After that, edit the site.conf file so that it looks like the following:

```
server {
    listen       80;
    server_name  localhost;

    root  /usr/share/nginx/html/site1/Shield\ Theme;

    location / {
        index  index.html index.htm;
    }

    error_page   500 502 503 504  /50x.html;
    location = /50x.html {
        root   /usr/share/nginx/html;
    }
}
```

Reload configuration and browse http://localhost:8006. Contrary to what you might have guessed, it throws a 404 error. What went wrong?

TROUBLESHOOTING TIPS

Try listing the directory and sure enough, it is there:

```
#ls /usr/share/nginx/html/site1/Shield\ Theme
assets  index.html
```

Instead of guessing around, you can take a few approaches to troubleshoot such issues without wasting time.

Approach 1: The first one is accessing the tail of the access logs like so:

```
#tail /var/log/nginx/access.log
/usr/share/nginx/html/site1/Shield\x5C Theme - / - GET / HTTP/1.1 - 404 - 570 -
```

Approach 2: Sometimes, you might find that a plain status code doesn't help as much. In that case, you can use a command-line utility called strace. If it is not available on the CentOS version you are using, download it using yum.

```
#sudo yum install -y strace
```

117

1. strace needs process id (PID) of the process you need to hook into. Use the
    following command to get the PID of the worker process.

```
# ps -aux | grep nginx
root      28524 0.0  0.2  48236 2052 ?        Ss   14:15   0:00 nginx: master process /usr/
sbin/nginx -c /etc/nginx/nginx.conf
nginx     28534 0.0  0.2  48240 2184 ?        S    14:18   0:00 nginx: worker process
```

2. After you get the PID, use strace as follows and refresh the URI again in your
    browser:

```
strace -p 28534 -e trace=file -f
```

3. Once you refresh the browser, strace should output a few lines like so:

```
Process 28534 attached
stat("/usr/share/nginx/html/site1/Shield\\ Theme/index.html", 0x7fffd772cb90) = -1 ENOENT
(No such file or directory)
stat("/usr/share/nginx/html/site1/Shield\\ Theme", 0x7fffd772cb90) = -1 ENOENT (No such file
or directory)
```

As you can see, this gives you a much clearer picture of what is going on. It seems like Nginx has issues
with parsing path with space.

Once you know the reason, fixing it is easy. Fix the site1.conf by changing it like so:

```
server {
    listen          80;
    server_name  localhost;

    root    "/usr/share/nginx/html/site1/Shield Theme";

    location / {
        index   index.html index.htm;
    }

    error_page   500 502 503 504   /50x.html;
    location = /50x.html {
        root    /usr/share/nginx/html;
    }
}
```

Now, the browser should be happy and it should render the site well (see Figure 6-9).

Figure 6-9. Site1 rendered using localhost:8006 as URI

Websites Using Different Names

Try to host site2 using the same concept, and with site2.conf (create a copy of site1.conf if you like and make the changes required) file as follows:

```
server {
    listen       80;
    server_name  localhost;

    root  "/usr/share/nginx/html/site2";

    location / {
        index  index.html index.htm;
    }

    error_page   500 502 503 504  /50x.html;
    location = /50x.html {
        root    /usr/share/nginx/html;
    }
}
```

It might look simple, but when you try reloading the configuration, it won't work and throw an error message instead:

```
#nginx -s reload
nginx: [warn] conflicting server name "localhost" on 0.0.0.0:80, ignored
```

What went wrong?

Reading the warning carefully reveals that the name localhost was used multiple times with the same port and Nginx ignored it. In other words, it means that you cannot use the same server_name to distinguish different websites for obvious reasons. Open site2.conf again and change server_name directive from localhost to 127.0.0.1. Leave everything as is.

```
server {
    listen        80;
        server_name         127.0.0.1;

    root   "/usr/share/nginx/html/site2";

    location / {
        index  index.html index.htm;
    }

    error_page   500 502 503 504   /50x.html;
    location = /50x.html {
        root    /usr/share/nginx/html;
    }
}
```

Reload the configuration and you will find that this time, both websites work (see Figure 6-10). You now have an interesting configuration here! It might confuse you, especially if you are coming from an IIS background. When you access localhost:8006 you get site1 but when you use 127.0.0.1, you get site2. But isn't localhost the same as 127.0.0.1? The answer lies in the fact that for Nginx, the look up and name matching happens in a little different manner. You will learn about it shortly in an upcoming section.

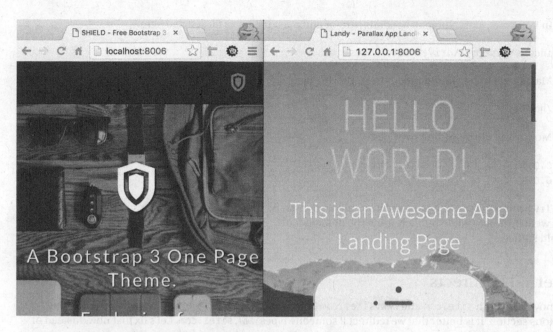

Figure 6-10. *Both site1 and site2 running in parallel*

Websites Using Domain Name

A typical web site will have a domain name like www.site1.com, but you can find many people type site1.com as well. From search engine optimization perspective (SEO), it is often considered better to have just one address. It can either be www.site1.com or site1.com, but it should be consistent and assuming site1.com is the chosen one, www.site1.com should redirect to site1.com. In this section, you start with making a basic change like the following for site1.conf:

```
server {
    listen        80;
    server_name   site1.com, www.site1.com;

    root  "/usr/share/nginx/html/site1/Shield Theme";

    ...output trimmed...
}
```

Reload the configuration and try browsing to the following URI:

```
http://site1.com
http://www.site.com
```

Did it work?

Well, it won't because site1.com is not a valid domain name and your operating system tried to fetch the address for site1.com thinking it actually exists. In reality, you will need to buy a domain name called site1.com from a domain registrar and map it directly to the public IP of your server. For testing purposes, you can create host entries to fool your operating system into thinking that site1.com and site2.com points to 127.0.0.1.

121

In Windows, start Notepad as administrator and open the hosts file located here:

`C:\Windows\System32\drivers\etc\hosts`

Mac/Linux users should modify the following file:

`/etc/hosts`

Modify the file by adding two lines:

```
127.0.0.1               site1.com
127.0.0.1               site2.com
```

Try browsing the site again, and it should work now. As mentioned earlier, it doesn't really mean that your website is accessible publicly using the domain name, but for your machine and test purpose this should suffice.

Internal Redirects

You now have both `site.com` and `www.site1.com` pointing to the correct website. As pointed out in the previous section, it is better that we redirect if someone types `www.site1.com`. Let's fix that now. Instead of setting explicit locations, you can use two `server` blocks in the `site1.conf` file as follows:

```
server {
    listen      80;
    server_name www.site1.com;
    return      301 http://site1.com$request_uri;
}
server {
    listen      80;
    server_name site1.com;

    root  "/usr/share/nginx/html/site1/Shield Theme";

    location / {
        index  index.html index.htm;
    }

    error_page  500 502 503 504  /50x.html;
    location = /50x.html {
        root   /usr/share/nginx/html;
    }
}
```

The first server block simply returns a 301, which in HTTP means "Moved Permanently." Once the browser gets this output, it knows that it has to make another request, which in this case is this:

`http://site1.com$request_uri.`

The `$request_uri` is a variable and is present there to ensure that if someone asks for `http://www.site1.com/abc/foo`, they get redirected to `http://site1.com/abc/foo`. If you don't add `$request_uri`, you will end up redirecting the request to `http://site1.com` and this can confuse your visitors.

To make it even more robust, you can use $scheme://site1.com/$request_uri. $scheme is another variable that will ensure that the request gets routed to HTTP or HTTPS. The way it is configured now, if the page requested is https://www.site1.com/abc, it will get redirected to http://site1.com/abc, which is not good from a security perspective.

■ **Note**   The redirection set like this might not work in port-forwarding solutions that you have set up using VirtualBox. In the real world, where your public IPs are exposed and mapped to the domain name, the redirection will work just fine.

Sites Using Different Ports

In specific cases, you can have different parts of your application exposed on different ports. In that case, you can configure server blocks in a way that multiple server blocks with the same name exist, but are listening on different ports.

To enable this capability, you will need to use the listen port and do some extra tasks. First of all, update your site1.conf file so that it looks similar to the following:

```
server {
    listen      8080;
    server_name site1.com, www.site1.com;

    root /usr/share/nginx/html/site3;

    location / {
        index index.html index.htm;
    }

    error_page 500 502 503 504 /503.html;
    location = /50x.html{
        root /usr/share/nginx/html;
    }
}
server {
    listen      80;
    server_name  site1.com, www.site1.com;

    root  "/usr/share/nginx/html/site1/Shield Theme";

    location / {
        index  index.html index.htm;
    }

    error_page   500 502 503 504  /50x.html;
    location = /50x.html {
        root   /usr/share/nginx/html;
    }
}
```

Notice the subtle change in the `listen` directive. In the first server block, it is bound to port 8080, where as in the second block it is bound to port 80, which is the default port. Also notice that the first server block points to a different root (`/usr/share/nginx/html/site3`). You can have a totally different application hosted here. For now, simply create a directory called `site3` (at `/usr/share/nginx/html`), and create a text file called `index.html` with some text.

Before you check it from your host server, check it locally from the guest using `curl`:

```
#curl localhost:8080
hello from site 3!
```

If you get an output locally, you have done well, and you can now expose your website outside your guest server. But before you do that, open port 8080 using the following command:

```
#firewall-cmd --permanent --zone=public --add-port=8080/tcp
#firewall-cmd --reload
```

With firewall ports opened, it is time to add one more forwarding rule to forward a request to the internal port. Use Figure 6-11 to ensure you have added the new rule correctly.

Name	Protocol	Host IP	Host Port	Guest IP	Guest Port
HTTP - WFE1	TCP	127.0.0.1	8006	10.0.2.6	80
HTTP - WFE1 - Site 3	TCP	127.0.0.1	8016	10.0.2.6	8080
HTTP - WFE2	TCP	127.0.0.1	8007	10.0.2.7	80
SSH - WFE1	TCP	127.0.0.1	3026	10.0.2.6	22
SSH - WFE2	TCP	127.0.0.1	3027	10.0.2.7	22

Figure 6-11. *Adding port-forwarding rule for Site3 (HTTP - WFE1 - Site 3)*

Once the rules are set, you should be able to browse to `http://site1.com:8016` and get your page back from `site3`.

Wildcard Mapping

You can also have server blocks set up with wildcards. In simple words, you can have a server block handle request to `blog.site1.com`, `mobile.site1.com`, etc. by changing the server_name to `*.site1.com`. You can even use wildcard (*) as a prefix or a suffix. Hence, `*.site1.com` or `www.site1.*` will equate to `blog.site1.com` or `www.site1.co.us` respectively.

Blocking Access

Right now if you try accessing the site using 127.0.0.1 or site1.com, both will work and you will get the same website. If you want to block access to 127.0.0.1 but allow access to site1.com, you can add additional blocks to take care of it like so:

```
server {
    listen       80;
    server_name  127.0.0.1;
    return       444;
}
server {
    listen       80;
    server_name  site1.com;

    root  "/usr/share/nginx/html/site1/Shield Theme";
    ...output trimmed...
}
```

Return code 444 is a special part of Nginx's nonstandard code that closes the connection.

Domain Name Mapping

You have already seen that adding a host header helps you resolve a name like www.site.com to your Nginx server. This approach wouldn't be of help if you really want to take your website online. If you really want to take your web server online, you will need to buy a domain name from one of the domain name registrars. There are plenty of them available and a simple Internet search will take you to the most famous ones. Typically, you buy the name for a year (or multiple years) and map the name on the portal of the website you purchased it from. For example, if you use GoDaddy.com to buy your domain, you can log in at their portal and configure the domain name so that it points to your public IP (Figure 6-12).

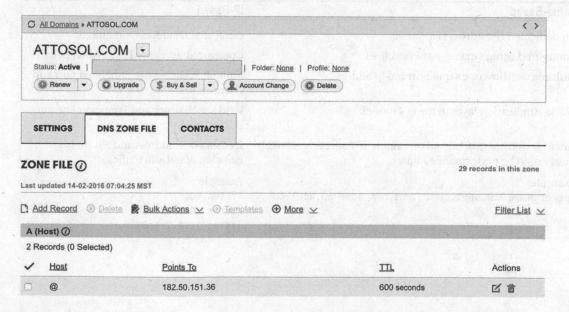

Figure 6-12. *GoDaddy's portal for managing a domain name. Try pinging attosol.com*

A lot goes behind the scene when you type a name in your browser and hit enter. Here is the very simplistic gist of it:

1. Your browser asks the Operating System to resolve the hostname.

   a. Operating system checks what the name resolves to using the hosts files. If the host files don't have an entry, it checks your locally configured DNS servers.

   b. Operating system returns the IP address corresponding to the hostname to the browser. So far, by creating the entries for site1.com point to 127.0.0.1, you have been using host files to your advantage. This is to ensure that your operating system doesn't search the DNS servers at all, since it is able to find the entries in the host file.

2. The browser creates an HTTP request with information like host header.

3. The browser then sends the HTTP request.

4. The server at the IP address receives the request from the browser (including the hostname).

5. The server then processes the request and sends the response back to the client.

IP-Based Hosting

So far in this chapter, you have been using server_name to distinguish between server blocks. This approach is the most common approach since it allows you to share the IP address of the server. There is another kind of configuration that can be classified into IP-based hosting. Table 6-2 differentiates and highlights the differences between them.

Table 6-2. *Difference between Name-based and IP-based hosting*

Name-Based	IP-Based
No dedicated IP address is required.	Dedicated IP address is required.
Configured using server_name directive.	Configured using the listen directive.
Multiple websites use same port and ip address.	Multiple websites use individual port and IP addresses.
Works Application layer in the OSI model.	Works at Network and Transport layer in the OSI model.
Since all websites are hosted on a single IP address and NIC, there could be performance impact.	Dedicated IP address and NIC helps isolation of website traffic.
Example: server_name www.app1.com *.app1.com someapp.app1.com;	Example: listen 80; listen 10.0.2.4:80; listen 10.0.2.5:8080;

Mixed Name-Based and IP-Based Servers

Take a look at a more practical example where both name-based and IP-based addresses are used. In the following configuration, Nginx first tests the IP address and port of the request against the listen directive. It then matches the host header of the request with the server_name. If the server name is not found, the request is mapped to the default_server. If the default_server is not mentioned, the first server block takes care of the request.

```
server {
    listen      10.0.2.6:80;
    server_name site1.net www.site1.net;
    ...
}
server {
    listen      10.0.2.6:80 default_server;
    server_name site1.org www.site1.org;
    ...
}
server {
    listen      10.0.3.6:80 default_server;
    server_name site1.com www.site1.com;
    ...
}
server {
    listen      10.0.3.6:80;
    server_name site1.biz www.site1.biz;
    ...
}
```

Common Configuration Mistakes

This section goes over some common errors many users make and then offers suggestions on how to avoid or fix them.

Let's Use 777

When a configuration doesn't work as it is expected to, some administrators take a shortcut (i.e., chmod 777). NO, just don't do that ever! It has been already explained earlier in the chapter that it is better to not troubleshoot by the trial-and-error method. Try to find out what is wrong by using logs and tools that are suitable to the situation.

Root Inside Location Block

Notice the use of multiple root directives in the following configuration. It is a perfectly valid configuration, but it is not a good configuration. It creates two problems. The first problem is that you now have to add a root to every location block you add, which adds a lot of unnecessary lines in your configuration. The second problem is that if you don't provide a root block to the location block, it will not have any root.

```
server {
    server_name www.site1.com;
    location / {
        root /usr/share/nginx/html;
        # [...]
    }
    location /somewhere {
        root /usr/share/nginx/html;
        # [...]
    }
}
```

You should refactor the previous configuration like so:

```
server {
    server_name www.site1.com;
    root /usr/share/nginx/html;
    location / {
        # [...]
    }
    location /somewhere {
        # [...]
    }
}
```

Monolithic Configuration Files

If you like, you can keep adding your server blocks to the default.conf file. It is perfectly okay if you intend to host only one application on the server. However, it is often not the case. Hence it is strongly advised to keep different configuration files for different domain names. It will make your administration tasks a lot easier and will eventually save you a lot of time scrolling up and down finding the correct server blocks.

Unnecessary Complications

There are multiple ways to achieve the same result in Nginx. Whenever you have to use if directives or redirections, evaluate if your approach is correct and determine if there is a better way. Ask questions and visit forums if there is any confusion. There might be easier and more efficient solutions that might not cross your mind. A lot of times it is found that the configuration contains unnecessary processing blocks inside a server block that could have been easily avoided using another server block. For instance, if you take a look at the following configuration, you will find two server blocks. The primary task of the first server block is to redirect to the second server block. You may ask how is it more efficient?

```
server {
    server_name www.site1.com;
    return 301 $scheme://site1.com$request_uri;
}
server {
    server_name site1.com;
    # [...]
}
```

To answer the efficiency question, take a look at the larger picture about how a request actually reaches your server. Primarily, outside visitors are likely to use a search engine to reach your website. While indexing, search engines will easily understand that you prefer site1.com over www.site1.com. Thus, most people will not hit the first server block at all. It also implies that the redirection code is not executed to process your request at all!

Contrast this situation to an alternate configuration where location blocks are used in the second server block and there is just one server block taking care of all requests. Now, your redirection code is evaluated EVERY time any request comes in. This leads to unnecessary evaluation of a URI that could have been easily avoided by using two server blocks as shown in this example.

Listening on Hostname

You should never listen on hostname. It can cause binding issues during the restarts of the server. Use IP instead of hostnames.

```
server {
    # Bad > listen site1.com:80;
    #Good > listen 127.0.0.1:80;
    # [...]
}
```

Summary

Nginx is very flexible and there are often multiple ways of achieving a task. It can be both good and bad, depending on your knowledge about the subject. Luckily, the community is vibrant and all you have to do when, in doubt, is to ask!

In this chapter you have learned the finer nuances about hosting multiple websites on the same Nginx server. You should be fairly comfortable now about the name-based and IP-based hosting options. Hopefully the common tasks and configurations mentioned in this chapter will help you configure your server with ease. Last but not least, you should now be aware of some of the most common configuration mistakes made by web administrators. Knowing the dangers, as they say, is the first step in order to avoid them.

CHAPTER 7

■ ■ ■

Nginx and Dynamic Content

This chapter will take your knowledge level deeper by providing insights into serving dynamic content. Please keep in mind that hosting dynamic content directly with Nginx is not possible. This is to say that Nginx worker processes will not load the processing modules in its own memory address space to serve the pages. The idea is to proxy the content to the components that do the actual processing of your requests. As limiting as it sounds, it has its own good side effects. The primary benefit is that the slowness caused by dynamic sites cannot directly affect Nginx. It has powerful routing and proxy capabilities that will tremendously benefit you as a web administrator.

This chapter might not appeal to you if you are not familiar with developer technologies and you can skip it if you like. However, you don't need to be intimidated by the code and other details if you choose to read through, since the samples will be fairly straight forward for you to understand. The idea is not to dive too much into code but instead to show you just a few samples so that you get the gist of how Nginx can be helpful in accelerating your applications. For brevity, only CentOS-related directions are provided. Conceptually, it won't be very different for other distros. Without further ado, let us begin.

Sudo Scare

In chapter 6 one of the things you learned about was not using the root account due to multiple reasons. To that effect, you created a user called user1. But this user is quite powerless at the moment. Check it out by doing the following:

- Start by logging in as user1 like so: ssh -p 3026 user1@127.0.0.1.

- Try running the following command and notice how it tries to scare you:

```
[user1@wfe1 ~]$ sudo yum -y install php56
[sudo] password for user1:
user1 is not in the sudoers file.  This incident will be reported.
```

- It basically says that user1 is not allowed to do sudo.

- Since you know you can trust user1, you can add him to the sudoers list by using visudo.

- Type su and hit enter to get into the root prompt.

- Type visudo and hit enter again. It will open the file (/etc/sudoers) in vi editor and allow you to edit it.

© Rahul Soni 2016
R. Soni, *Nginx*, DOI 10.1007/978-1-4842-1656-9_7

■ **Caution**   Even though you can edit the file directly, you should avoid doing it, since `visudo` validates the file when you exit. If you choose to use any other editor, you may end up making a bad mistake and locking yourself out of the server. It is extremely important that you exercise caution while adding users to the sudoers list.

- After the file is open, look for a line that says root ALL=(ALL) ALL and add your user in the next line.

```
## Allow root to run any commands anywhere
root    ALL=(ALL)       ALL
user1   ALL=(ALL)       ALL
```

- Save the file and type exit to get back from the `root` prompt to the `user1` prompt.

- sudo should now work for the commands.

Installing MySQL

Now that the user is in the sudoers list, you can install some software to complete the LEMP (Linux, eNginx, MySQL, and PHP) stack. Let us start with MySQL. MySQL is an open source relational database management system (RDBMS). In July 2013, it was the second most widely used RDBMS, just behind SQLite.

■ **Note**   SQLite is deployed with every Android and iPhone device along with the Chrome and Firefox browsers. In the second quarter of 2013 alone, 213 million smartphones shipped, of which 200 million were Android and iOS.

Log in on to your wfe1.localdomain server using ssh -p 3026 user1@127.0.0.1. To install MySQL server, you need to first download the Yum repository. The following link contains information about different versions that are available: http://dev.mysql.com/downloads/repo/yum/. Visit the link and find the version you are interested in. For CentOS, you can pick RHEL 7's download link which can be found here: http://dev.mysql.com/downloads/file.php?id=450705.

■ **Note**   that these links might change over a period of time, and in future you will most likely have later versions, so it would be better to visit the page and get the latest links before you execute the commands that follow.

1. Install wget so that you can download anything from the server directly instead of uploading the file using FTP.

```
sudo yum install -y wget
```

2. Now, use wget to download the repository and use the rpm (RPM Package Manager) utility to manage the file you just downloaded as follows:

```
sudo wget http://dev.mysql.com/get/mysql57-community-release-el7-7.noarch.rpm
sudo rpm -Uvh mysql57-community-release-el7-7.noarch.rpm
```

3. Time to install MySQL. Execute the following command:

```
sudo yum install -y mysql-community-server
```

4. A bunch of files will be downloaded and installed for you due to the yum (and other package managers') goodness that comes with Linux.

5. Once the setup is done, you can start the MySQL service like so:

```
sudo service mysqld start
sudo service mysqld status
```

6. During the installation the server is initialized and an SSL certificate and key files are generated in the data directory. Along with that, a superuser account 'root'@'localhost' is created. If you try to connect using mysql -u root command, you will get the following error (and you can easily figure out that it is because you haven't provided any password):

```
ERROR 1045 (28000): Access denied for user 'root'@'localhost' (using password: NO)
```

7. Since the install never really asked for a password, how would you know what the password is? The answer to this is simple. It is because there is a temporary password allocated during the installation process. You can retrieve that and as you can guess, change it immediately so that you have a strong password in place. To retrieve the password, use the following command:

```
sudo grep 'temporary password' /var/log/mysqld.log
--- 1 [Note] A temporary password is generated for root@localhost: gj>jwax<uOrT
```

8. Connect to MySQL using mysql -u root -p and type in the temporary password. This will allow you to enter the MySQL console. To change the temporary password, use the following command:

```
mysql> ALTER USER 'root'@'localhost' IDENTIFIED BY 'P@ssword1!';
Query OK, 0 rows affected (0.00 sec)
```

9. Try typing simple commands and you can start talking to your MySQL server.

```
mysql> show databases;
+--------------------+
| Database           |
+--------------------+
| information_schema |
| mysql              |
| performance_schema |
| sys                |
+--------------------+
4 rows in set (0.00 sec)
```

10. Type quit; at the prompt and you will be back to your user prompt.

Before you proceed with installing PHP and other Nginx configuration on WFE1, you may want to clean up what you might have done in the previous chapter. This is simply to avoid any confusion:

```
sudo rm -rf site1 site2 site3
sudo rm -f /etc/nginx/conf.d/site*.conf
```

Also remove the host name entries from your host file that you might have created during the previous chapter.

Installing PHP

Let us install PHP next. PHP originally stood for Personal Home Page, but of late it is referred to as Hypertext Preprocessor. It is a server-side scripting language designed for web development. It is one of the core standing pillars for the LAMP (Linux, Apache, MySQL, and PHP) or LEMP (Linux, Nginx, MySQL, and PHP) stack. Please keep in mind that there are multiple options for running PHP. The most common options available to you are mod_php, FastCGI, and PHP-FPM.

- mod_php is the built-in version available only for Apache. Installing it is easy, and its ease of use coupled with tight integration is probably the most common reason to deploy mod_php. However, it forces every Apache child to use more memory and needs a restart of Apache to read an updated php.ini file.

- FastCGI is a pretty generic protocol available on most platforms including Windows IIS. It is an improvisation over the earlier variation of Common Gateway Interface (CGI) that reduces the overheads by spinning up one process for multiple requests. You might be already aware that CGI used one process per request and it was not as scalable for extremely busy sites. FastCGI has a smaller memory footprint than mod_php and has more configuration options.

- PHP-FPM is an alternative for PHP FastCGI implementation and is the newest kid on the block. It can be used with any web server that is compatible with FastCGI and plays well with Nginx too. It gives you a lot of configuration options and it really shines in multiple areas, especially related to availability. You can start different processes with different settings and different php.ini options. This means you can have multiple processes serving different versions of PHP in case your application is not compatible with a specific PHP version.

In this book, you will be using PHP-FPM. To install it, you will need to first add the yum repository followed with yum install like so:

```
sudo rpm -Uvh https://dl.fedoraproject.org/pub/epel/epel-release-latest-7.noarch.rpm
sudo rpm -Uvh https://mirror.webtatic.com/yum/el7/webtatic-release.rpm
sudo yum install -y php56w-fpm php56w-opcache php56w-mysql
```

This will install your php-fpm service, and you can start using it for applications that are written in PHP. To start, stop, or restart the service use the commands respectively:

```
sudo service php-fpm start
sudo service php-fpm stop
sudo service php-fpm restart
```

To view the status, run the following command and notice how it shows a green circle to the left of service name:

```
sudo service php-fpm status
Redirecting to /bin/systemctl status  php-fpm.service
●php-fpm.service - The PHP FastCGI Process Manager
   Loaded: loaded (/usr/lib/systemd/system/php-fpm.service; disabled; vendor preset:
disabled)
   Active: active (running) since Tue 2016-03-08 02:10:35 EST; 1s ago
 Main PID: 2665 (php-fpm)
   Status: "Ready to handle connections"
   CGroup: /system.slice/php-fpm.service
           ├─2665 php-fpm: master process (/etc/php-fpm.conf)
           ├─2666 php-fpm: pool www
           ├─2667 php-fpm: pool www
           ├─2668 php-fpm: pool www
           ├─2669 php-fpm: pool www
           └─2670 php-fpm: pool www
```

To view the version of PHP, you can use the following command:

```
php -v
PHP 5.6.18 (cli) (built: Feb  4 2016 22:08:11)
Copyright (c) 1997-2016 The PHP Group
Zend Engine v2.6.0, Copyright (c) 1998-2016 Zend Technologies
    with Zend OPcache v7.0.6-dev, Copyright (c) 1999-2016, by Zend Technologies
```

■ **Tip**   Even though Nginx+Apache+mod_php combination works, Nginx+PHP-FPM happens to be more performant due to architectural differences of PHP-FPM. It is a good idea to evaluate your application against the latter technology combination to gain high performance from your web servers.

Let's configure Nginx to test if PHP works by default. As discussed in chapter 6, start by creating a configuration file for the test site by copying the /etc/nginx/conf.d/default.template:

```
sudo cp /etc/nginx/conf.d/default.template /etc/nginx/conf.d/test.conf
```

Modify the test.conf file so that it looks like the following:

```
server {
    listen       80;
    server_name  localhost;

    root    /usr/share/nginx/html;

    location / {
        index  index.html index.htm;
    }

    # pass the PHP scripts to FastCGI server listening on 127.0.0.1:9000
    location ~ \.php$ {
        fastcgi_pass    127.0.0.1:9000;
        fastcgi_index   index.php;
        fastcgi_param   SCRIPT_FILENAME  $document_root$fastcgi_script_name;
        include         fastcgi_params;
    }
}
```

In the previous configuration block, the last location block is what does the real magic from PHP perspective.

- The location route matches all routes that end with a .php.

- The fastcgi_pass directive tells Nginx to pass on the request to the specified address. If you like, you can have another server just to serve PHP requests. In this configuration however, since the php_fpm service is running locally, the request gets routed to that process on the same server instead on port 9000.

- fastcgi_index directive sets a file name that will be appended after a URI that ends with a slash, in the value of the $fastcgi_script_name variable.

- fastcgi_param sets the parameter for the SCRIPT_FILENAME. In the current block if the request is for /page.php the SCRIPT_FILENAME variable will be $document_root/ page.php, but if the request is just for / the SCRIPT_FILENAME will be $document_ root/index.php. $document_root variable is equal to the root directive set inside your location or server block.

- The include directives initialize a bunch of other parameters and is set in a file located at /etc/nginx/fastcgi_params. It is a good idea to keep all parameters related to fastcgi grouped in a single file.

```
fastcgi_param   QUERY_STRING        $query_string;
fastcgi_param   REQUEST_METHOD      $request_method;
fastcgi_param   CONTENT_TYPE        $content_type;
fastcgi_param   CONTENT_LENGTH      $content_length;

fastcgi_param   SCRIPT_NAME         $fastcgi_script_name;
fastcgi_param   REQUEST_URI         $request_uri;
fastcgi_param   DOCUMENT_URI        $document_uri;
fastcgi_param   DOCUMENT_ROOT       $document_root;
fastcgi_param   SERVER_PROTOCOL     $server_protocol;
fastcgi_param   HTTPS               $https if_not_empty;

fastcgi_param   GATEWAY_INTERFACE   CGI/1.1;
fastcgi_param   SERVER_SOFTWARE     nginx/$nginx_version;

fastcgi_param   REMOTE_ADDR         $remote_addr;
fastcgi_param   REMOTE_PORT         $remote_port;
fastcgi_param   SERVER_ADDR         $server_addr;
fastcgi_param   SERVER_PORT         $server_port;
fastcgi_param   SERVER_NAME         $server_name;

# PHP only, required if PHP was built with --enable-force-cgi-redirect
fastcgi_param   REDIRECT_STATUS     200;
```

Now it's time to test if PHP is working. Create a file at /usr/share/nginx/html/test.php and paste the following code in it. The first line reads the server variables and the second line displays tabular information about PHP itself.

```
<?php var_export($_SERVER)?>
<?php phpinfo() ?>
```

Browse to http://localhost:8006/test.php and you should be able to see a page that looks similar to Figure 7-1.

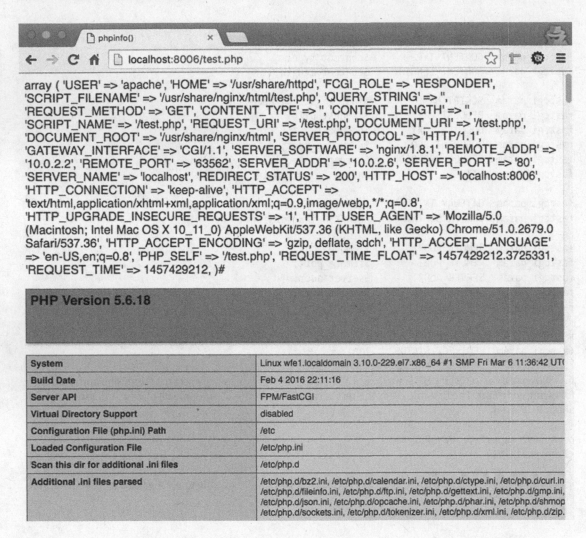

Figure 7-1. *Output of test.php*

This is great! Your server can now host PHP pages and output dynamic pages for you.

Notice the USER is Apache in Figure 7-4. Why would that be so? Well, the reason is that by default the configuration file for php-fpm is configured so that the process is executed as apache. Run the command ps -aux | grep php and you will find that the php-fpm process is running as apache.

```
ps -aux | grep php
root      2665  0.0  1.9 393584 20292 ?         Ss    02:10   0:00 php-fpm: master process
(/etc/php-fpm.conf)
apache    2666  0.0  0.4 393584  4908 ?         S     02:10   0:00 php-fpm: pool www
apache    2667  0.0  0.4 393584  4908 ?         S     02:10   0:00 php-fpm: pool www
apache    2668  0.0  0.4 393584  4908 ?         S     02:10   0:00 php-fpm: pool www
apache    2669  0.0  0.4 393584  4908 ?         S     02:10   0:00 php-fpm: pool www
apache    2670  0.0  0.4 393584  4908 ?         S     02:10   0:00 php-fpm: pool www
user1     2702  0.0  0.0 112612   736 pts/0     S+    02:17   0:00 grep --color=auto php
```

In contrast `ps -aux | grep nginx` will tell you that the process for Nginx is running as `nginx`.

```
ps -aux | grep nginx
nginx    953  0.0  0.1  48268  1904 ?       S    Mar07  0:00 nginx: worker process
user1   2705  0.0  0.0 112612   736 pts/0   R+   02:20  0:00 grep --color=auto nginx
```

To change the user, you can edit the configuration file `sudo vi /etc/php-fpm.d/www.conf` and change the line that reads user = apache to user = nginx and group = apache to group = nginx. Restart the service by typing the following command.

```
sudo service php-fpm restart
```

If you refresh the page, you will now see that the settings have taken affect and you are being served a page with `'USER'=>'nginx'`. You can also check the output of `ps -aux | grep php` and confirm that the process is indeed running as `nginx`.

Your `wfe1.localdomain` server can be considered fully setup as a LEMP stack server. You can now set up dynamic applications on it.

■ **Caution**   Once you have tested the test.php, it is a good practice to remove the file since it can be used by malicious users for gathering system information.

Configure Nginx for WordPress

WordPress is the world's most commonly used content management system based on PHP and MySQL. More than 60 million websites use WordPress as their content management system. It is open source and the application files are installed on a web server. You can also host your blog or site using WordPress.com, but in our context we will be dealing only with the self-hosting option of WordPress.

In the previous chapter you have already downloaded the zipped version of the repository from Github located at `https://github.com/attosol/nginx`. You will find a folder called `/dynamic/wordpress-4.4.2`. This folder contains version 4.4.2 of WordPress. WordPress is known for easy installation steps. So, let us quickly install WordPress and see it in action by following these steps:

1. Log in to the MySQL prompt using `mysql -u root -p`.

2. To create a database, use the following command where `wpsite` is the name of the database:

```
CREATE DATABASE wpsite
```

3. Grant all privileges to a user account using the following command where `wpuser` is the name of the user and P@ssword1! is your strong password. Change the password as you deem fit and run the command:

```
GRANT ALL PRIVILEGES on wpsite.* TO wpuser@localhost IDENTIFIED BY "P@ssword1!";
```

4. Upload the files using an FTP client as shown in Figure 7-2. Create a new folder called WordPress and upload all the content from `/dynamic/wordpress-4.4.2`.

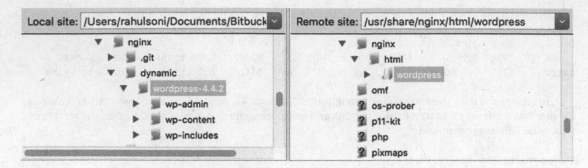

Figure 7-2. *Uploading content to WFE1 server*

5. Remove your test.conf file that you created from the default.template a while ago in this chapter:

```
sudo rm -f /etc/nginx/conf.d/test.conf
```

6. Create a copy of the default.template file like so:

```
sudo cp /etc/nginx/conf.d/default.template /etc/nginx/conf.d/wpsite.conf
```

7. Make your look as follows and reload using sudo nginx -s reload:

```
server {
    listen        80;
    server_name  localhost;

    root    /usr/share/nginx/html/wordpress;

    location / {
        index  index.php index.html index.htm;
    }

    # pass the PHP scripts to FastCGI server listening on 127.0.0.1:9000
    location ~ \.php$ {
        fastcgi_pass    127.0.0.1:9000;
        fastcgi_index   index.php;
        fastcgi_param   SCRIPT_FILENAME  $document_root$fastcgi_script_name;
        include         fastcgi_params;
    }
}
```

8.   Although not mandatory, it is a good idea to check if your database is up and connecting well from PHP. It is actually fairly simple. Create a file in your /usr/share/nginx/html/wordpress directory called dbtest.php and write the following text:

```
<?php
  $db=mysql_connect('localhost', 'wpuser', 'P@ssword1!');
  if (!$db) echo "connection failed";
  else echo "connection succeeded";
?>
```

9.   If you browse to http://localhost:8006/dbtest.php you should see "connection succeeded" message. If you don't see it, something is missing and you are advised to cross check before proceeding ahead.

10. Time for some cool stuff. Type http://localhost:8006/index.php in your browser. It should take you to the famous 5-minute WordPress installation page, which looks similar to Figure 7-3:

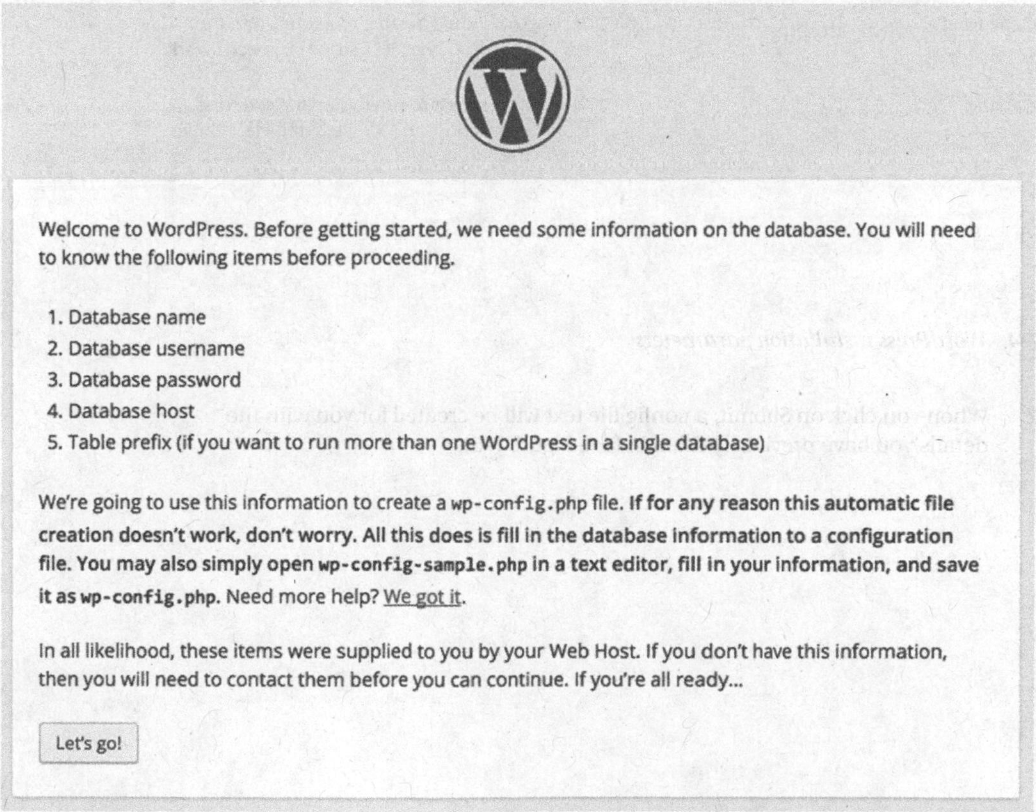

Welcome to WordPress. Before getting started, we need some information on the database. You will need to know the following items before proceeding.

1. Database name
2. Database username
3. Database password
4. Database host
5. Table prefix (if you want to run more than one WordPress in a single database)

We're going to use this information to create a wp-config.php file. **If for any reason this automatic file creation doesn't work, don't worry. All this does is fill in the database information to a configuration file. You may also simply open wp-config-sample.php in a text editor, fill in your information, and save it as wp-config.php.** Need more help? <u>We got it.</u>

In all likelihood, these items were supplied to you by your Web Host. If you don't have this information, then you will need to contact them before you can continue. If you're all ready...

Let's go!

Figure 7-3. WordPress installation page. Click Let's go!

11. You will be presented a screen that will ask for the parameters that you have already set up. Provide the details as you see in Figure 7-4 and click Submit.

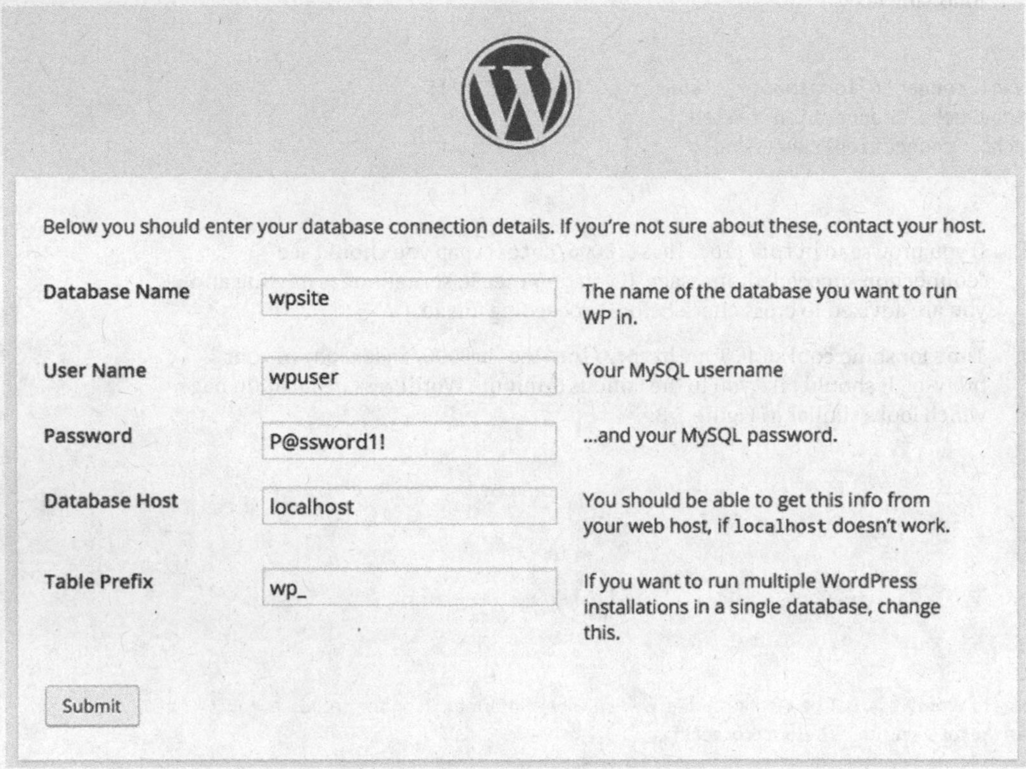

Figure 7-4. *WordPress installation parameters*

12. When you click on Submit, a config file text will be created for you with the details you have previously filled in (see Figure 7-5).

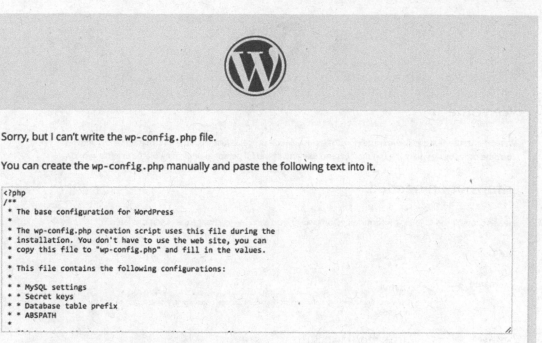

Sorry, but I can't write the wp-config.php file.

You can create the wp-config.php manually and paste the following text into it.

```php
<?php
/**
 * The base configuration for WordPress
 *
 * The wp-config.php creation script uses this file during the
 * installation. You don't have to use the web site, you can
 * copy this file to "wp-config.php" and fill in the values.
 *
 * This file contains the following configurations:
 *
 * * MySQL settings
 * * Secret keys
 * * Database table prefix
 * * ABSPATH
 *
```

After you've done that, click "Run the install."

Run the install

Figure 7-5. Configuration file created by WordPress installation

13.   Copy the entire text and paste it in a file created at /usr/share/nginx/html/
      wordpress/wp-config.php.

■ **Tip**   There is another way in which you can do the previous few steps related to WordPress. All you will
need is to create a copy of the wp-config-sample.php as wp-config.php and make the necessary changes in
the file. If you do that, your WordPress setup will start with the step you see in Figure 7-5.

---

14.   After that, click on Run the install button (Figure 7-5). And you will be presented
      the final screen for WordPress setup. It is that simple!

15.   Click on Install WordPress and you are all set with your website. To login to your
      website, you now have to go to http://localhost:8006/wp-admin/index.php
      and type in the Username and Password that you have configured in Figure 7-6.

Welcome

Welcome to the famous five-minute WordPress installation process! Just fill in the information below and you'll be on your way to using the most extendable and powerful personal publishing platform in the world.

Information needed

Please provide the following information. Don't worry, you can always change these settings later.

Site Title	My Site!!!
Username	Rahul
	Usernames can have only alphanumeric characters, spaces, underscores, hyphens, periods, and the @ symbol.
Password	HI0p2RZQX2*5j#Q0Su 👁 Hide
	Strong
	Important: You will need this password to log in. Please store it in a secure location.
Your Email	rahul@attosol.com
	Double-check your email address before continuing.
Search Engine Visibility	☐ Discourage search engines from indexing this site
	It is up to search engines to honor this request.

Install WordPress

Figure 7-6. *WordPress setup - Final Step*

Create your posts and try browsing to http://localhost:8006 and you will be glad to see your website online. Often the WordPress administrators change the Settings ➤ Permalink in the WordPress Administration Dashboard to Post Name or one of the other options as shown in Figure 7-7.

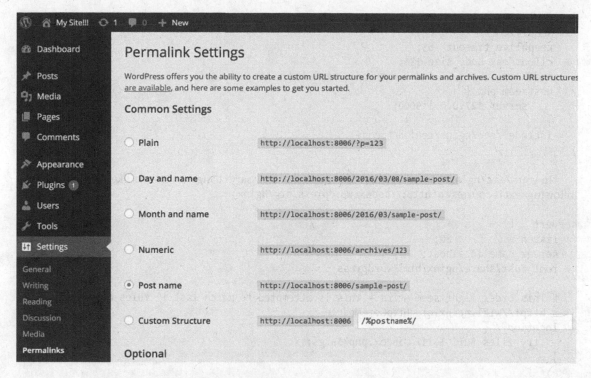

Figure 7-7. Changing Settings to get cleaner URL in WordPress

The moment you change the settings here, your home will continue to work but the cleaner URIs (for example, http://localhost:8006/test-post-1) will fail. This is because of the way the URI is mapped in the Nginx configuration. To fix such issues, change your /etc/nginx/nginx.conf file to look like the following:

```
user  nginx;
worker_processes  1;
error_log  /var/log/nginx/error.log warn;
pid        /var/run/nginx.pid;

events {
    worker_connections  1024;
}

http {
    include         /etc/nginx/mime.types;
    default_type    application/octet-stream;
    log_format      main  '$remote_addr - $remote_user - [$time_local] - $document_root -
    $document_uri - '
                    '$request - $status - $body_bytes_sent - $http_referer';
```

```
    access_log             /var/log/nginx/access.log  main;
    sendfile               on;
    keepalive_timeout 65;
    client_max_body_size 13m;
    index                  index.php index.html index.htm;
    upstream php {
        server 127.0.0.1:9000;
    }
    include /etc/nginx/conf.d/*.conf;
}
```

In your /etc/nginx/conf.d/wpsite.conf make the necessary changes so it looks like the following (the following text is courtesy of http://codex.wordpress.org/Nginx):

```
server{
    listen            80;
    server_name localhost;
    root /usr/share/nginx/html/wordpress;

    # This order might seem weird - this is attempted to match last if rules below fail.
    # http://wiki.nginx.org/HttpCoreModule
    location / {
        try_files $uri $uri/ /index.php?$args;
    }

    # Add trailing slash to */wp-admin requests.
    rewrite /wp-admin$ $scheme://$host$uri/ permanent;

    # Directives to send expires headers and turn off 404 error logging.
    location ~* ^.+\.(ogg|ogv|svg|svgz|eot|otf|woff|mp4|ttf|rss|atom|jpg|jpeg|gif|png|ico|zip
|tgz|gz|rar|bz2|doc|xls|exe|ppt|tar|mid|midi|wav|bmp|rtf)$ {
        access_log off;
        log_not_found off;
        expires max;
    }

    # Uncomment one of the lines below for the appropriate caching plugin (if used).
    #include global/wordpress-wp-super-cache.conf;
    #include global/wordpress-w3-total-cache.conf;

    #Pass all .php files onto a php-fpm/php-fcgi server.
    location ~ [^/]\.php(/|$) {
        fastcgi_split_path_info ^(.+?\.php)(/.*)$;
        if (!-f $document_root$fastcgi_script_name) {
            return 404;
        }
        include fastcgi_params;
        fastcgi_index index.php;
        fastcgi_param SCRIPT_FILENAME $document_root$fastcgi_script_name;
        fastcgi_pass php;
    }
}
```

Quite a number of new directives have come to play in the configuration just covered. In Table 7-1, let us look at the ones that have not yet been discussed.

Table 7-1. *Important Directives at play in the mysite.conf file*

Directive	Description
worker_connections	Sets the maximum number of simultaneous connections that can be opened by a worker process. This number includes all connections like connection with proxied servers as well as clients. Also remember that simultaneous connections cannot exceed the current limit on the maximum number of open files (worker_rlimit_nofile).
default_type	This directive defines the default MIME type of a response. It is set to application/octet-stream by default in this case. This implies that the server can send any binary file. For example, the server can emit a zip file and it will be appropriately handled by the client since it knows that the type of the file is binary.
client_max_body_size	Defines the maximum size allowed for the request body. If the size increases the configured limits, it sends an error code 413, which means Request Entity Too Large. In this configuration it is set to 13MB. Depending on your content type, you should tweak it.
upstream	This directive is used to group servers in a block making your configuration more readable and manageable. If you provide multiple servers, the requests get distributed in a round-robin load balanced fashion. In this configuration, a php upstream is defined with just one server inside it.
try_files	Tells Nginx to try finding the files in specified order. In the current configuration it searches for $uri, $uri/, /index.php?$args.
rewrite	Checks for a specific regular expression and redirects if found. Here, it checks for /wp-admin$ and appends a forward slash ($scheme://$host$uri/ permanent;) whenever the URI contains wp-admin.
log_not_found	Since it turned to off in this configuration, Nginx won't log errors if files are not found.
expires	This directive enables Nginx to send an Expires and Cache-Control response header. This is a very crucial directive since you can save a lot of bandwidth if the directive is enabled and set to max. By setting it max, you are effectively telling the client and proxy servers to cache the files for as long as possible.
fastcgi_split_path_info	This directive defines a regular expression based on which the request gets split. The former part of the split string becomes $fastcgi_script_name and the latter becomes $fastcgi_path parameter, which can be subsequently used. If the URI is /page.php/post/001, $fastcgi_script_name will contain /page.php while $fastcgi_path_info will be equal to /post/001.
fastcgi_pass	This directive sets the address of a FastCGI server. It can be a domain name or an IP address. In this case it sets it to php, which is the name of the upstream block.

The MEAN Stack

A stack called MEAN (Mongo, Express, Angular, and Node) is becoming increasingly popular among the full-stack web developers. These web developers are often called full-stack developers because the entire technology stack, from database (MongoDB) to back end (Node.JS + Express.JS) to front end (Angular.JS) uses JavaScript. Even though they can use the MEAN stack to handle all requests, it often makes sense to accelerate the entire application using Nginx as front end. In the remainder of this chapter you will see how to set up a MEAN stack and start a sample web application.

Installing MongoDB

MongoDB is a very popular database choice these days. It is a cross-platform and document-oriented database. In the NoSQL database world, MongoDB absolutely shines. Since WFE1 has been allocated for MySQL, you can use WFE2 for MongoDB. In production, you will most likely have dedicated database servers. For the lab setup however, you should be good to go. To install MongoDB, use the following steps:

1. Create a file called /etc/yum.repos.d/mongodb-org-3.2.repo and write the following text in it:

```
[mongodb-org-3.2]
name=MongoDB Repository
baseurl=https://repo.mongodb.org/yum/redhat/$releasever/mongodb-org/3.2/x86_64/
gpgcheck=0
enabled=1
```

2. Execute the following command to install MongoDB:

```
sudo yum install -y mongodb-org
```

Again, covering all topics about Mongo, or MEAN for that matter, is outside the scope of this book, but there is a bare minimum you need to know so that at least you can start up the server and fire away some commands.

3. MongoDB comprises of multiple components, but for testing the waters, you need to learn just a couple of them. mongod is the daemon that can be considered as the Mongo server. The mongo command, often known as mongo shell, is the client that connects to the mongo server and is very similar to MySQL command line conceptually. You can start the mongo server using this:

```
sudo service mongod start
```

4. Now, simply type mongo and you should be able to connect to the server. Typing mongo invokes the mongo shell, which is fairly simple to use once you learn it.

■ **Tip** Note that it is possible that you get the following error while trying to invoke Mongo. The error happens if your locale settings are broken.

```
Failed global initialization: BadValue Invalid or no user locale set. Please ensure LANG
and/or LC_* environment variables are set correctly.
```

You can fix this error by manually setting the variable (export LC_ALL=C) before you start the Mongo shell.

---

5. You can view the version of MongoDB by typing `version()` in the mongo shell. Try the following commands in order and you can see how intuitive it is:

```
> use foo
switched to db foo
> db
foo
> db.users.insert({"name":"mongo", "about":"rocks!"})
WriteResult({ "nInserted" : 1 })
> db.users.find()
{ "_id" : ObjectId("56e7f53b569a00edf1c98a9b"), "name" : "mongo", "about" : "rocks!" }
> quit()
```

You can learn more about MongoDB at `http://www.mongodb.org`. In fact, they even run regular courses for free where you can learn about it and get certified if you wish to. For more information about their courses, please visit `http://university.mongodb.com/courses`.

Installing Node.JS

Node.js is an extremely powerful, open source, cross-platform runtime environment for developing server-side web applications. Although it is not a JavaScript framework, many of its modules are written in JavaScript. The runtime environment interprets JavaScript using Google's V8 JavaScript engine. Of late, it has become very popular among web developers. Learn more at `http://nodejs.org`.

Installing Node is much more straightforward. Run the following command one by one, and by the end of the third command, you will have NodeJS installed on your server.

```
sudo curl --silent --location https://rpm.nodesource.com/setup_4.x | sudo bash -
sudo yum -y install nodejs
sudo yum -y install gcc-c++ make
```

You can test if Node is installed correctly by running the following command:

```
node -v
v4.4.0
```

Installing Express.JS

They say Express and Node are like twins that are joined at the hip. Technically though, consider Express. js as a Node.js web application server framework. It serves as the back end for Node.js and comes with a plethora of plug-ins for various aspects, like parsing a cookie or a request body, authentication and much more. It can be installed by executing npm (Node Package Manager) commands. To install it globally on the server, type `sudo npm install express -g`. Learn more at `http://expressjs.com`.

Installing Angular.JS

This portion is usually done in the application side using the npm install command. The npm install command reads the dependencies and installs everything that is needed by the server. Angular, as such, is not something that is installed. Consider it a JavaScript framework for the client side. It is simply downloaded at the client side and provides a huge amount of functionality like data binding, routing and a lot more. To learn more about it visit `http://angularjs.org`.

Creating a MEAN Application

Building a MEAN application is fun. So, instead of giving you a sample, this section will show you how you can type a few more commands and set up an application with basic scaffolding.

1. To ensure that npm is the latest version, install it using the following command:

```
sudo npm -g install npm
```

2. Next, install express generator. This will help you start an application quickly with basic scaffolding.

```
sudo npm install express-generator -g
```

3. Create an application and run using the following commands. Yes, it is that simple!

```
express myapp
cd myapp
npm install
```

4. You can very well run the application using npm start at this moment. But that is not a good idea since the process runs as a foreground application. Running this application using a package called pm2 helps in production scenarios. Install it by using the following command:

```
sudo npm install pm2 -g
```

5. Once done, you can now execute your application using the following:

```
pm2 start bin/www.
[PM2] Starting bin/www in fork_mode (1 instance)
[PM2] Done.
```

• To view all applications hosted using pm2, you can use pm2 list. (see Figure 7-8).

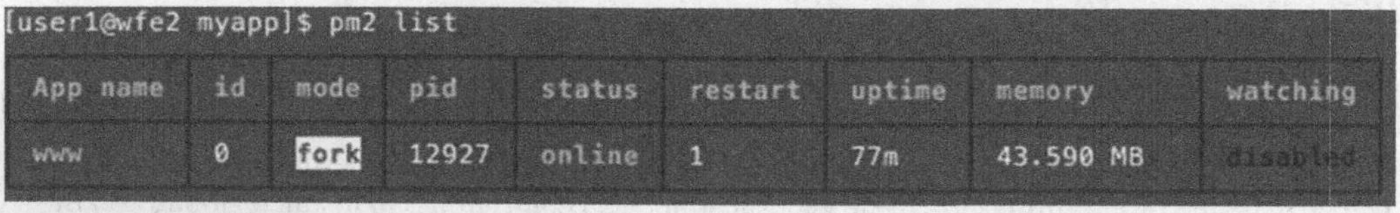

App name	id	mode	pid	status	restart	uptime	memory	watching
www	0	fork	12927	online	1	77m	43.590 MB	disabled

Figure 7-8. *PM2 List*

6. The App name can be used to view details about the application. As you can see in Figure 7-9, the PID is 12927 and the application name is www. You can redeploy your code and simply run pm2 restart www to restart this application. It keeps running the application in background mode.

7. To view the application details, use pm2 show www.

8.   To stop the application, use pm2 stop www.

9.   To learn more about pm2, visit http://pm2.keymetrics.io/.

Okay, so now that the application is running in the background, you can do curl localhost:3000 to view the output. It will be a very html output on the command line.

Configure Nginx for MEAN Stack

The Node application that is running needs to be exposed using Nginx. Recall that this application is just the beginning of the MEAN stack. It doesn't even use MongoDB or Angular yet. But for the purpose of this book, it should suffice. You simply need to know the pattern for managing and hosting such applications. Typically, the application files will be given to you just like you have them in the myapp directory.

1.   For simplicity clean up any other conf file in /etc/nginx/conf.d and create a new configuration file as follows:

```
sudo cp /etc/nginx/conf.d/default.template /etc/nginx/conf.d/node.conf
```

2.   Edit the node.conf file so that it looks like so:

```
upstream nodeapp {
    server    127.0.0.1:3000;
}


server {
    listen      80;
    server_name localhost;
    root        /usr/share/nginx/html;

    location / {
      proxy_pass http://nodeapp;
    }
}
```

Notice the usage of upstream directive. The Express application was listening on port 3000, hence server directive inside upstream will route the traffic there.

Inside the server block, there is location directive that uses proxy_pass to redirect the traffic upstream using the http://nodeapp address. You will learn more about these directives in chapter 8.

Try browsing http://localhost:8007 and instead of getting the page you might get an error saying 502 Bad Gateway. The error in the error.log is typically like the following:

```
[crit] 13535#0: *43 connect() to 127.0.0.1:3000 failed (13: Permission denied) while
connecting to upstream, client: 127.0.0.1, server: localhost, request: "GET / HTTP/1.1",
upstream: "http://127.0.0.1:3000/", host: "localhost"
```

If you don't get this error, you are good to go! However, in case you get the error, most likely it is happening due to SELinux. To troubleshoot this, install setroubleshoot, using: sudo yum install setroubleshoot.

3.   After the package installs, execute the following command:

```
sudo cat /var/log/audit/audit.log | grep nginx | grep denied | audit2allow -M mynginx
```

Finally, execute `sudo semodule -i mynginx.pp` and the problem should be resolved. Check by browsing `http://localhost:8007`.

Summary

In this chapter you have learned various important things about hosting dynamic applications with Nginx. The chapter started with setting up a LEMP stack by installing the appropriate packages for MySQL and PHP. Post that, you learned about installation, configuration, and some finer nuances of WordPress administration on Nginx. Later in this chapter, you learned about the basics of MEAN stack and how easy it is to configure it using Nginx. You will be learning more about performance fine-tuning for dynamic applications and load balancing in the coming chapters.

CHAPTER 8

■ ■ ■

Load Balancing with Nginx

So far in this book, you have seen the power of Nginx as a web server. However, Nginx is much more than that. It is frequently used as a proxy server. A proxy server's job is to front end the request and pass it on to the proxied server, which is also known as an upstream server. The upstream server processes the request and sends the response back to the Nginx server, which further relays the response to the clients who made the request. You may think, why do you need to complicate things as much? Wouldn't it make the processing slower because of the number of hops? This chapter focuses on answers to similar questions, and you will learn about setting up servers based on different scenarios.

Defining High Availability

Let's begin with the fundamentals of high availability. A system can be considered highly available if it is continuously operational as long as desired. That is easier said than done. There are basically three main aspects that you need to consider while designing a highly available system.

1. Eliminate a single point of failure. In simple words, it means that you should design your system such that failure at a specific point doesn't bring down the entire system. In a web server context, it means that having just one server, serving your requests for www.yoursite.com is not recommended. Even though you can have multiple worker processes for Nginx, it doesn't take care of scenarios where a server has to be patched for security and rebooted. Also, it doesn't take care of hardware or network failures. Having a single server serving your web pages, hence, can become a single point of failure and should be avoided.

2. Reliable failover. In simplistic terms, a failover implies that if one of the servers goes down, another one takes its place without the end user noticing the disruption in service. Consider a car. If one of the tires gets punctured, even though you have an extra tire , it takes a while to manually change it. You can say that the failover is reliable, but it isn't quick. In today's world, for a busy e-commerce website, slow failover means revenue loss that could run in millions. It is to be noted that the revenue loss here is not only from the lost business, but also due to the lack of trust that ensues following a major failure.

3. Failure detection at run time. No system is 100 percent perfect. Although, if monitored well, it can appear to be 100 percent reliable. High-availability design suggests that you create the system in such a way that failure could be detected and fixed with time in hand. However, it is easier said than done.

© Rahul Soni 2016
R. Soni, *Nginx*, DOI 10.1007/978-1-4842-1656-9_8

All the three points mentioned above sound pretty obvious, but designing such a system is hard. In fact, very hard! As an engineer or architect, you will be often asked to maintain a Service Level Agreement (SLA) in terms of percentage of uptime. Take a look at Table 8-1.

Table 8-1. *Service Level Agreement Chart*

Availability %	Downtime per year	Downtime per day
99% (two nines)	3.65 days	14.4 mins
99.9% (three nines)	8.76 hours	1.44 mins
99.99% (four nines)	52.56 mins	8.66 seconds
99.999% (five nines)	5.26 mins	864.3 milliseconds
99.9999% (six nines)	31.5 seconds	86.4 milliseconds

That's right: it is just 31.5 seconds per year for a six niner SLA. In today's world, 4 nines and 5 nines have almost become a norm for major cloud providers, and 100 percent is not farfetched either. See Figure 8-1.

▾ ▦ **Compute**

Service Name	Status	30 Day Availability	*1 block = 1 mins*	Outages	Regions	▲ Downtime/Region	Total
Amazon EC2	♠	100%	‖‖‖‖‖‖‖‖‖‖‖‖‖‖	0	10	None	None
Rackspace Cloud Servers	♠	100%		0	6	None	None
StratoGen VMware Cloud	♠	100%	‖‖‖‖‖‖‖‖‖‖‖‖‖‖	1	5	None	None
Joyent Cloud	♠	100%		0	4	None	None
UpCloud	♠	100%	‖‖‖‖‖‖‖‖‖‖‖‖‖‖	0	4	None	None
Gandi Cloud VPS	♠	100%		0	2	None	None
GoDaddy Cloud	♠	•100%	‖‖‖‖‖‖‖‖‖‖‖‖‖‖	0	2	None	None
Hosting.com	♠	100%		0	2	None	None
Liquid Web Storm Servers	♠	100%	‖‖‖‖‖‖‖‖‖‖‖‖‖‖	0	2	None	None
Phoenix NAP Cloud	⚠	100%		0	2	None	None
Cloudhelix VMware Cloud Hosting	♠	100%	‖‖‖‖‖‖‖‖‖‖‖‖‖‖	0	1	None	None
Colosseum Cloud	♠	100%		0	1	None	None
GMO Cloud - US	♠	100%	‖‖‖‖‖‖‖‖‖‖‖‖‖‖	0	1	None	None
KT ucloud	♠	100%		0	1	None	None
M9 Systems	♠	100%	‖‖‖‖‖‖‖‖‖‖‖‖‖‖	0	1	None	None
NetHosting Cloud	♠	100%	‖‖‖‖‖‖‖‖‖‖‖‖‖‖	0	1	None	None

Figure 8-1. *Service status by different cloud providers (courtesy: https://cloudharmony.com/status-group-by-regions)*

Load Balancing for High Availability

When you manage web servers, one of your primary duties is to maintain a specific SLA. As discussed in the previous section, keeping a server running 24x7x365 becomes crucial. At the same time, patching the server regularly is equally important. Sometimes, patching requires you to reboot the server before the settings take effect. During the rebooting process, the website remains down. Ask yourself, what if the server doesn't come up after the reboot or a system failure occurs due to hardware? Scary, right? To avoid such scenarios, you set up a load balancer. Figure 8-2 shows what the network would look like.

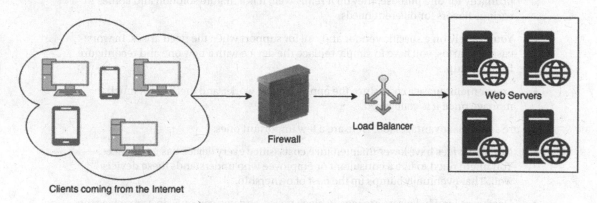

Clients coming from the Internet

Figure 8-2. *A typical network load balancer in action*

As you can see, this setup doesn't have web server as a single point of failure any more. You now have four web servers handling the load from various clients. It is the responsibility of the load balancer to appropriately route the Internet traffic to one of the web servers, retrieve the response from the web server, and return it back to the client. It takes care of bullet #1 discussed in the high-availability section.

Regarding bullet #2, if your application is designed in such a way that the entire application is deployed in one web server, you are good to go and will not have to worry about failover. This is because, if one server goes down, the Network Load Balancer (NLB) will detect it, and won't route the traffic to the server that is down. Quite often, the "entire application in one server" is not practical and the servers have to be created based on the role that it serves. So, in effect, you will have a set of database servers, another set of application servers, and yet another set of front-end servers. The front end in this case doesn't have a single point of failure (the rest of the system has not been drawn in the figure for brevity). The idea is to avoid single point of failures at all levels.

Bullet #3, that is, failure detection, is what helps the load balancer determine which server is down. Ideally, you should have a monitoring solution that keeps monitoring the logs, service levels, and other server vitals to ensure everything runs smoothly in a production farm. The monitoring solution typically has an alerting mechanism that alerts the administrators when the server starts showing signs of stress.

■ **Note**   The network diagram in Figure 8-2 might look robust, but it is not. That is because the load balancer and firewall has now become a single point of failure. You can design them to be fault tolerant by making them failover smoothly in case of issues. However, this won't be covered in this book since it is out of its scope.

Hardware Load Balancer

As the name suggests, a hardware load balancer is a device that is installed in a datacenter and does the job of splitting traffic. Since the decision is made at the electronics level, it happens to be extremely fast. Moreover, the failure rates are low, too. There are multiple vendors like F4, Cisco, Citrix, etc., who provide the hardware. Typically, the configuration is done through a console or a web interface.

Some benefits of using a hardware load balancer include the following:

- It helps generate excellent statistics out of the box. Since the devices are made primarily for one purpose, they do it really well. It is a mature solution and comes in various flavors for different needs.

- You can rely on a specific vendor and call for support when the need arises. In worst-case scenarios, you have to simply replace the device with a new one and reconfigure from backup.

- Lower maintenance costs since the appliance just works, and there is not much to manage once it is configured.

There are some disadvantages too. Here are a few important ones:

- Not all devices have lower maintenance costs, since every device has its nuances. You might need to hire a consultant or employee who understands these devices well. That eventually bumps up the cost of ownership.

- Hardware load balancers are mostly black boxes, and you can only do as much as the console or the API allows. Beyond that, you might have to evaluate another device that has bigger/better feature sets.

- The devices are generally quite costly, and needs you to have a datacenter that you control. In today's world, a lot is being migrated to the cloud and if you have a solution that is deployed mostly in the cloud, a hardware NLB is out of the race.

Software Load Balancer

With time, the load balancers have evolved. They are often referred to as *Application Delivery Controllers* (ADC) and they do much more than traffic routing. The load balancer is not just a black box as it once was, and it has to be a lot more scalable due to the goals of today's massively scalable applications. The future is software, and right from servers, to switches, firewalls, routers, and load balancers, the inclination has been toward a software solution due to various reasons. With the advent of cloud computing this inclination is turning even more toward a software solution. Primarily, it helps in the long run if you are not stuck with a proprietary hardware and its limitations.

Nginx can help you load balance your traffic and much more. There are some very good reasons why you should use Nginx as a software load balancer.

Flexibility

This is the most important reason why you may want to use a software load balancer. Please keep in mind that installing a hardware load balancer requires a lot more work than a software load balancer. A software load balancer can be used anywhere including containers, hypervisors, commodity hardware, and even in the cloud!

Cost

Nginx provides a software-based application delivery platform that load balances HTTP and TCP applications at a fraction of the cost compared to hardware solutions. The open source version is free, and the paid version Nginx PLUS offers 24x7 support at a much lower cost factor.

Sizing

You buy what you need in case of a software LB, whereas, you have to appropriately size for the requirements and often keep an additional buffer for growth. In effect, when it comes to hardware LB, you buy more than what you need to begin with. Sizing correctly is not an easy task and you often undersize or oversize, and this leads to complications in the running deployment. Even if you have purchased it just right, you will have to make the payment up front for the need that you might have had *after* three or five years, based on your initial estimate.

Application vs. Network

The guiding force behind the purchase of a hardware LB is often the network setup. In comparison, software LB is often preferred if you think more about your application and its scalability. This becomes even more important if your application is modern and geared toward cloud deployment.

Elasticity

A software LB is elastic in the sense that you can easily provision bigger servers or spawn additional ones during the spikes. With hardware LB, you will always have to consider the spikes in your sizing calculation and buy appropriately. In effect, it means more resources blocked than you would need on average, and you will end up paying for the resources that you never really utilized.

Consider Figure 8-3. Assume that the average number of hits you anticipate is around 5K per minute throughout the year. Due to a marketing campaign or any other reason you happened to see a spike that took the number of requests to 8K+ per minute. In this case, a hardware LB might start throttling or might even fail to respond appropriately. The solution is to buy the device appropriately considering the maximum throughput that you anticipate. This also implies that you will end up paying for a device that handles more concurrent requests (8K per min), whereas your average is much less (just 5K per minute).

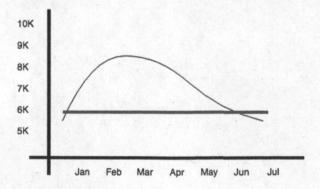

Figure 8-3. *Sales spike between Jan to May*

Easy Deployment

Setting up a software LB is much simpler and easier than hardware LB. Additionally, a software LB is same whether it runs on a bare metal server, virtual server, container, or cloud. The functionality and configuration method doesn't change. This is not the case with hardware load balancers. Every device is different and has different requirements and capacities. Maintenance requires specific knowledge of the given hardware and the variety of choices makes it even more difficult to evaluate different devices.

Multi-Tenancy

If you have multiple applications, buying a different hardware LB for each application might be too expensive. To counter that, sharing the LB between multiple applications also means that one noisy application can negatively impact others. Software LB can be easily multi-tenanted, and it turns out to be a lot more effective in the long run since it doesn't suffer from a *noisy-neighbor* issue.

Load Balancing in Nginx

Now that you have learned about the basics of load balancing and advantages of using a software load balancer, let's move forward and work on the Nginx servers you already created in the previous chapters.

Clean Up the Servers

Before setting up anything new, clean up the previous applications so that you can start afresh. This is to keep things simpler. You will be settings up applications in different ways in the upcoming sections of this chapter. The idea is to give you information about different scenarios from a practical perspective.

1. Log on to the WFE1 using `ssh -p 3026 user1@127.0.0.1`

2. Remove everything from the Nginx home directory.

```
sudo rm -rf /usr/share/nginx/html/*
```

3. Reset your configuration (`sudo vi /etc/nginx/nginx.conf`) to the following:

```
user  nginx;
worker_processes  1;
error_log  /var/log/nginx/error.log warn;
pid        /var/run/nginx.pid;

events {
    worker_connections  1024;
}
```

```
http {
    include             /etc/nginx/mime.types;
    default_type        application/octet-stream;
    log_format          main '$remote_addr - $remote_user - [$time_local] - $document_root -
    $document_uri - '
                        '$request - $status - $body_bytes_sent - $http_referer';

    access_log          /var/log/nginx/access.log  main;
    sendfile            on;
    keepalive_timeout   65;
    index               index.html index.htm;
    include /etc/nginx/conf.d/*.conf;
}
```

4. Now, remove the entries in conf.d by using the following command:

```
sudo rm -f /etc/nginx/conf.d/*.conf
```

5. Repeat the steps for WFE2.

Create Web Content

Let's create some content so that it is easy to identify which server served the request. In practical situations, the content on the WFE1 and WFE2 will be same for the same application. Run the following command on both WFE1 and WFE2:

```
uname -n | sudo tee /usr/share/nginx/html/index.html
```

This command is pretty straightforward. It uses the output of uname -n and dumps it in a file called index.html in the default root location of Nginx. View the content and ensure that the output is different on both the servers.

```
$cat /usr/share/nginx/html/index.html
wfe1.localdomain
```

■ **Tip**   The tee command reads from the standard input and writes to standard output as well as files. It is handy, since it shows you the output along with creating the file at the same time.

Configure WFE1 and WFE2

The content is available on both servers now, but since you have already cleaned up the configuration you will need to re-create the configuration file by using the following command:

```
sudo cp /etc/nginx/conf.d/default.template /etc/nginx/conf.d/main.conf
```

The command will create a copy of the configuration for a default website. If you recall, the default. template contained the following text:

```
server {
    listen       80;
    server_name  localhost;

    location / {
        root   /usr/share/nginx/html;
        index  index.html index.htm;
    }
    error_page   500 502 503 504  /50x.html;
    location = /50x.html {
        root   /usr/share/nginx/html;
    }
}
```

- Restart the service: sudo systemctl restart nginx.

- Repeat the steps on WFE2.

- Once done, you should be able to execute curl localhost on both servers, and you should get output as wfe1.localdomain and wfe2.localdomain respectively. Notice that even though the request is same (curl localhost), the output is different. In practice, the output will be the same from both servers.

Set Up NLB Server

Setting up an NLB server is no different than setting up a regular web server. The installation steps are similar to what you have learned already. The configuration, however, is different and you will learn about it in the upcoming sections.

1. Create a new virtual machine called NLB.

2. Set up a NAT configuration as you have learned in previous chapters. It should look similar to Figure 8-4.

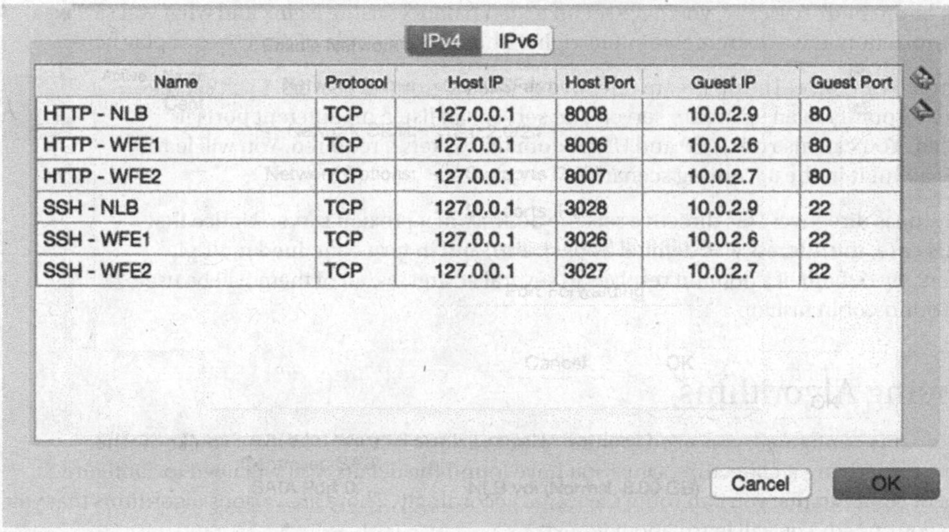

		IPv4	IPv6			
Name	Protocol	Host IP	Host Port	Guest IP	Guest Port	
HTTP - NLB	TCP	127.0.0.1	8008	10.0.2.9	80	
HTTP - WFE1	TCP	127.0.0.1	8006	10.0.2.6	80	
HTTP - WFE2	TCP	127.0.0.1	8007	10.0.2.7	80	
SSH - NLB	TCP	127.0.0.1	3028	10.0.2.9	22	
SSH - WFE1	TCP	127.0.0.1	3026	10.0.2.6	22	
SSH - WFE2	TCP	127.0.0.1	3027	10.0.2.7	22	

Cancel   OK

Figure 8-4. Network configuration for NLB with two WFEs

3. Install Nginx (refer to chapter 2) on the NLB server.

4. Since it is a new server, when you execute `curl localhost`, you will see the default welcome page. You can ignore it for the time being.

5. Open the configuration file (`/etc/nginx/conf.d/default.conf`) and make the changes as follows:

```
upstream backend{
        server 10.0.2.6;
        server 10.0.2.7;
}

server {
    listen        80;
    location / {
        proxy_pass http://backend;
}
```

6. Restart the service.

7. Try the following command a few times and notice how it gives you output from WFE1 and WFE2 in an alternate fashion.

```
[root@nlb ~]# curl localhost
wfe1.localdomain
[root@nlb ~]# curl localhost
wfe2.localdomain
[root@nlb ~]# curl localhost
wfe1.localdomain
[root@nlb ~]# curl localhost
wfe2.localdomain
```

So, what just happened? Basically, you have set up a load balancer using Nginx and what you saw was the load balancer in action. It was extremely simple, right? There are a couple of directives at play here.

- upstream directive: The upstream directive defines a group of servers. Each server directive points to an upstream server. The server can listen on different ports if needed. You can also mix TCP and UNIX-domain sockets if required. You will learn more about it in the upcoming scenarios.

- proxy_pass directive: This directive sets the address of a proxied server. Notice that in this case, the address was defined as back end, and in turn contained multiple servers. By default, if a domain resolves to several addresses, all of them will be used in a round-robin fashion.

Load Balancing Algorithms

When a load balancer is configured, you need to think about various factors. It helps if you know the application and its underlying architecture. Once you have found the details, you will need to configure some parameters of Nginx so that you can route the traffic accordingly. There are various algorithms that you can use based on your need. You will learn about it next.

Round Robin

This is the default configuration. When the algorithm is not defined, the requests are served in round-robin fashion. At a glance, it might appear way too simple to be useful. But, it is actually quite powerful. It ensures that your servers are equally balanced and each one is working as hard.

Let's assume that you have two servers, and due to the nature of your application you would like three requests to go to the first server (WFE1) and one request to the second server (WFE2). This way, you can route the traffic in a specific ratio to multiple servers. To achieve this, you can define weight to your server definitions in the configuration file as follows.

```
upstream backend{
        server 10.0.2.6 weight=3;
        server 10.0.2.7 weight=1;
}

server {
    listen       80;
    location / {
        proxy_pass http://backend;
    }
}
```

Reload Nginx configuration and try executing curl localhost multiple times. Note that three requests went to the WFE1 server, whereas one request went to WFE2.

```
[root@nlb ~]# curl localhost
wfe1.localdomain
[root@nlb ~]# curl localhost
wfe1.localdomain
[root@nlb ~]# curl localhost
wfe1.localdomain
[root@nlb ~]# curl localhost
wfe2.localdomain
```

Least Connected, Optionally Weighted

In scenarios where you cannot easily determine the ratio or weight, you can simply use the least connected algorithm. It means that the request will be routed to the server with the least number of active connections. This often leads to a good load-balanced performance. To configure this, you can use the configuration file like so:

```
upstream backend{
        least_conn;
        server 10.0.2.6 weight=1;
        server 10.0.2.7 weight=1;
}
```

Without a load testing tool, it will be hard to determine the output using command line. But the idea is fairly simple. Apart from the least number of active connections, you can also apply weight to the servers, and it would work as expected.

IP Hash

There are quite a few applications that maintain state on the server: especially the dynamic ones like PHP, Node, ASP.NET, and so on. To give a practical example, let's say the application creates a temporary file for a specific client and updates him about the progress. If you use one of the round-robin algorithms, the subsequent request might land on another server and the new server might have no clue about the file processing that started on the previous server. To avoid such scenarios, you can make the session sticky, so that once the request from a specific client has reached a server, Nginx continues to route the traffic to the same server. To achieve this, you must use ip_hash directive like so:

```
upstream backend{
        ip_hash;
        server 10.0.2.6;
        server 10.0.2.7;
}
```

The configuration above ensures that the request reaches only one specific server for the client based on the client's IP hash key. The only exception is when the server is down, in which case the request can land on another server.

Generic Hash

A hash algorithm is conceptually similar to an IP hash. The difference here is that for each request the load balancer calculates a hash that is based on the combination of text and Nginx variables that you can specify. It sends all requests with that hash to a specific server. Take a look at the following configuration where hash algorithm is used with variables $scheme (for http or https) and $request_uri (URI of the request):

```
upstream backend{
        hash $scheme$request_uri;
        server 10.0.2.6;
        server 10.0.2.7;
}
```

Bear in mind that a hash algorithm will most likely not distribute the load evenly. The same is true for an IP hash. The reason why you still might end up using it is because of your application's requirement of a sticky session. Nginx PLUS offers more sophisticated configuration options when it comes to session persistence. The best use case for using hash is probably when you have a dynamic page that makes data intensive operations that are cachable. In this case, the request to that dynamic page can go to one server only, which caches the result and keeps serving the cache result, saving the effort required at the database side and on all the other servers.

Least Time (Nginx PLUS), Optionally Weighted

Nginx PLUS has an additional algorithm that can be used. It is called the least time method where the load balancer mathematically combines two metrics for each server—the current number of active connections and a weighted average response time for past requests —and sends the request to the server with the lowest value. This is a smarter and more effective way of doing load balancing with heuristics.

You can choose the parameter on the least_time directive, so that either the time to receive the response header or the time to receive the full response is considered by the directive. The configuration looks like so:

```
upstream backend{
        least_time (header | last_byte);
        server 10.0.2.6 weight=1;
        server 10.0.2.7 weight=1;
}
```

Most Suitable Algorithm

There is no silver bullet or straightforward method to tell you which method will suit you best. There are plenty of variables that need to be carefully determined before you choose the most suitable method. In general, least connections and least time are considered to be best choices for the majority of the workloads.

Round robin works best when the servers have about the same capacity, host the same content, and the requests are pretty similar in nature. If the traffic volume pushes every server to its limit, round robin might push all the servers over the edge at roughly the same time, causing outages.

You should use load testing tools and various tests to figure out which algorithm works best for you. One thing that often helps you make good decision is the knowledge of the application's underlying architecture. If you are well aware about the application and its components, you will be more comfortable in doing appropriate capacity planning.

You will learn about load testing tools, performance, and benchmarking in the upcoming chapters.

Load Balancing Scenarios

So far in this chapter you have seen an Nginx load balancer routing to the back-end Nginx servers. This is not a mandatory requirement. You can choose Nginx to route traffic to any other web server. As a matter of fact, that is what is done mostly in practical scenarios and as far as the request is HTTP based, it will just work. Nginx routes the request based on the mapped URI. You can use Nginx easily to front end the PHP, ASP. NET, Node.js, or any other application for that matter and enjoy the benefits of Nginx as you will see in the upcoming scenarios.

Nginx Routing Request to Express/Node.js

If you recall, in the previous chapter you configured Nginx for MEAN stack. Assuming WFE1 and WFE2 are hosting applications based on MEAN stack and the application is running on port 3000, your NLB server's configuration will look like the following:

```
upstream nodeapp {
        server 10.0.2.6:3000;
        server 10.0.2.7:3000;
}

server {
    listen       80;
    server_name  localhost;

    location / {
       proxy_pass http://nodeapp;
    }
}
```

A common mistake that usually happens is that the additional ports are not opened in the firewall. So, you need to ensure that ports are opened explicitly by using the following command on both WFE1 and WFE2:

```
[user1@wfe1 ~]$ sudo firewall-cmd --permanent --add-port=3000/tcp
success
[user1@wfe1 ~]$ sudo firewall-cmd --reload
success
```

Once you have opened the ports, Nginx will start routing the request successfully. Note that the opened ports are not exposed to the Internet. It is just for Nginx that is load balancing the requests.

Passing the HOST Header

Since everything has been working in these simple demos, it might mislead you into thinking that all you need to pass to the back-end server is the URI. For real world applications you might have additional information in request headers that—if missed—will break the functionality of the application. In other words, the request coming from Nginx to the back-end servers will look different than a request coming directly from the client. This is because Nginx makes some adjustments to headers that it receives from the client. It is important that you are aware of these nuances.

- Nginx gets rid of any empty headers for performance reasons.

- Any header that contains an underscore is considered invalid and is eventually dropped from the headers collection. You can override this behavior by explicitly setting underscores_in_headers on;

- The "HOST" header is set to the value of $proxy_host, which is a variable that contains the domain name of IP address grabbed from the proxy_pass definition. In the configuration that follows, it will be backend.

- Connection header is added and set to close.

You can tweak the header information before passing on by using the proxy_set_header directive. Consider the following configuration in the NLB:

```
upstream backend{
        server 10.0.2.6;
        server 10.0.2.7;
}

server {
    listen        80;

    location / {
        proxy_set_header HOST $host;
        proxy_pass http://backend;
    }
}
```

In the previous configuration, an explicit HOST header has been set using proxy_set_header directive. To view the effect, follow these steps:

- Ensure that your NLB configuration appears as the previous configuration block. Restart Nginx service.

- On WFE1, change the nginx.conf (sudo vi /etc/nginx/nginx.conf) such that the log_format has an additional field called $host as follows:

```
log_format          main  '$host - $remote_addr - $remote_user - [$time_local] - $document_
root - $document_uri - $request - $status - $body_bytes_sent - $http_referer';
```

- Save the file and exit. Restart Nginx service.
- Switch back to NLB and make a few requests using curl localhost
- View the logs on the WFE1 using sudo tail /var/log/nginx/access.log -n 3.

```
[user1@wfe1 ~]$ sudo tail /var/log/nginx/access.log -n 3
localhost - 10.0.2.9 - - - - /usr/share/nginx/html - /index.html - GET / HTTP/1.0 - 200 - 17 - -
localhost - 10.0.2.9 - - - - /usr/share/nginx/html - /index.html - GET / HTTP/1.0 - 200 - 17 - -
localhost - 10.0.2.9 - - - - /usr/share/nginx/html - /index.html - GET / HTTP/1.0 - 200 - 17 - -
```

- As you can see, the requests had localhost as the hostname and it is because you have used proxy_set_header HOST $host.

- To view what the result would have looked like without this header change, comment the line in NLB's configuration:

```
location / {
    # proxy_set_header HOST $host;
    proxy_pass http://backend;
}
```

- Restart Nginx on NLB and retry curl localhost a few times.

- If you view the logs on WFE1 using the tail command, you should see an output similar to this:

```
localhost - 10.0.2.9 - - - - /usr/share/nginx/html - /index.html - GET / HTTP/1.0 - 200 - 17 - -
backend - 10.0.2.9 - - - - /usr/share/nginx/html - /index.html - GET / HTTP/1.0 - 200 - 17 - -
backend - 10.0.2.9 - - - - /usr/share/nginx/html - /index.html - GET / HTTP/1.0 - 200 - 17 - -
```

- Notice the last couple of lines where the hostname appears as back end. This is the default behavior of Nginx if you don't set the HOST header explicitly. Based on your application, you might need to set explicitly or ignore this header in the NLB configuration.

Forwarding IP Information

Since the requests are forwarded to the back end, it has no information about where the requests have actually come from. To the back-end servers, it knows the NLB as the client. There are scenarios where you might want to log information about the actual visitors. To do that, you can use proxy-set-header just as you did in the previous example but with different variables like so:

```
location / {
    proxy_set_header HOST $proxy_host;
    proxy_set_header X-Real-IP $remote_addr;
    proxy_set_header X-Forwarded-For $proxy_add_x_forwarded_for;
    proxy_pass http://backend;
}
```

In this configuration apart from setting HOST header, you are also setting the following headers:

- X-Real-IP is set to $remote_addr variable that contains the actual client IP.

- X-Forwarded-For is another header set here, which contains $proxy_add_x_forwarded_for. This variable contains a list of $remote_addr - client IPs - separated by a comma.

- To log the actual client IP, you should now modify the log_format to include $http_x_real_ip variable that contains the real client IP information.

- By default, X-Real-IP is stored in $http_x_real_ip. You can change this behavior by using - real_ip_header X-Forwarded-For; - in your http, location or server directive in order to save the value of X-Forward-For header instead of X-Real-IP header.

Buffering

As you can guess, with an NLB in between the real back-end server, there are two hops for every request. This may adversely affect the client's experience. If the buffers are not used, data that is sent from the back-end server immediately gets transmitted to the client. If the clients are fast, they can consume this immediately and buffering can be turned off. For practical purposes, the clients will typically not be as fast as the server in consuming the data. In that case, turning buffering on will tell Nginx to hold the back-end data temporarily, and feed that data to the client. This feature allows the back ends to be freed up quickly since they have to simply work and ensure that the data is fed to Nginx NLB. By default, buffering is on in Nginx and controlled using the following directives:

- proxy_buffering: Default value is on, and it can be set in http, server, and location blocks.

- proxy_buffers *number size*: proxy_buffers directive allows you to set the number of buffers along with its size for a single connection. By default, the size is equal to one memory page, and is either 4K or 8K depending on the platform.

- proxy_buffer_size *size*: The headers of the response are buffered separately from the rest of the response. This directive sets that size, and defaults to proxy_buffers size.

- proxy_max_temp_file_size *size*: If the response is too large, it can be stored in a temporary file. This directive sets the maximum size of the temporary file.

- proxy_temp_file_write_size *size*: This directive governs the size of data written to the file at a time. If you use 0 as the value, it disables writing temporary files completely.

- proxy_temp_path *path*: This directive defines the directory where temporary files are written.

Nginx Caching

Buffering in Nginx helps the back-end servers by offloading data transmission to the clients. But the request actually reaches the backend server to begin with. Quite often, you will have static content, like 3rd party JavaScript libraries, CSS, Images, PDFs, etc. that doesn't change at all, or rarely changes. In these cases, it makes sense to make a copy of the data on the NLB itself, so that the subsequent requests could be served directly from the NLB instead of fetching the data every time from the backend servers. This process is called caching.

To achieve this, you can use the proxy_cache_path directive like so in the HTTP block:

```
proxy_cache_path path levels=1:2 keys_zone=my_cache:10m max_size=10g inactive=60m
```

Before you use this directive, create the path as follows and set appropriate permissions:

```
mkdir -p /data/nginx/cache
chown nginx /data/nginx/cache
chmod 700 /data/nginx/cache
```

- Levels define the number of subdirectories Nginx will create to maintain the cached files. Having a large number of files in one flat directory slows down access, so it is recommended to have at least a two-level directory hierarchy.

- keys_zone defines the area in memory which contains information about cached file keys. In this case a 10MB zone is created and it should be able to hold about 80,000 keys (roughly).

- max_size is used to allocate 10GB space for the cached files. If the size increases, cache manager process trims it down by removing files that were used least recently.

- inactive=60m implies the number of minutes the cache can remain valid in case it is not used. Effectively, if the file is not used for 60 minutes, it will be purged from the cache automatically.

By default, Nginx caches all responses to requests made with the HTTP GET and HEAD methods. You can cache dynamic content too where the data is fetched from a dynamic content management system, but changes less frequently, using fastcgi_cache. You will learn about caching details in chapter 12.

Server Directive Additional Parameters

The server directive has more parameters that come in handy in certain scenarios. The parameters are fairly straightforward to use and simply require you to use the following format:

```
server address [parameters]
```

You have already seen the server address in use with weight. Let's learn more about some additional parameters.

- max_fails=number: Sets the number of unsuccessful attempts before considering the server unavailable for a duration. If this value is set to 0, it disables the accounting of attempts.

- fail_timeout=time: Sets the duration in which max_fails should happen. For example, if max_fails parameter is set to 3, and fail_timeout is set to 10 seconds, it would imply that there should be 3 failures in 10 seconds so that the server could be considered unavailable.

- backup: Marks the server as a backup server. It will be passed requests when the primary servers are unavailable.

- down: Marks the server as permanently unavailable.

- max_conns=number: Limits the maximum number of simultaneous active connections. Default value of 0 implies no limit.

Configure Nginx (PLUS) for Heath Checks

The free version of Nginx doesn't have a very important directive, and it is called health_check. This feature is available in Nginx PLUS, and enabling it gives you a lot of options related to health of the upstream servers.

- interval=time: Sets the interval between two health checks. The default value is 5 seconds and it implies that the server checks the upstream servers every 5 seconds.

- fails=number: If the upstream server fails x number of times, it will be considered unhealthy. The default value is 1.

- passes=number: Once considered unhealthy, the upstream server needs to pass the test x number of times before it could be considered healthy. The default value is 1.

- uri = path: Defines the URI that is used to check requests. Default value is /.

- match=name: You can specify a block with its expected output in order the test to succeed. In the following configuration, the test is to ensure that the output has a status code of 200, and the body contains "Welcome to nginx!"

```
http {
    server {
        location / {
            proxy_pass http://backend;
            health_check match=welcome;
        }
    }

    match welcome {
        status 200;
        header Content-Type = text/html;
        body ~ "Welcome to nginx!";
    }
}
```

- If you specify multiple checks, any single failure will make the server be considered unhealthy.

Activity Monitoring in Nginx (PLUS)

Nginx PLUS includes a real-time activity monitoring interface that provides load and performance metrics. It uses a RESTful JSON interface, and hence it is very easy to customize. There are plenty of third-party monitoring tools that take advantage of JSON interface and provide you a comprehensive dashboard for performance monitoring.

You can also use the following configuration block to configure Nginx PLUS for status monitoring.

```
server {
    listen 8080;
    root /usr/share/nginx/html;

    # Redirect requests for / to /status.html
    location = / {
        return 301 /status.html;
    }

    location = /status.html { }

    location /status {
        allow x.x.x.x/16; # permit access from local network
        deny all; # deny access from everywhere else

        status;
    }
}
```

Status is a special handler in Nginx PLUS. The configuration here is using port 8080 to view the detailed status of Nginx requests. To give you a better idea of the console, the Nginx team has set up a live demo page that can be accessed at `http://demo.nginx.com/status.html`.

Summary

In this chapter, you have learned about the basic fundamentals of high availability and why it matters. You should also be comfortable with the basic concepts about hardware and software load balancing. Nginx is an awesome product for software load balancing and you have learned about how easily you can set it up in your web farm. The architecture of Nginx allows you to have a very small touch point for front-end servers, and the flexibility ensures that you can customize it precisely based on your requirements. You can scale out your farm easily with Nginx, and use Nginx PLUS to achieve even more robustness in your production farm when the need arises.

CHAPTER 9

■■■

Log Analysis, Monitoring, and Automation

If you are a web hosting provider, setting up web servers will be a fairly repetitive task to the extent that you might want to automate the whole process of creating and configuring the website. However, if you have a few websites to manage, setting up a web server and hosting your application will often be relatively straightforward. Once you have set up the web server, the changes in the configuration will be rare and only on a need basis. A typical web administrator spends far more time maintaining the web farm than configuring it. This chapter focuses on maintaining the web server. You will learn about log gathering, analysis, monitoring, and automation.

Error Log

While processing the requests, it is possible that the request is not honored for several reasons. As a visitor, these error messages can be pretty generic. Most browsers have an in-built error messages template that is used regardless of the web server it requested from. So, in case your (any) web server responds with status code 404, it is possible that the browser shows an in-built custom error message. This is done for consistency, so that even the layman can understand what the error message means.

As an administrator though, the generic error message doesn't help much. If you find errors while browsing your website, you will have to troubleshooting using *error logs*. Nginx writes information about the issues it encountered while processing a request in an error log. The logging mechanism is smart and has various levels. The levels ensure that you log only as much as needed on a regular basis. You must understand that logging is a cost, and it uses resources.

It is a good idea to log at higher level in production and lower levels during development. Take a look at Figure 9-1 to understand about levels. Emergency (emerg) is the highest level of error message that you shouldn't ignore at all. Most emerg level errors will cause service issues and the Nginx service will not even start. Alert (alert) is the second highest level of error followed by critical (crit), error, warning (warn), notice, information (info), and debugging (debug).

© Rahul Soni 2016
R. Soni, *Nginx*, DOI 10.1007/978-1-4842-1656-9_9

Figure 9-1. *Error levels in Nginx*

If you set the error logging to warn, you are telling Nginx to log any error message that has a level of warning or above. In essence, warn, error, crit, alert, and emerg messages will all be logged if you choose *warn* as the error logging method.

To configure error log, you will need to use the `error_log` directive in main, HTTP, mail, stream, server, or location block as follows:

```
error_log  /var/log/nginx/error.log info;
```

If you restart the Nginx service now, you should be able to see logs in /var/log/nginx/error.log.

Try doing as follows so that you learn about different entries that get logged during reload of a configuration (`sudo nginx -s reload`).

1. Edit your Nginx configuration file and ensure that the error_log directive is set to info level.

2. Read the log file using `sudo tail /var/log/nginx/error.log`:

3. Note the time stamp so that you can compare the additional logs that have appeared after you have entered the following command:

```
sudo nginx -s reload
```

4. Read the log again, using `sudo tail /var/log/nginx/error.log -n 50`:

```
[notice] 13300#0: signal process started
[notice] 13281#0: signal 1 (SIGHUP) received, reconfiguring
[notice] 13281#0: reconfiguring
[notice] 13281#0: using the "epoll" event method
[notice] 13281#0: start worker processes
[notice] 13281#0: start worker process 13301
[notice] 13285#0: gracefully shutting down
[notice] 13285#0: exiting
[notice] 13285#0: exit
[notice] 13281#0: signal 17 (SIGCHLD) received
[notice] 13281#0: worker process 13285 exited with code 0
[notice] 13281#0: signal 29 (SIGIO) received
```

Notice, that the log entry is marked [notice] as the log levels, and it emits a bunch of lines telling exactly what Nginx has done. Try running different commands, and check the logs again to see various entries being logged. It is a good way of learning and understanding the underlying concepts.

174

> ■ **Note** By default, you can use all levels except debug. For debug level to work, you must use --with-debug while building Nginx. Refer to chapter 2 for more information about setting up Nginx using different switches. You can use nginx -V to determine if your Nginx binary was built with debug module.

The configuration file can have multiple error_log directives, and the one declared at the lowest level of hierarchy overrides the configuration on the higher level. If there are multiple error_log directives at a level, the logs are written to all specified log files.

Access Log

Access log is another log that Nginx creates while serving requests. Where error logs contain service-related information, access logs contain information about client requests. Every request is logged right after it is processed.

1. Start by typing nginx -V to view the path of access logs and error logs and find the values of --error-log-path (for error logs) and --http-log-path (for access logs):

```
$nginx -V
nginx version: nginx/1.8.1
built by gcc 4.8.3 20140911 (Red Hat 4.8.3-9) (GCC)
built with OpenSSL 1.0.1e-fips 11 Feb 2013
TLS SNI support enabled
configure arguments: --prefix=/etc/nginx --sbin-path=/usr/sbin/nginx --conf-path=/etc/
nginx/nginx.conf --error-log-path=/var/log/nginx/error.log --http-log-path=/var/log/nginx/
access.log --pid-path=/var/run/nginx.pid --lock-path=/var/run/nginx.lock --http-client-body-
temp-path=/var/cache/nginx/client_temp --http-proxy-temp-path=/var/cache/nginx/proxy_temp
--http-fastcgi-temp-path=/var/cache/nginx/fastcgi_temp --http-uwsgi-temp-path=/var/cache/
nginx/uwsgi_temp --http-scgi-temp-path=/var/cache/nginx/scgi_temp --user=nginx --group=nginx
--with-http_ssl_module --with-http_realip_module --with-http_addition_module --with-http_
sub_module --with-http_dav_module --with-http_flv_module --with-http_mp4_module --with-
http_gunzip_module --with-http_gzip_static_module --with-http_random_index_module --with-
http_secure_link_module --with-http_stub_status_module --with-http_auth_request_module
--with-mail --with-mail_ssl_module --with-file-aio --with-ipv6 --with-http_spdy_module
--with-cc-opt='-O2 -g -pipe -Wall -Wp,-D_FORTIFY_SOURCE=2 -fexceptions -fstack-protector-
strong --param=ssp-buffer-size=4 -grecord-gcc-switches -m64 -mtune=generic'
```

2. Open nginx.conf file, and remove log_format related lines if any.

3. Reload the configuration and execute curl http://localhost.

4. View the access logs, by using the following command:

```
$sudo tail /var/log/nginx/access.log
127.0.0.1 - - [actual_request_time] "GET / HTTP/1.1" 200 17 "-" "curl/7.29.0"
```

5. This format is the default format and is referred to as combined format that appears automatically if you do not specify any specific log format. The combined format contains information about $remote_addr $remote_user [$time_local] $request $status $body_bytes_sent $http_referer $http_user_agent. In the previous command you can see that the request is a GET request for the root (/) location and was done using curl.

If you need to, you can change the format using log_format and specify more or less variables based on your requirement. A list of all variables in Nginx can be viewed at http://nginx.org/en/docs/varindex.html. The following snippet shows how you can declare a log_format as per your need, followed by access_log directive. Note that the log_format has a name called main, and this is the name provided in the access_log directive in addition to the file name.

```
log_format  main  '$remote_addr - $remote_user [$time_local] "$request" '
                  '$status $body_bytes_sent "$http_referer" '
                  '"$http_user_agent" "$http_x_forwarded_for"';

access_log  /var/log/nginx/access.log  main;
```

Some of the important variables used in log_format are as follows:

- $bytes_sent: Total number of bytes sent to a client.

- $request_time: Total time taken to process a request. If a request is taking longer time, you should try to figure out the root cause for it. This variable contains information about time elapsed since the first bytes were read by the client, until the time the last byte was consumed.

- $status: Contains the status code of the response. It is important that you scan your log files periodically to check if the requests are being served as per your application design. 5xx related errors are the ones that should be fixed as soon as possible, since it implies that your server (or application) was not able to handle the request gracefully. In general:

  - 2xx means success

  - 3xx means redirection

  - 4xx means errors due to client

  - 5xx means errors due to the server

What to Log?

The logging configuration is so simple that it is easy to goof up. It might seem productive to log as much as possible, but in production scenarios where thousands of connections are handled every second, logging more can slow your web server down. This slowness is not because of the actual *writing* process, but more because of the evaluation of variables. Bear in mind that the variables in Nginx are evaluated at runtime for *every* request.

Your application, budget, and other requirements determine what to log and what not to. For example, if bandwidth is costly and of concern to you, it would be prudent to log compression ratio, so that you can log the details and analyze it later.

In simple words, every field that is logged using log_format will have a cost and you should think about how you plan to consume the log in future. If you can't imagine a reason for logging a counter, you should not log it to begin with. This will save you both disk space and processing time.

Because you can configure logging in `http`, `server` and `location` blocks, you can fine tune it at various levels as per your requirement.

A common mistake that is often committed is to log at a much lower level than necessary. If you are running an application in production after thorough testing, you might want to log errors at a higher level, like error or crit. That way, you can safely ignore the logs at lower levels. During the development and troubleshooting process, it makes a lot of sense to keep the logging level low, so that you can minutely analyze the logs.

To summarize, be wise while logging and don't log for logging sake.

Log Buffers

You can buffer the logs in memory before it is written to the disk. The `access_log` directive allows you to set the buffer size. If the logs are buffered, data is written to the file when one of the following conditions is true:

- The next line doesn't fit the buffer.

- The buffered data is older than the flush parameter. (the flush parameter in the access_log specifies how frequently the logs should be flushed to the disk).

- The worker process is shutting down or reopening the log files.

Conditional Log

If the traffic to your website is huge, you may not want to log the successes at all. It is possible in Nginx to do conditional logging. Once enabled, the request will not be logged if the condition evaluates to 0 or an empty string. The following configuration snippet is pretty smart if you think about it.

```
map $status $loggable{
        ~^[23]  0;
        default 1;
}
access_log /var/log/nginx/access.log  combined if=$loggable;
```

At first, the map directive creates variables whose values depend on certain factors. In this case, $status is taken as input and $loggable is the output. The regular expression is used to match $status and evaluate if the status starts with 2xx or 3xx, in which case it sets the $loggable to 0. Otherwise, the $loggable is set to 1. In the access_log directive, $loggable variable is evaluated using the `if` directive. If the value is 0, it is not logged and vice versa.

Log Compression

`access_log` directive provides a very neat way to compress the logs. It is as easy as appending another parameter to the directive like so:

```
access_log /log_path/log.gz combined gzip=1 flush=10m
```

In this case, the logs are compressed before being written to the file. gzip=1 implies that the level of compression is at least 1, and hence it is fastest. You can change the level to a maximum of 9, which would imply best compression but slowest. Generally, the higher the compression level, the more CPU Nginx consumes. The gzipped files get saved in the same location as access log and can be viewed with zcat like so:

```
sudo zcat /var/log/nginx/access.log-xxxxxx.gz
```

If the file is large, you can pipe the output to more or less as follows:

```
sudo zcat /var/log/nginx/access.log-xxxxxx.gz | more
sudo zcat /var/log/nginx/access.log-xxxxxx.gz | less
```

■ **Tip**   more is an older command that allows only forward scrolling and is available on most platforms. Less, on the other hand, is a newer command with a lot of functionality including backward scrolling. Read more about them in the main pages.

Syslog

If you have multiple servers emitting logs, it can be quite painful to individually log in on every server and analyze the logs. Syslog is a widely accepted utility that provides a way for networked servers to send event messages to a central logging server. Nginx can take advantage of syslog by using syslog: prefix in error_log and access_log directives.

In the following example, the access log is written to a syslog server using an IPv6 address on port 8080. The entries are tagged with text nginx_fe1 so that every line has this text. This will help you isolate logs from various servers even though they are stored in the same file.

```
access_log syslog:server=[xxx:xx::1]:8080,facility=local7,tag=nginx_fe1,severity=info;
```

Syslog protocol utilizes numerical facility listed below (default value is local7 as used in the previous configuration block):

```
 0 kernel messages
 1 user-level messages
 2 mail system
 3 system daemons
 4 security/authorization messages
 5 messages generated internally by syslogd
 6 line printer subsystem
 7 network news subsystem
 8 UUCP subsystem
 9 clock daemon
10 security/authorization messages
11 FTP daemon
12 NTP subsystem
13 log audit
14 log alert
15 clock daemon
```

```
16 local use 0 (local0)
17 local use 1 (local1)
18 local use 2 (local2)
19 local use 3 (local3)
20 local use 4 (local4)
21 local use 5 (local5)
22 local use 6 (local6)
23 local use 7 (local7)
```

Analyze Logs

Analyzing a log is a time-consuming process, and you have multiple tools and utilities that can help in faster log analysis. One of the simplest and least effective ways is to cat the log file, simply because the log files are usually big. There are various free and commercial tools available for this job. You will learn about some of the free tools in this section.

tail

You have been already using tail so far in this book so you must be pretty familiar with the basic syntax already. By default, `tail` command prints the last 10 lines of the file to a standard output. There are some interesting parameters that you should be aware of:

- tail /access.log -c 500: will read the last 500 bytes of the log file

- tail /access.log -n 50: will read the last 50 lines of the log file

- tail /access.log -f: will keep listening to the log file and emit the latest lines as they appear. This comes in handy when you want to troubleshoot an issue in production. You can run this command before you try to reproduce the issue. Since the command keeps emitting the output as it appears, it will make your troubleshooting experience a lot smoother because you will not have to repeat the command again and again to view the latest entries.

ngxtop

Available as an open source project, ngxtop parses your access log and outputs useful metrics from your web server. It is very similar to `top` command.

A sample output of top command:

```
$top
top - 05:31:06 up 14 days, 19:48,  2 users,  load average: 0.00, 0.01, 0.05
Tasks:  91 total,   2 running,  89 sleeping,   0 stopped,   0 zombie
%Cpu(s):  0.0 us,  0.0 sy,  0.0 ni,100.0 id,  0.0 wa,  0.0 hi,  0.0 si,  0.0 st
KiB Mem :  1017160 total,   140920 free,   309768 used,   566472 buff/cache
KiB Swap:   839676 total,   839252 free,      424 used.   483480 avail Mem
```

```
 PID USER   PR  NI    VIRT    RES    SHR S %CPU %MEM     TIME+ COMMAND
   1 root   20   0  208216   6948   2540 S  0.0  0.7   0:43.27 systemd
   2 root   20   0       0      0      0 S  0.0  0.0   0:00.14 kthreadd
   3 root   20   0       0      0      0 S  0.0  0.0   0:04.41 ksoftirqd/0
   5 root    0 -20       0      0      0 S  0.0  0.0   0:00.00 kworker/0:0H
   6 root   20   0       0      0      0 S  0.0  0.0   0:02.72 kworker/u2:0
   7 root   rt   0       0      0      0 S  0.0  0.0   0:00.00 migration/0
   8 root   20   0       0      0      0 S  0.0  0.0   0:00.00 rcu_bh
   9 root   20   0       0      0      0 S  0.0  0.0   0:00.00 rcuob/0
```

If you have been following along in this book so far, you must be working on CentOS, and it doesn't have pip installed by default. pip is a package management system (just like yum) used to install and manage software packages written in Python. Ngxtop is written in Python and you need to install it.

1. Use the following command to download it:

```
sudo curl "https://bootstrap.pypa.io/get-pip.py" -o "get-pip.py" -k
```

2. Install it:

```
sudo python get-pip.py
```

3. Check if it is installed properly by executing pip --help

4. You can view the version by executing the following:

```
pip -V
pip 8.1.2 from /usr/lib/python2.7/site-packages (python 2.7)
```

5. Now that pip is installed, use it to install ngxtop:

```
sudo pip install ngxtop
```

Time to execute ngxtop!
If you execute it locally, you will see the output that follows in Figure 9-2.

```
[user1@wfe1 ~]$ sudo ngxtop

running for 102 seconds, 0 records processed: 0.00 req/sec

Summary:
|   count |   avg_bytes_sent |   2xx |   3xx |   4xx |   5xx |
|---------+------------------+-------+-------+-------+-------|
|       0 |                  |     0 |     0 |     0 |     0 |

Detailed:
| request_path  | count  | avg_bytes_sent  | 2xx   | 3xx   | 4xx   | 5xx   |
|---------------+--------+-----------------+-------+-------+-------+-------|
```

Figure 9-2. Nginx top output

In a production box, you will see a more comprehensive output. To get a feel of it, let it run locally and hit the website using a browser from your host machine (http://127.0.0.1:8006).

Soon, you will start seeing additional information as you can see in Figure 9-3. This can be very helpful in production scenarios if you have long-running requests. You can quickly fire up the ngxtop command and get a gist of what's going on. Keep in mind though that this utility is designed to run for shorter periods of time just like the top command for troubleshooting and monitoring purposes. You will need to use other software in case you want to do detailed analysis for a longer period of time.

```
[user1@wfe1 ~]$ sudo ngxtop

running for 556 seconds, 25 records processed: 0.04 req/sec

Summary:
|   count | avg_bytes_sent |  2xx |  3xx |  4xx |  5xx |
|---------+----------------+------+------+------+------|
|      25 |        215.400 |   15 |    1 |    9 |    0 |

Detailed:
| request_path  | count | avg_bytes_sent |  2xx |  3xx |  4xx |  5xx |
|---------------+-------+----------------+------+------+------+------|
| /             |    16 |         15.938 |   15 |    1 |    0 |    0 |
| /favicon.ico  |     9 |        570.000 |    0 |    0 |    9 |    0 |
```

Figure 9-3. Nginx top output with data

Official home page: https://github.com/lebinh/ngxtop

There is some output taken directly from their home page, to give you a gist of what kind of information you can get using this tool.

- View top source IPs of clients:

```
$ ngxtop top remote_addr
running for 20 seconds, 3215 records processed: 159.62 req/sec
top remote_addr
| remote_addr     | count |
|-----------------+-------|
| 118.173.177.161 |    20 |
| 110.78.145.3    |    16 |
| 171.7.153.7     |    16 |
| 180.183.67.155  |    16 |
| 183.89.65.9     |    16 |
| 202.28.182.5    |    16 |
| 1.47.170.12     |    15 |
| 119.46.184.2    |    15 |
| 125.26.135.219  |    15 |
| 125.26.213.203  |    15 |
```

- List 4xx or 5xx responses with HTTP referrer

```
$ ngxtop -i 'status >= 400' print request status http_referer
running for 2 seconds, 28 records processed: 13.95 req/sec
```

```
request, status, http_referer:
| request   |   status | http_referer   |
|-----------+----------+----------------|
| -         |      400 | -              |
```

GoAccess

GoAccess is another web log analyzer and much more functional than ngxtop. It is an open source project that allows you to view logs interactively and runs directly in the terminal. Apart from view the logs in the terminal, it also allows you to create HTML reports for the logs. You can read more about it at `https://github.com/allinurl/goaccess`. The list of features it provides is pretty impressive:

- General statistics, bandwidth, etc.

- Time taken to serve the request (useful to track pages that are slowing down your site)

- Metrics for cumulative, average, and slowest running requests

- Top visitors

- Requested files and static files

- 404 or Not Found

- Hosts, Reverse DNS, IP Location

- Operating Systems

- Browsers and Spiders

- Referring Sites and URLs

- Key Phrases

- Geo Location - Continent/Country/City

- Visitors Time Distribution

- HTTP Status Codes

- Metrics per Virtual Host

- Ability to output HTML, JSON, and CSV

- Tailor GoAccess to suit your own color taste/schemes

- Incremental log processing

- Support for large datasets and data persistence

- Support for HTTP/2 and IPv6

- Output statistics to HTML

It supports nearly all web log formats:

- Amazon CloudFront (Download Distribution)

- AWS Elastic Load Balancing

- Combined Log Format (XLF/ELF) Apache | Nginx

- Common Log Format (CLF) Apache

- Google Cloud Storage

- Apache virtual hosts

- Squid Native Format

- W3C format (IIS)

You can view the details in a colored format directly on the terminal or create HTML reports as can be seen in Figures 9-4 and 9-5 respectively.

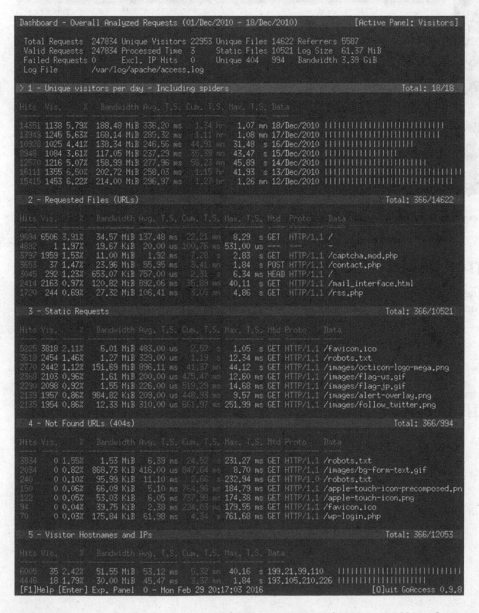

Figure 9-4. *goaccess output in a terminal (courtesy:* `https://github.com/allinurl/goaccess`*)*

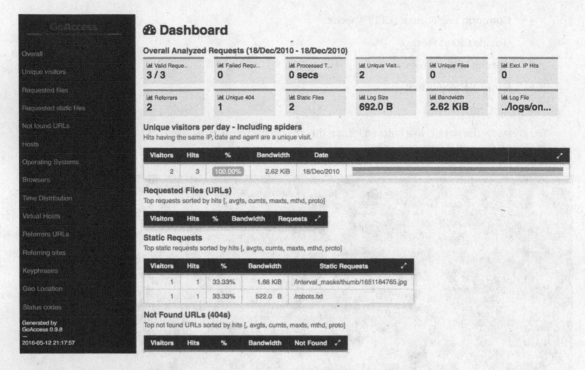

Figure 9-5. goaccess HTML report sample (courtesy: https://goaccess.io/goaccess_html_report.html)

Custom Error pages

If your visitors request a page that doesn't exist, by default, a plain looking and boring error message is displayed like the one you see in Figure 9-6.

Figure 9-6. Default error messages

There are other scenarios where it could be a lot more cryptic. To view it in practice, follow along these steps to learn how you can customize and show a much more informative error messages when something goes wrong.

1. Start by modifying the config file so that you can reproduce errors easily. In the following config, there is a path setup (http://localhost/testing) that would error out on purpose since the path doesn't exist.

```
server {
    listen       80;
    server_name  localhost;

    location / {
        root    /usr/share/nginx/html;
        index   index.html index.htm;
    }

    location /testing {
        fastcgi_pass unix:ooops;
    }
}
```

2. Reload configuration and execute curl localhost/testing.

```
$ curl localhost/testing
<html>
<head><title>502 Bad Gateway</title></head>
<body bgcolor="white">
<center><h1>502 Bad Gateway</h1></center>
<hr><center>nginx/1.8.1</center>
</body>
</html>
```

3. If this error was thrown to your visitor, he would hardly understand what it means. Try another request with curl localhost/nopage, and you will see another message similar to this with a different code.

4. In the following configuration error_page directive has been used. The directives talk about the error code and the corresponding route that should take care of the particular status code. For instance, when a page could not be found, a 404 error would be thrown and eventually handled by /custom_4xx.html route. Similarly, any server-related error (5xx) will be handled by /custom_5xx.html route.

```
server {
    listen       80;
    server_name  localhost;

    location / {
        root    /usr/share/nginx/html;
        index   index.html index.htm;
    }
```

```
location /testing {
    fastcgi_pass unix:ooops;
}

error_page  404            /custom_4xx.html;
error_page 500 502 503 504 /custom_5xx.html;

location = /custom_4xx.html {
    root /usr/share/nginx/html;
}

location = /custom_5xx.html {
    root /usr/share/nginx/html;
}
}
```

5. Once this configuration is saved, you must create the files custom_4xx.html and custom_5xx.html in the root specified (the files must have read permissions for the Nginx process account). Here is what the text looks like:

```
$ sudo cat /usr/share/nginx/html/custom_4xx.html
<h1>Sorry, the page could not be found</h1>
<p>Please ensure that you have typed the address correctly.</p>
$ sudo cat /usr/share/nginx/html/custom_5xx.html
<h1>Sorry, we couldn't process the request</h1>
<p>There seems to be an error. Please report it at contact@oursite.com if you continue to
see this.</p>
```

6. The error details are still bland and you can definitely customize it further. Be creative! With the error pages in place, try to repeat the following commands:

```
$ curl localhost/foo
<h1>Sorry, the page could not be found</h1>
<p>Please ensure that you have typed the address correctly.</p>
$ curl localhost/testing
<h1>Sorry, we couldn't process the request</h1>
<p>There seems to be an error. Please report it at contact@oursite.com if you continue to
see this.</p>
```

7. This is pretty great. But there is a small catch. Try hitting the following URI:

```
$ curl localhost/custom_5xx.html
<h1>Sorry, we couldn't process the request</h1>
<p>There seems to be an error. Please report it at contact@oursite.com if you continue to
see this.</p>
```

8. This route now functions as if it was a normal page. This behavior is normally not desired. To avoid these routes from working directly, you should mark these locations with an additional directive called `internal` like so:

```
location = /custom_4xx.html {
    root /usr/share/nginx/html;
    internal;
}

location = /custom_5xx.html {
    root /usr/share/nginx/html;
    internal;
}
```

9. Reload the configuration and try again:

```
curl localhost/custom_5xx.html
<h1>Sorry, the page could not be found</h1>
<p>Please ensure that you have typed the address correctly.</p>
```

10. Wait. The page requested was `custom_5xx.html`, but the result is from `custom_4xx.html`. Don't let this confuse you. What basically happened was that because of the `internal` directive, Nginx refused to return the page `custom_5xx.html` directly and errored out. To refuse it, Nginx threw error 404 and lied to the visitor that the page doesn't exist. Since 404 status code was mapped to custom_4xx.html, you saw the result from that page instead.

Benchmark

If you run a web server, it helps to know how it is performing. Even more, you need to know how much load it can possibly handle under stress. If your website appears on the news headlines for good reasons, you will definitely not want it to crash when all eyes are on it. To put the problem in simpler words, how would you plan the deployment in a predictable way?

Benchmarking tests help you derive conclusions and make business decisions. It should provide you performance-related numbers from multiple perspectives. The benchmarking exercise is comprised of various tests that yield results that can later be analyzed. It can be a pretty extensive process depending on how complex your application is. At the minimum, you should be informed about the following:

- Average Number of Users: You must find out the average number of users the servers can handle easily. If you expect 1000+ concurrent users, you should ensure that the tests put the appropriate load and the server stays up for a considerable amount of time.

- Performance Under Load: You must find out how does your server behave under stress? Are there areas of your application that show slowness? If the service goes down, does it come back up automatically? Do the requests hang and don't respond at all? What kind of errors do the end users see when there is a lot of load on the server?

- Hard Limits: This is something that is better *known* in advance than *discovered* late in production. For example, if you have an application that deals with file paths, it is better if you know well in advance that there is a limit to the path name length. Not knowing limitations of the hardware or software may become a recipe for disaster. It is possible that you don't hit the hard limits, but it helps if you are aware of it, so that you can plan the architecture appropriately. Load testing increases the load until the point the servers start failing. In that case, if you know the numbers you become aware of the hard limits of your server (or application) and you can plan well in advance, should such a need arise.

Apache Benchmark

Apache Benchmark (ab) is a nifty utility used for benchmarking. It is free, open source, and quite powerful. Follow these steps in order to use it:

1. Install it using yum `install ab`.

2. It is better to run ab from a different server than the server that is being tested. You can run it on your host server as well. A sample command and its output can be seen in the following code listing. (k parameter tells ab to use keep alive connections, c implies the number of requests to make concurrently. In this case 90 keep alive concurrent connections are to be used for a total of 10000 requests).

```
$ ab -kc 90 -n 10000 http://127.0.0.1:8006/index.htm
This is ApacheBench, Version 2.3 <$Revision: 1663405 $>
Copyright 1996 Adam Twiss, Zeus Technology Ltd, http://www.zeustech.net/
Licensed to The Apache Software Foundation, http://www.apache.org/

Benchmarking 127.0.0.1 (be patient)
Completed 1000 requests
Completed 2000 requests
Completed 3000 requests
Completed 4000 requests
Completed 5000 requests
Completed 6000 requests
Completed 7000 requests
Completed 8000 requests
Completed 9000 requests
Completed 10000 requests
Finished 10000 requests

Server Software:        nginx/1.8.1
Server Hostname:        127.0.0.1
Server Port:            8006

Document Path:          /index.htm
Document Length:        108 bytes
```

```
Concurrency Level:      90
Time taken for tests:   1.900 seconds
Complete requests:      10000
Failed requests:        0
Non-2xx responses:      10000
Keep-Alive requests:    9902
Total transferred:      2829510 bytes
HTML transferred:       1080000 bytes
Requests per second:    5262.02 [#/sec] (mean)
Time per request:       17.104 [ms] (mean)
Time per request:       0.190 [ms] (mean, across all concurrent requests)
Transfer rate:          1454.00 [Kbytes/sec] received

Connection Times (ms)
              min  mean[+/-sd] median   max
Connect:        0    1   25.1      0    1135
Processing:     0   15  120.6      1    1471
Waiting:        0   15  120.6      0    1471
Total:          0   16  133.6      1    1892

Percentage of the requests served within a certain time (ms)
  50%      1
  66%      1
  75%      1
  80%      1
  90%      1
  95%      1
  98%     35
  99%    781
 100%   1892 (longest request)
```

Some observations that you should notice:

- 5262 requests were served every second.

- The output shows connection times split into four areas: connect, processing, waiting, and total.

- There is no good or bad result, since it is primarily based on your requirements.

- You should repeat this test with different parameters to find out the results.

- It is a good practice to test various pages under different loads.

- When in doubt, test again.

- Test, test, test… is the basic mantra when it comes to benchmarks. Test as much as possible and make judicious decisions based on your requirement.

JMeter

The ab utility simply downloads the file. It is good for testing pages in silos and will give you results about how many of those requests could be served from a page download perspective. You can run the test for static file, images, PHP. and pretty much any URI. However, if the HTML page contains certain scripts, ab will not be able to tell you how long the page took to *render*.

Although this book will not cover load testing it is worth mentioning that JMeter is another fantastic tool that can help you a lot. It is a pure Java application designed to load test functional behavior and measure performance. You can record tests and execute them later with various load parameters. You can learn more about it from `http://jmeter.apache.org`.

Cloud-Based Benchmarking

While doing load testing it is often found that the server is way more powerful than the client, and the client is not able to make as many requests as the server is able to serve. To test such massive web servers and farms, you need to have equally powerful test servers. With the advent of cloud computing, this has become a lot simpler. There are many service providers who provide a cloud-based testing approach if your website is public. You schedule a test and the cloud service takes care of the rest. It makes a number of requests to your servers from different locations and returns informative results. `http://loader.io` is one good example of such a kind of service and has a free option as well. Quite a few cloud-based testing services have come up to make your job easier from a load testing perspective.

Baseline

People often confuse between benchmark and baseline since they are actually similar but distinct activities. You can consider baselining as an activity that yields result that you can refer to at a later point. Let's assume your server takes 110 seconds to boot up on a regular day. After a patch, you reboot it and it takes a much longer time, say, 200 seconds. If you haven't baselined the server on a regular day and already knew that 110 seconds is your baseline, it would become difficult for you to say that 200 seconds is *longer*. Baseline provides that reference point.

In contrast you benchmark your servers to compare the results. For instance, you can use results from a benchmark on a server to compare to another server and comment "this server is slower than the other by factor X."

In essence, baseline is about identifying an approved state, where as benchmarking is assessing the relative performance.

Monitoring

Even after all the preparation, gathering logs, baselining, and benchmarking, when your application is in production it might just crash. Monitoring of a web server is paramount and apparently you can never monitor enough. A web server is like a mid-air flight. If you don't monitor the vitals constantly, major accidents can happen. Aggressive monitoring and alert mechanism helps you in fixing the issues during the flight. It is impossible to monitor the servers manually, and you should choose your tools wisely.

Nginx PLUS

While configuring load balancing in chapter 8, you have already learned about Nginx PLUS and its monitoring capabilities. Nginx team has provided a sample configuration that can be download using curl directly. Run the following command:

```
curl https://www.nginx.com/resource/conf/status.conf | sudo tee status.conf
sudo mv status.conf /etc/nginx/conf.d/
```

The commands will create a status.conf file that will work only if you have Nginx PLUS binaries. The status.conf that was downloaded looks as follows and is well commented (for further details refer to https://www.nginx.com/blog/live-activity-monitoring-nginx-plus-3-simple-steps). You will learn about basic authentication in chapter 10:

```
# This is an example of Live Activity Monitoring (extended status) feature configuration
# Created by NGINX, Inc. for nginx-plus-r6

# Documentation: http://nginx.org/r/status

# In order to enable this configuration please move this file to /etc/nginx/conf.d
# and reload nginx:
# mv /etc/nginx/conf.d/status.conf.example /etc/nginx/conf.d/status.conf
# nginx -s reload

# Note #1: enable status_zone directive for http and tcp servers.
# For more information please see http://nginx.org/r/status_zone

# Note #2: enable zone directive for http and tcp upstreams.
# For more information please see http://nginx.org/r/zone

server {
        # Status page is enabled on port 8080 by default.
        listen 8080;

        # Status zone allows the status page to display statistics for the whole server
        block.
        # It should be enabled for every server block in other configuration files.
        status_zone status-page;

        # In case of nginx process listening on multiple IPs you can restrict status page
        # to single IP only
        # listen 10.2.3.4:8080;

        # HTTP basic Authentication is enabled by default.
        # You can add users with any htpasswd generator.
        # Command line and online tools are very easy to find.
        # You can also reuse your htpasswd file from Apache web server installation.
        #auth_basic on;
        #auth_basic_user_file /etc/nginx/users;
```

```
# It is recommended to limit the use of status page to admin networks only
# Uncomment and change the network accordingly.
#allow 10.0.0.0/8;
#deny all;
# NGINX provides a sample HTML status page for easy dashboard view
root /usr/share/nginx/html;
location = /status.html { }

# Standard HTTP features are fully supported with the status page.
# An example below provides a redirect from "/" to "/status.html"
location = / {
        return 301 /status.html;
}

# Main status location. HTTP features like authentication, access control,
# header changes, logging are fully supported.
location /status {
        status;
        status_format json;
}
}
```

Automation

There are many manual tasks that are supposed to be executed repeatedly (or in a fixed frequency) in a web farm. They say, to err is human, and human errors can only be avoided if you can avoid the use of humans! As web administrators, you wouldn't want to err either by forgetting to back up periodically, or archiving the logs, or any similar mundane but important task. If you know something is important, it is a good idea to automate it.

Let's say you want to delete log files older than 10 days. To achieve this, you can use the following command:

```
find /var/log/nginx -type f -mtime +10
```

The command finds all files that are older than 10 days:

```
/var/log/nginx/access.log-20160306.gz
/var/log/nginx/error.log-20160306.gz
/var/log/nginx/access.log-20160307.gz
/var/log/nginx/error.log-20160307.gz
/var/log/nginx/access.log-20160308.gz
/var/log/nginx/error.log-20160308.gz
/var/log/nginx/access.log-20160309.gz
/var/log/nginx/error.log-20160309.gz
```

If you are satisfied with the output, you can add an -exec parameter and process it appropriately. Hence, to delete this, you can use the following command:

```
sudo find /var/log/nginx -type f -mtime +10 -exec rm {} \;
```

In this command, you are trying to find files (-type f) that are older than 10 days and remove that file. You can do additional things such as using bash script if you like. The core idea is to finalize the activity that you would like to do every day (or at any specific interval for that matter).

Once the script is ready, you will need to schedule it so that it is executed automatically as per your requirements. crontab can be of great help here, since it contains a list of commands that you want to be executed. crontab stands for cron table, since it uses the scheduler called cron. You need to do the following to register this command so that it is executed automatically.

1. Type crontab -e. This will open vi editor and you can edit it as you would edit any other file. Every line is an additional task and lines prefixed with # are considered comments.

2. There are six distinct pieces of information that have to be included in every line separated by a space. The first five pieces of information tell cron when to run it, and the last one tells what to run. The pieces are as follows in order (* in the crontab entry signifies every):

   a. A number, a list of numbers (ex. 10, 20, 30) or a range of numbers (ex. 10–20) that represents minutes of the hour.

   b. A number, a list of numbers, or a range that represents hour of the day.

   c. A number, a list of numbers, or a range that represents days of the month.

   d. A number, a list of numbers, or a range that represents months of the year.

   e. A number, a list of numbers, or a range that represents days of the week.

   f. Actual command or bash script that needs to be executed.

3. If you write the following line as one of the entries, it will execute the command and delete the older logs every night at 1 a.m.:

```
0 1 * * * /path/to/script/remove_old_logs.sh
```

4. Exit the editor and create a new file at path that you have mentioned in the crontab list entry, and cron will take care of the rest.

Some additional sample entries:

```
# Run something every minute
* * * * * /path/to/script/every_minute.sh

# Run something every hour starting 9AM and ending at 6PM every day
0 9-18 * * * /path/to/script/every_hour.sh

# Run something every night at 11:30PM
30 23 * * * /path/to/script/every_night_at_specific_time.sh

# Run something every Sunday at 1 AM
0 1 * * Mon /path/to/script/every_monday_morning.sh
```

Summary

In this chapter you have learned about the usage of error logs and access logs. You should be able to comfortably analyze what kind of information you need to log and how much to log. You have also learned about log analysis using tools. Do ensure that you baseline your servers and benchmark new servers appropriately whenever you need to scale up or scale out. Don't forget to customize your error pages and use the monitoring tools pragmatically in production. Automation is good, and you should try to automate as much as possible to reduce human errors.

CHAPTER 10

■ ■ ■

SSL, Security, and Authentication

The only truly secure system is one that is powered off, cast in a block of concrete and sealed in a lead-lined room with armed guards.

—Gene Spafford

If your public website is completely static, your exposure is less. But the moment you step in the world of dynamic web applications, complexities arise. How would you authenticate your clients? How would you authorize them? How will your customers know that the website they are viewing is actually coming off your web servers and there is nobody between you and your client playing the spoilsport? How will you ensure that nobody sees the password while the packets are en route? This chapter deals with some of these questions and talks about how and why you should secure the website.

Tools to Protect Network Traffic

Before you learn about how to fix the problem, you should be aware of the complexity of the problem. Your requests that get routed from your browser to the destined server have multiple parties in between. Anyone who has access to these servers can run certain tools and capture the network traffic. If the connection is not private, they can read the packets pretty easily. The tools might have a complex interface to the non-informed audience, but for the network experts the output is pretty easy to read. There are a variety of tools available to sniff network traffic.

Capturing Network Traffic with Wireshark

One of the most famous tools for capturing network traffic is Wireshark. It is available on most platforms and can be downloaded from www.wireshark.org. Once you have downloaded and installed it, you can start sniffing data packets sent on the network. Figure 10-1 shows a snapshot of what it looks like. You should try capturing real traffic and play around to get a better grasp of the tool.

When you start a basic network capture using Wireshark, it presents a dialog box showing the interfaces installed on your system. Figure 10-1 shows the interfaces found on a MacBook Pro. For your practice, you can capture Loopback interface so that your requests to http://127.0.0.1:8006/ can be captured. Using an interface like WiFi will capture everything going to your WiFi router and the output may be overwhelming to start with.

© Rahul Soni 2016
R. Soni, *Nginx*, DOI 10.1007/978-1-4842-1656-9_10

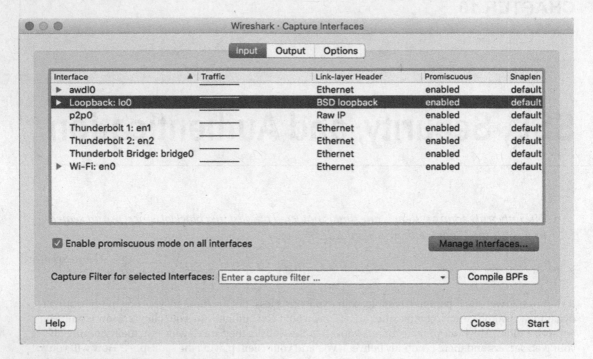

Figure 10-1. *Wireshark - Capture Interfaces*

After the capture was started, an HTTP request was sent using a browser for http://127.0.0.1:8006 (WFE1). Figure 10-2 gives you a glimpse of what it looks like.

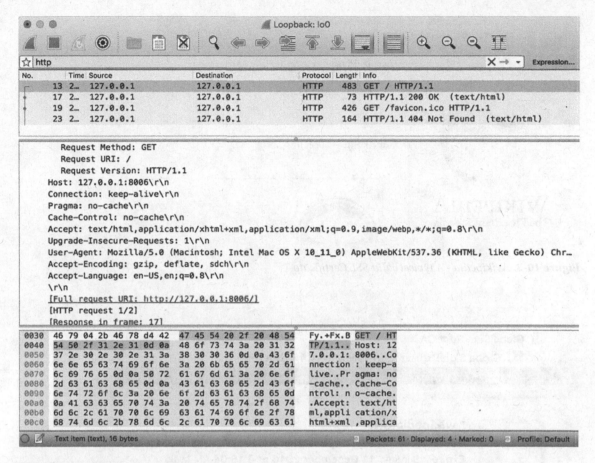

Figure 10-2. *Wireshark - Sample Output*

If you notice carefully, you can easily read the packets as if it was normal text. The packets shown in Figure 10-2 show that the request is made to http://127.0.0.1:8006. It also shows all the request headers. The subsequent packets show that the response was a Status code HTTP/1.1 200 OK. This information might look trivial at first glance, since the page is a static web page. However, if the page was in HTML form, you could have seen all the fields (including password) in clear text!

Needless to say, that would be a very risky proposition. So, *the real danger* is that your traffic on the wire is not safe. There are many hops between your operating system and the web servers and anyone capturing a network trace poses risk for your data.

Using Secure HTTP

When an end user browses the Internet, he may or may not have noticed the S in HTTPS:// in the URI. It would be rather hard to educate everyone about the secure (HTTPS = HTTP Secure) protocol. In general, the browsers behave a certain way to alarm or not alarm the users based on conditions that you will learn about shortly. Consider Figure 10-3. It shows https in green color. If a user clicks and views the detail of the certificate, he will find out more details about the website (Figure 10-4). Based on this information, he may or may not want to proceed to the website, especially if it is a bank's website or anything private. It is difficult to remember the URIs for each bank and hence the certificates instill a trust factor in the visitor's mind.

Figure 10-3. *Wikipedia - A typical valid SSL Certificate*

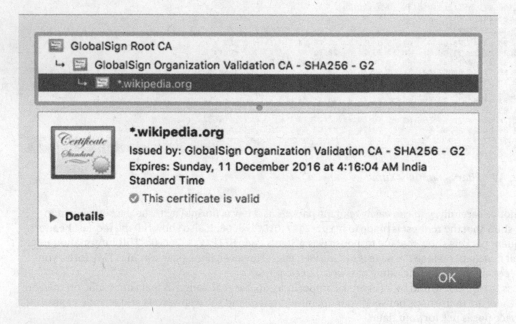

Figure 10-4. *Wikipedia - Certificate details*

If you go to www.godaddy.com, you will find that the certificate reveals even more details (Figure 10-5) about it and the address bar itself shows the name of the website. Fundamentally, both the certificates (the one for Wikipedia and GoDaddy) do the same stuff from encryption perspective. The difference lies in the trust factor and ease of use for the end users. The companies who sell certificates price their products according to the verification they do before they provide a certificate.

Figure 10-5. *GoDaddy - Certificate Details with green bar in the browser*

The documentation required varies for different kinds of certificates that you intend to buy for your website. A basic certificate that verifies your domain name is the cheapest one to buy. But the other options require more documentation and are costlier depending on your choice.

Notice the missing green padlock that you found in Figures 10-4 and 10-5. Figure 10-6 shows a site without any certificate.

wfe1 .localdomain

Figure 10-6. *WFE1 without certificate*

Contrast the situation to the one in Figure 10-7. If you visit a bank's site that looks like the one in Figure 10-7, you will most likely not proceed. Technically, there is no issue with the website. If you click on Advanced and proceed, the website will render just fine. Still, the trust factor is completely missing here. Even to the less informed this kind of message is a deterrent.

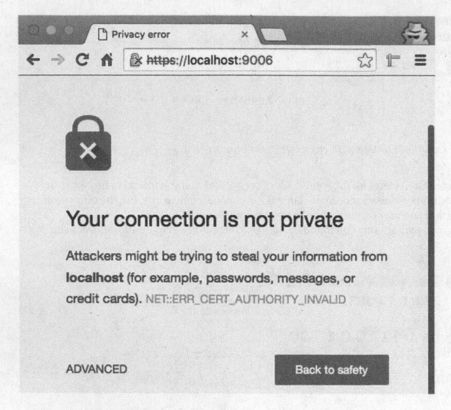

Figure 10-7. *Non-Trusted certificate*

The point that can be summarized from the discussion so far is that the web is an insecure place and the green padlock brings a little order to the chaos. The secret sauce is an SSL certificate, which you will learn about next.

SSL Encryption

SSL stands for Secure Socket Layer and helps in establishing an encrypted connection between the client browser (or any other client application) and the server. This *secure* connection ensures that the conversation remains private and integral. Please note that HTTPS simply adds an additional layer to the commonly understood HTTP protocol. It has two primary purposes:

- Verify and ensure that you are talking to the server that you think you are talking to. (Recall the trust section discussed just prior to this section.)

- Ensure that only the server can read what you send and only you can read what the server has sent back.

Behind the scenes, very clever public key algorithm ensures that the two purposes are met and the shared information is never leaked. If somebody tries to capture network traces for SSL traffic, he will be disappointed since it won't capture anymore cleartext traffic.

Enabling SSL Nginx

You can enable SSL for Nginx using `openssl` command. For a production scenario you will need to create a certificate request and follow a different procedure that will be detailed in a later section. In this section, you will create a self-signed certificate for testing purposes.

A self-signed certificate is a special kind of certificate issued by the entity to identify itself. A certificate can be created for free, but since it is trusted only by itself, it defeats the overall purpose of certification and identification of the correct server publicly. Hence, it is not recommended to use a self-signed certificate in production at all. That said, they come in handy during testing of different scenarios. You can create as many as you like and you have full control over it. Once you are satisfied with the self-signed certificate, you can proceed toward buying an actual certificate from a renowned certificate provider.

To create a self-signed certificate, do as follows:

- Logon to WFE1

```
ssh -p 3026 user1@127.0.0.1
```

- Create a directory to hold all SSL-related files

```
sudo mkdir /etc/nginx/ssl
```

- Use the following command to create a private key and a certificate:

```
sudo openssl req -nodes -days 3650 -x509 -newkey rsa:2048 -keyout /etc/nginx/ssl/private.key
-out /etc/nginx/ssl/cert.crt
Generating a 2048 bit RSA private key
.............................................................................................
.....................................................++++
.++++
writing new private key to '/etc/nginx/ssl/private.key'
-----
You are about to be asked to enter information that will be incorporated
into your certificate request.
What you are about to enter is what is called a Distinguished Name or a DN.
There are quite a few fields but you can leave some blank
For some fields there will be a default value,
If you enter '.', the field will be left blank.
-----
Country Name (2 letter code) [XX]:IN
State or Province Name (full name) []:
Locality Name (eg, city) [Default City]:
Organization Name (eg, company) [Default Company Ltd]:Rahul Soni
Organizational Unit Name (eg, section) []:
Common Name (eg, your name or your server's hostname) []:localhost
Email Address []:
```

- The previous command starts by creating a private.key followed with a self-signed certificate stored in cert.crt.

- req implies that it is a request.

- -nodes tells openssl to avoid using a passphrase for the certificate.

- -days 3650 requests a self-signed certificate for 10 years.

- -x509 tells it to create a self-signed certificate instead of a certificate request.

- -newkey rsa:2048 implies that you want to create a new certificate and a key file at the same time. rsa switch tells it to keep the key at 2048 bits long.

- -out decides the location where the certificate will be created.

- Set up SSL using your config file. Modify your /etc/nginx/conf.d/main.conf file as follows:

```
server {
    listen        80;
    server_name  localhost;

    listen 443 ssl;
    ssl_certificate /etc/nginx/ssl/cert.crt;
    ssl_certificate_key /etc/nginx/ssl/private.key;

    location / {
        root    /usr/share/nginx/html;
        index   index.html index.htm;
    }
}
```

- The cert.crt file is the public component that is sent to every client that connects to the server.

- The private.key file should be restricted since it is private to the server. However, Nginx's master process must have read access to the file.

- Set up Port Forwarding so that the requests can be routed to your WFE1. See Figure 10-8.

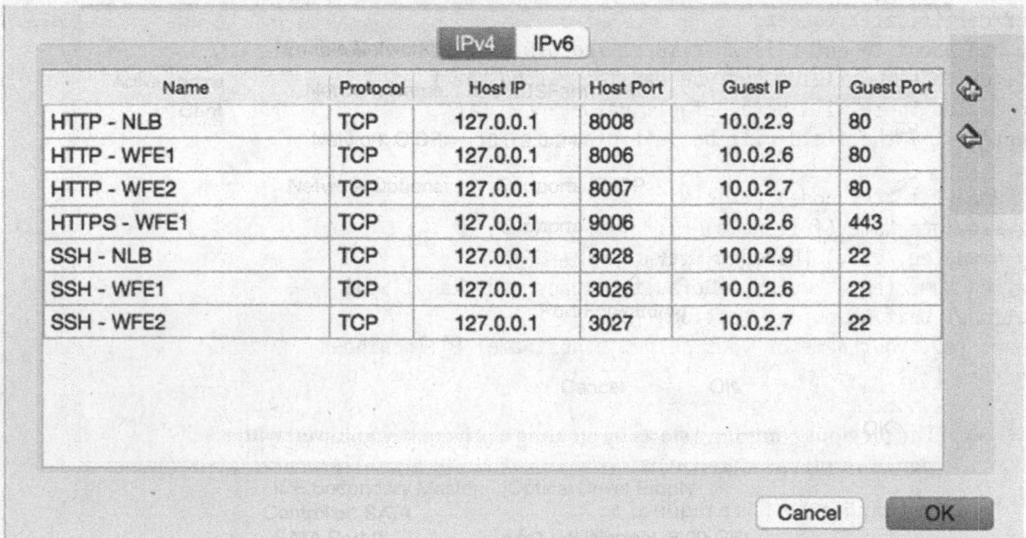

Name	Protocol	Host IP	Host Port	Guest IP	Guest Port
HTTP - NLB	TCP	127.0.0.1	8008	10.0.2.9	80
HTTP - WFE1	TCP	127.0.0.1	8006	10.0.2.6	80
HTTP - WFE2	TCP	127.0.0.1	8007	10.0.2.7	80
HTTPS - WFE1	TCP	127.0.0.1	9006	10.0.2.6	443
SSH - NLB	TCP	127.0.0.1	3028	10.0.2.9	22
SSH - WFE1	TCP	127.0.0.1	3026	10.0.2.6	22
SSH - WFE2	TCP	127.0.0.1	3027	10.0.2.7	22

Figure 10-8. *Port forwarding for WFE1 (Notice the new entry with Guest Port 443)*

- Open the firewall ports on WFE1 for outside access:

```
sudo firewall-cmd --permanent --add-port=443/tcp
```

- Restart firewall:

```
sudo systemctl restart firewalld
```

- Restart your Nginx services and try accessing the website using https://127.0.0.1:9006 and you will be shown an error like the one in Figure 10-7. Click on Advanced and then click "Proceed to localhost (unsafe)." Viewing the details of the certificate will reveal why this error happened. Figure 10-9 clearly exposes the fact that the root certificate is not trusted. This goes on to say that just having an SSL certificate is not enough. You should buy certificates from renowned authorities that are globally trusted on all operating systems.

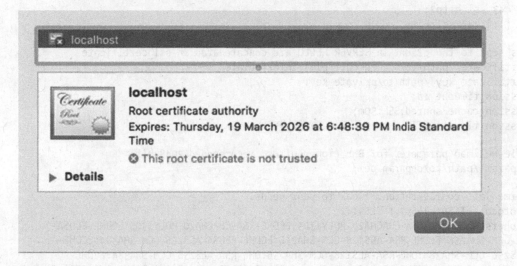

Figure 10-9. *Certificate appears bad since the root is not trusted*

Optimizing HTTPS Servers

Encrypting and decrypting traffic is a CPU-consuming operation and hence adds overhead to the processing, especially from a CPU perspective. You must enable keepalive connections to send several requests over one connection since SSL handshake is among the most intensive operation. If you turn off the keepalive option, every request will require an addition SSL handshake, which would be counterproductive.

Similarly, the SSL sessions are stored in a cache that is shared between workers. It is a good idea to use ssl_session_directive and increase the default value of 5 minutes. 1MB of the cache contains about 4000 sessions, so you can increase the allocated value as well. The following directives can be used in the http block of the config file. As can be seen, the memory is increased to 10MB and timeout is increased to 15 minutes.

```
ssl_session_cache    shared:SSL:10m;
ssl_session_timeout 15m;
```

Another fantastic tool you can use is SSL Config Generator, found at https://mozilla.github.io/server-side-tls/ssl-config-generator/. You can create an SSL config easily and tweak the details as you find fit. A sample Nginx configuration taken from the website looks as follows:

```
server {
    listen 80 default_server;
    listen [::]:80 default_server;

    # Redirect all HTTP requests to HTTPS with a 301 Moved Permanently response.
    return 301 https://$host$request_uri;
}

server {
    listen 443 ssl http2;
    listen [::]:443 ssl http2;

    # certs sent to the client in SERVER HELLO are concatenated in ssl_certificate
    ssl_certificate /path/to/signed_cert_plus_intermediates;
    ssl_certificate_key /path/to/private_key;
    ssl_session_timeout 1d;
    ssl_session_cache shared:SSL:50m;
    ssl_session_tickets off;

    # Diffie-Hellman parameter for DHE ciphersuites, recommended 2048 bits
    ssl_dhparam /path/to/dhparam.pem;

    # intermediate configuration. tweak to your needs.
    ssl_protocols TLSv1 TLSv1.1 TLSv1.2;
    ssl_ciphers 'ECDHE-ECDSA-CHACHA20-POLY1305:ECDHE-RSA-CHACHA20-POLY1305:ECDHE-ECDSA-
AES128-GCM-SHA256:ECDHE-RSA-AES128-GCM-SHA256:ECDHE-ECDSA-AES256-GCM-SHA384:ECDHE-
RSA-AES256-GCM-SHA384:DHE-RSA-AES128-GCM-SHA256:DHE-RSA-AES256-GCM-SHA384:ECDHE-
ECDSA-AES128-SHA256:ECDHE-RSA-AES128-SHA256:ECDHE-ECDSA-AES128-SHA:ECDHE-RSA-AES256-
SHA384:ECDHE-RSA-AES128-SHA:ECDHE-ECDSA-AES256-SHA384:ECDHE-ECDSA-AES256-SHA:ECDHE-
RSA-AES256-SHA:DHE-RSA-AES128-SHA256:DHE-RSA-AES128-SHA:DHE-RSA-AES256-SHA256:DHE-RSA-
AES256-SHA:ECDHE-ECDSA-DES-CBC3-SHA:ECDHE-RSA-DES-CBC3-SHA:EDH-RSA-DES-CBC3-SHA:AES128-
GCM-SHA256:AES256-GCM-SHA384:AES128-SHA256:AES256-SHA256:AES128-SHA:AES256-SHA:DES-CBC3-
SHA:!DSS';
    ssl_prefer_server_ciphers on;

    # HSTS (ngx_http_headers_module is required) (15768000 seconds = 6 months)
    add_header Strict-Transport-Security max-age=15768000;

    # OCSP Stapling ---
    # fetch OCSP records from URL in ssl_certificate and cache them
    ssl_stapling on;
    ssl_stapling_verify on;
```

```
## verify chain of trust of OCSP response using Root CA and Intermediate certs
ssl_trusted_certificate /path/to/root_CA_cert_plus_intermediates;

resolver <IP DNS resolver>;

....
}
```

Creating a Certificate Request

A Certificate Request (CSR) is a file containing the information that is required to request a certificate—both public information that anyone browsing your website will be able to see, as well as private information, like a private key, that only you will have access to.

You can use the openssl command to create a certificate request based on your needs. Be extremely careful about the files it generates. You need to properly back it up and copy on all servers where you want SSL to work. This is because running the following command generates a private key only on one server. If you have a web farm, you will need to ensure that the private key is appropriately copied and that permissions are explicitly granted on all servers.

```
sudo openssl req -new -newkey rsa:2048 -nodes -keyout /etc/nginx/ssl/mydomain.key -out /etc/
nginx/ssl/mydomain.csr
[sudo] password for user1:
Generating a 2048 bit RSA private key
...........................................................................+++
..................+++
writing new private key to '/etc/nginx/ssl/mydomain.key'
-----
You are about to be asked to enter information that will be incorporated
into your certificate request.
What you are about to enter is what is called a Distinguished Name or a DN.
There are quite a few fields but you can leave some blank
For some fields there will be a default value,
If you enter '.', the field will be left blank.
-----
Country Name (2 letter code) [XX]:IN
State or Province Name (full name) []:WB
Locality Name (eg, city) [Default City]:KK
Organization Name (eg, company) [Default Company Ltd]:Attosol Technologies
Organizational Unit Name (eg, section) []:
Common Name (eg, your name or your server's hostname) []:*.attosol.com
Email Address []:contact@attosol.com

Please enter the following 'extra' attributes
to be sent with your certificate request
A challenge password []:
An optional company name []:
```

Most certificate providers will ask you to open the file in a text editor or simply send the public key to them in order for them to create a certificate for you. The rest of it is mostly paperwork. Once they are sure that you are who you say you are, they will certify you and provide a globally recognizable and trusted certificate that will be made available for download. Installation and configuration of the certificate is the same as for a self-signed certificate.

You can buy certificates from many authorities. The top four combined, however, make up about 94 percent of the total market share as listed in Table 10-1 (as per the W3Techs Survey 2015).

Table 10-1. *Top Certificate Providers*

Name	Website	Market Share
Comodo	https://ssl.comodo.com	41%
Symantec (acquired Verisign)	https://www.symantec.com/website-security	30%
GoDaddy	https://www.godaddy.com/web-security	13%
GlobalSign	https://www.globalsign.com/en/	10%

There is a new authority called Let's Encrypt that provides free certificates and is worth checking out. More details can be found at https://letsencrypt.org.

Web Server Security

Typically, applications have their own authentication and authorization methods and are used to restrict access to certain areas of the application. The web server also has ways to restrict access.

■ **Authorization** An operation to ensure that you can only do as much as it is allowed. For example, the server knows that you are X, but it might have a constraint that you are not authorized to modify a file. Authorization comes into effect after you are authenticated.

Creating the Password File

Nginx requires you to use a password file in the following format:

```
name1:password1
name2:password2
```

and so on. The names can be cleartext, but the password needs to be in an encrypted state. You can use openssl command line to create the file as follows:

- -n ensures that the user name (user1) is written on the same line without a new line character.

```
sudo sh -c "echo -n 'user1:' >> /etc/nginx/.pwd"
```

- You can add your password now:

```
sudo sh -c "openssl passwd -apr1 >> /etc/nginx/.pwd"
Password:
Verifying - Password:
```

- To view the output, use the following command:

```
cat /etc/nginx/.pwd
user1:$apr1$/X48Flid$dOhTdQqWPyMMmFR2m/Nh/O
```

- You can add more users as needed using the same set of commands.

Configuring Nginx Password Authentication

Now that the password file is set up, you can edit your Nginx configuration file like the following. Notice how the location block now mentions auth_basic and auth_basic_user_file directives. Reload the configuration and your website should now be protected. See Figure 10-10. If the password is entered incorrectly, or if you click cancel, the page results in an error as you can see in Figure 10-11.

```
server {
    listen        80;
    server_name  localhost;

    listen 443 ssl;
    ssl_certificate /etc/nginx/ssl/cert.crt;
    ssl_certificate_key /etc/nginx/ssl/private.key;

    location / {
        root    /usr/share/nginx/html;
        index  index.html index.htm;
        auth_basic "Authentication Required";
        auth_basic_user_file /etc/nginx/.pwd;
    }
}
```

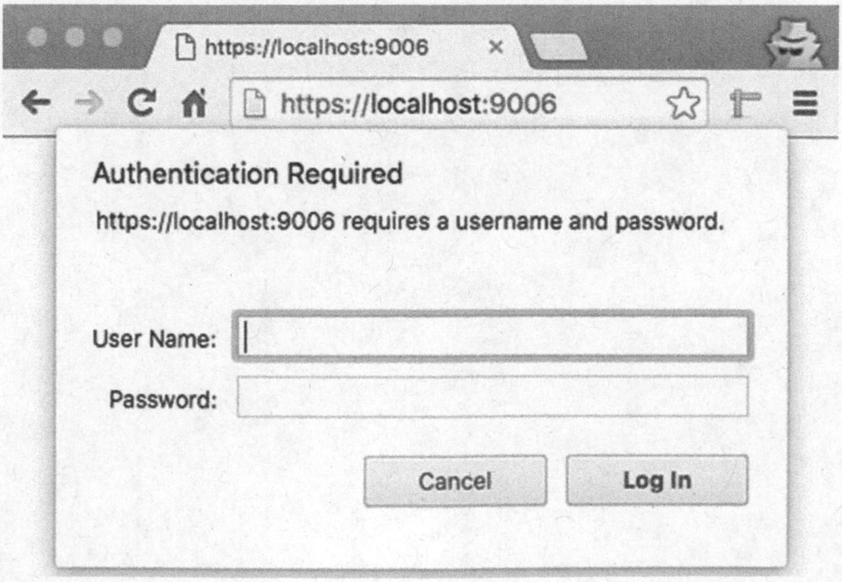

Figure 10-10. *Authentication Prompt after the configuration*

207

401 Authorization Required

nginx/1.8.1

Figure 10-11. *Failure to provide a valid password results in an error message*

Summary

Security should be taken very seriously. In this chapter, you have learned about how network sniffing can lead to security attacks and data theft. Based on your business you must decide on the kind of certificate you want to purchase. People trust a website based on its certificate, and a broken or expired certificate can create unnecessary hassles for your visitors. You must configure the certificates carefully and keep proper backups of the private keys. Last but not least, if your application doesn't have an authentication and authorization module, you can quickly restrict specific portions of your website using basic authentication.

CHAPTER 11

■ ■ ■

Upgrading and Migrating

Web technologies are evolving at a rapid pace and so is Nginx. Upgrading server-side software can be tricky, especially if the server is currently in use. If you have a web farm, you might not feel comfortable with the idea of upgrading the web servers while the visitors are still connected to it. However, with upgrades you get new features and bug fixes, and quite often the pain of upgrading is worth the effort. In this chapter you will learn about upgrading your web server in ways that shorten or remove the downtime. You will learn about the options available to you so that you can exercise them in different scenarios.

Controlling Nginx

To quickly reiterate, Nginx has one master process and one or more worker processes. If caching is enabled, the cache loader and cache manager processes also run at startup. The master process reads and evaluates the configuration files, and also maintains the worker processes. It is the worker process that does the actual processing of the requests. To stop or start Nginx, you send signals to the master process. When you run a command like nginx -s signal you basically tell the master process about your intentions.

There are four signals allowed:

1. quit: Shut down Nginx gracefully.

2. reload: Reload the configuration file in case you have made any changes and want them to come into effect. If the master process is not running, this command will simply error out because there is no process to honor this command. The reload command ensures a smooth completion of the old connections.

3. reopen: Reopen the log files is useful in scenarios where you have want to move the write cursor to the end of the file. Now, why would you do that? There are utilities that regularly truncate the log files and create archives of what's been truncated. So, if you use one such utility or you have edited the logs directly, you should reopen the log files to avoid any log corruption. Reopening puts the write marker to the end of the log file.

4. stop: Shut down Nginx immediately. The difference between stop and quit is that quit is graceful but stop is not. When you say quit, Nginx finishes serving the open connections before it is shut down. stop, on the other hand, terminates all connections immediately.

© Rahul Soni 2016
R. Soni, *Nginx*, DOI 10.1007/978-1-4842-1656-9_11

The process id (PID) is written in a file called `nginx.pid`, usually located in `/var/run/nginx.pid`. Execute a cat command as follows and notice that the PID is same the running process.

```
$ cat /var/run/nginx.pid '
9920
$ ps -aux | grep nginx
root      9920  0.0  0.1  57792  1280 ?        Ss   06:55   0:00 nginx: master process /usr/
                                                                 sbin/nginx -c /etc/nginx/nginx.conf
nginx     9922  0.0  0.1  58176  1964 ?        S    06:55   0:00 nginx: worker process
nginx     9923  0.0  0.1  57960  1708 ?        S    06:55   0:00 nginx: cache manager process
```

If you stop nginx (`nginx -s stop`), the nginx.pid file gets deleted. But if you reload the configuration (`nginx -s reload`), you will find that the file keep showing the old PID, proving that the master process was not recycled.

Command-Line Parameters

Before you could send a signal to Nginx, you must ensure that it is started. In the previous code block, you can see that `nginx` binary is located at `/usr/sbin/nginx`. To start Nginx use one of these methods:

- `/usr/sbin/nginx` or `nginx`
- `/usr/sbin/nginx -t -c /some/other/config.conf -g "worker_processes 2;"`
    - This command tells Nginx to test the configuration (-t) and load some other configuration file (-c). Apart from that, it also sets the worker_processes to 2 using the -g switch.
- `-?` `-h` prints the help.
- `-v` prints the version information.
- `-V` prints the version information along with compiler information and configuration parameters.

If you try to use a global parameter that already exists in the configuration file, you will get an error message like this:

```
sudo /usr/sbin/nginx -g "worker_processes 4;"
nginx: [emerg] "worker_processes" directive is duplicate in /etc/nginx/nginx.conf:2
```

The error message tells you the file due to which it failed. Edit the file and remove the worker_processes directive. Try the commands now:

```
$ sudo kill nginx
$ sudo /usr/sbin/nginx -g "worker_processes 4;"
$ ps -aux | grep nginx
root     10846  0.0  0.1  57796  1244 ?        Ss   12:02   0:00 nginx: master process /usr/sbin/
                                                                 nginx -g worker_processes 4;
nginx    10847  0.0  0.1  58176  1924 ?        S    12:02   0:00 nginx: worker process
nginx    10848  0.0  0.1  58176  1924 ?        S    12:02   0:00 nginx: worker process
nginx    10849  0.0  0.1  58176  1924 ?        S    12:02   0:00 nginx: worker process
nginx    10850  0.0  0.1  58176  1924 ?        S    12:02   0:00 nginx: worker process
nginx    10851  0.0  0.1  57960  1676 ?        S    12:02   0:00 nginx: cache manager process
nginx    10852  0.0  0.1  57960  1676 ?        S    12:02   0:00 nginx: cache loader process
```

Sure enough, it works and you can see all the processes. You can send signals to the master process or worker process in special cases:

```
sudo kill -SIGNAL $( cat /var/run/nginx.pid )
```

The -SIGNAL can be one of the following:

- TERM, INT: Fast Shutdown

- QUIT: Graceful Shutdown

- HUP: Start new worker processes with a new configuration, and gracefully shut down the existing worker processes. Notice the following commands. The command spawns 2 worker processes and the HUP signal kills all processes except master process. The PID 2405 doesn't change, but every other PID changes.

```
$ sudo kill nginx
$ sudo /usr/sbin/nginx -g "worker_processes 2;"
$ ps -aux | grep nginx
root      2405  0.0  0.1  57796  1140 ?        Ss   22:29   0:00 nginx: master process /usr/
                                                                 sbin/nginx -g worker_processes 2;
nginx     2406  0.0  0.1  58176  1920 ?        S    22:29   0:00 nginx: worker process
nginx     2407  0.0  0.1  58176  1920 ?        S    22:29   0:00 nginx: worker process
nginx     2408  0.0  0.1  57960  1672 ?        S    22:29   0:00 nginx: cache manager process
nginx     2409  0.0  0.1  57960  1672 ?        S    22:29   0:00 nginx: cache loader process

$ sudo kill -HUP $( cat /var/run/nginx.pid )
$ ps -aux | grep nginx
root      2405  0.0  0.2  57920  2692 ?        Ss   22:29   0:00 nginx: master process /usr/
                                                                 sbin/nginx -g worker_processes 2;
nginx     2415  0.0  0.2  58300  2048 ?        S    22:29   0:00 nginx: worker process
nginx     2416  0.0  0.2  58300  2048 ?        S    22:29   0:00 nginx: worker process
nginx     2417  0.0  0.1  58084  1796 ?        S    22:29   0:00 nginx: cache manager process
nginx     2418  0.0  0.1  58084  1796 ?        S    22:29   0:00 nginx: cache loader process
```

You should note that this behavior happens only when the new configuration is found valid. To test this, edit your nginx.conf file and purposely introduce some junk text so that the configuration file is corrupt. Try sending the HUP signal again followed with ps -aux as shown below. The kill command appeared to have worked correctly, but the ps command shows that all the worker processes has the same PID as before. Clearly, the kill command didn't kill the running worker processes and this is good. The reason is because the configuration file is faulty and you wouldn't want a faulty configuration bringing the existing processes down. Nginx is smart and it kills the existing set of worker processes only when it is convinced that the new worker processes have spun and started taking requests.

```
$ sudo kill -HUP $( cat /var/run/nginx.pid )
$ ps -aux | grep nginx
root      2405  0.0  0.2  57920  2700 ?        Ss   22:29   0:00 nginx: master process /usr/
                                                                 sbin/nginx -g worker_processes 2;
nginx     2415  0.0  0.2  58300  2048 ?        S    22:29   0:00 nginx: worker process
nginx     2416  0.0  0.2  58300  2048 ?        S    22:29   0:00 nginx: worker process
nginx     2417  0.0  0.1  58084  1796 ?        S    22:29   0:00 nginx: cache manager process
```

There is a small problem with the approach, though. Since the `kill` command didn't throw any error message, it becomes tricky to find out whether it actually worked and did what was intended. You can test the configuration with `nginx -t` before sending signals. Another approach would be to use `nginx -s reload`:

```
$ sudo nginx -s reload
nginx: [emerg] unknown directive "aslkdj" in /etc/nginx/nginx.conf:6
```

- USR1: Reopen log files.

- USR2: You can upgrade to a new binary on the fly using USR2 signal. This approach is quite fascinating and effective. It is good that Nginx has this feature since the Nginx binaries are monolithic. If you remember, you have to compile the binaries with different switches since Nginx cannot load the modules dynamically. If you need to add a new module or upgrade to a later version, it becomes easier to test with this approach.

■ **Note** Ensure that you have fixed the invalid configuration you introduced just a while ago.

- At first, replace the old binary with a new one after taking the backup of the existing one.

- Send USR2 signal `sudo kill -HUP $( cat /var/run/nginx.pid )`:

```
$ sudo kill -USR2 $( cat /var/run/nginx.pid )
```

- If you run the `ps` command again, you will find an output similar to the following. Notice how the previous configuration was used to launch another set of master processes and worker processes. The previous master process with the PID 2405 continues to run in parallel with PID 2519. The second master process launches another set of worker process, cache manager and the cache loader. This makes it possible to run two instances of Nginx in parallel, handling the incoming requests together.

```
$ ps -aux | grep nginx
root      2405  0.0  0.2  57920  2700 ?        Ss   22:29   0:00 nginx: master process /usr/
sbin/nginx -g worker_processes 2;
nginx     2415  0.0  0.2  58300  2048 ?        S    22:29   0:00 nginx: worker process
nginx     2416  0.0  0.2  58300  2048 ?        S    22:29   0:00 nginx: worker process
nginx     2417  0.0  0.1  58084  1796 ?        S    22:29   0:00 nginx: cache manager process
root      2518  0.0  0.3  57796  3700 ?        S    22:58   0:00 nginx: master process /usr/
                                                                sbin/nginx -g worker_processes 2;
nginx     2519  0.0  0.1  58176  1920 ?        S    22:58   0:00 nginx: worker process
nginx     2520  0.0  0.1  58176  1920 ?        S    22:58   0:00 nginx: worker process
nginx     2521  0.0  0.1  57960  1672 ?        S    22:58   0:00 nginx: cache manager process
nginx     2522  0.0  0.1  57960  1672 ?        S    22:58   0:00 nginx: cache loader process
```

- WINCH: Now that you have a new instance running, you can check the requests and test the new configuration. If all is well, you may proceed to kill the original set of worker processes by sending the WINCH signal. Notice how the worker processes are killed but the master process is not. At this point only the new worker processes are running with the new configuration.

```
$ sudo kill -WINCH 2405
$ ps -aux | grep nginx
root       2405  0.0  0.2  57920  2700 ?        Ss   22:29   0:00 nginx: master process /usr/
                                                                  sbin/nginx -g worker_processes 2;
root       2518  0.0  0.3  57796  3700 ?        S    22:58   0:00 nginx: master process /usr/
                                                                  sbin/nginx -g worker_processes 2;
nginx      2519  0.0  0.1  58176  1920 ?        S    22:58   0:00 nginx: worker process
nginx      2520  0.0  0.1  58176  1920 ?        S    22:58   0:00 nginx: worker process
nginx      2521  0.0  0.1  57960  1672 ?        S    22:58   0:00 nginx: cache manager process
```

- But what about the old master process - PID 2405? Well, it still exists because Nginx allows you to thoroughly test the new configuration before you kill the older one, which served you well.

- Successfully Upgraded: In this case, you can safely send the QUIT signal: sudo kill -QUIT 2405. Shortly, you will be left with only one master process that will be your upgraded Nginx binary.

- Upgraded with Issues: Revert back to the original configuration. Send the HUP signal: sudo kill -HUP 2405 and the previous configuration will come back to life. You should now have the previous configuration back up and running. You can send TERM or QUIT signal to the new one: sudo kill -QUIT 2518. You should remove the new binary and replace with the older one now and you will be good.

Migrating from Apache to Nginx

There is a stark difference between the architectures of Nginx and Apache. From the configuration files to the underpinning of processes and threads, the architectural differences make Nginx shine. The Nginx configuration files are simpler to manage and read. Generally, you can get more throughputs from the same hardware using Nginx.

If you are running Apache, you can adopt Nginx in two different ways. The first way is to use Nginx as a reverse proxy and gradually move toward full adoption. The other way is to migrate the configuration from Apache to Nginx at one shot. The second approach requires more planning and work, but gives the dividend right away. Based on the complexity of your setup, you may choose to take one route or the other.

Feature Comparison

In Table 11-1, you can find the core functional differences between Nginx and Apache. Before even trying to migrate, you must be aware of all functionalities required by your application and what is available in Nginx out of the box. If everything that you use in Apache is available in Nginx, then it is a no-brainer and a full configuration migration is more suitable. However, if there are certain components that are available only in Apache, it makes more sense to use Nginx as a reverse proxy and get the best of both worlds.

Table 11-1. *Feature comparision of Nginx and Apache*

Feature	Apache	Nginx
Architecture	*Synchronous*: Each request is handled by a separate thread or process and uses synchronous sockets. It is a blocking architecture. The resources are not released unless the data is consumed by the client. If there are a lot of clients connected, Apache will need to spawn more threads in order to process the requests.	*Event based*: Asynchronous sockets listen for the requests and the resources are released as quickly as possible. Once the client is ready for more data, another event triggers and the processing resumes. Inherently, Nginx doesn't like blocking its resources due to client's slowness. The intention is to serve as many requests, as quickly as possible.
Performance	Response times are slower and with more requests, it tends to get even slower.	Response times are much faster than Apache and wins hands down. It is one of the primary reasons why people switch to Nginx.
Portability	Apache is more portable and runs under almost all major OS, including Linux, OSX, Windows, Unix, BSD, Solaris, and more.	Nginx is less portable than Apache. It shines best on *nix platform. It is available on Windows but not suitable for production.
Created	1994	2002
Language used	C	C & C++
Module	Modules can be loaded dynamically in Apache and it makes it easier to add/remove/test different modules.	Modules require a recompile of the binary. Before version 1-9-11, it couldn't be dynamically loaded, but this is changing fast. With the latest versions of Nginx, you will have more support for dynamic modules. You can read about it at `www.nginx.com/blog/dynamic-modules-nginx-1-9-11/`.
Hardware Requirement	Due to the architecture, lesser RAM can create a bottleneck for processing requests since the requests are not released quickly.	RAM requirement is comparatively lower due to more efficient request handling. You can get a lot more mileage from commodity hardware.
CGI Support	Most CGI protocols work with Apache because of module architecture.	Supports FastCGI, uWSGI, SCGI via modules that are included by default at compile time.
Configuration Files	XML based.	Text based.
Application Configuration	Allows individual configuration file per folder using .htaccess. This has its benefits as well as problems since the .htaccess files have to be individually managed.	No support for .htaccess files. The configuration is done using server blocks. As discussed earlier in this book, you can create and load multiple server blocks from the main configuration file. This approach is very effective, since every server block can be maintained as a separate file with as much configuration details as needed. It makes portability easier.

(continued)

Table 11-1. (*continued*)

Feature	Apache	Nginx
Modules Ecosystem	Apache has been around for a longer time and has a definite edge here. It has hundreds of modules.	Nginx has around 100+ modules available for your use. But there is still room for improvement.
General Ecosystem and Documentation	Apache has the edge here too. It has a large number of useful software that is extremely straightforward to use for Apache. An example is WordPress.	It requires a little extra work to set up and configure most third-party software that became wildly successful, like WordPress. Although possible, the process is sometimes painful due to a variety of platforms available and lack of documentation.
Support	Apache is a wildly successful product and the community is vibrant. There is hardly anything that you can ask and not get a decent answer.	Nginx is becoming more popular every day and the community is growing. The overall support, however, is still weaker in comparison to Apache due to the sheer number of Apache users out there. Don't let this discourage you, since there is an official support available with Nginx PLUS and the community is growing every day.

Configuration Comparison

You have already been working with Nginx configuration files in this book. A typical Apache configuration file, in contrast, looks similar to the following:

```
Listen 80
Listen 8080

<VirtualHost 172.20.30.40:80>
    ServerName www.example.com
    DocumentRoot "/www/domain-80"
</VirtualHost>

<VirtualHost 172.20.30.40:80>
    ServerName www.example.org
    DocumentRoot "/www/otherdomain-80"
</VirtualHost>
```

Based on the previous code, you must have already noticed that Apache uses XML format. The XML files are not very human readable, especially if it gets nested. Nginx provides a welcome change to this.

VirtualHost in Apache can be migrated to the server blocks with ease. PHP is handled in a different manner in Nginx and has been already explained in chapter 7. The glaring absence that causes the most amount of work during migration is .htaccess. Apache allows you to set folder level settings using a file that is called .htaccess. This file can be found at various levels and the last ones read are given precedence. Consider Figure 11-1. The .htaccess at /app/images will be read after /app. If the same setting is defined at both /app and /app/images, the latter would be given priority.

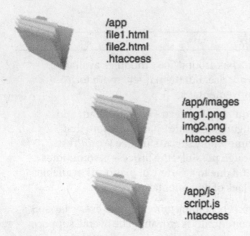

/app
file1.html
file2.html
.htaccess

/app/images
img1.png
img2.png
.htaccess

/app/js
script.js
.htaccess

Figure 11-1. *Directory heirarchy with .htaccess files*

In Apache, the .htaccess file is used for multiple purposes:

- Access and authentication rules for specific directories
- Setting flags for various modules
- Define rewriting rules

There is no equivalent to .htaccess in Nginx. That said, you can always find solutions by using different directives in different Nginx blocks.

Summary

Nginx has a very effective and robust upgrade method. If you plan properly you can have zero downtime for your web servers. When it comes to migrating, there is unfortunately no direct path available to migrate from Apache. But the thumb rule of migration is quite simple. Migrate whatever you can, and use Nginx to augment the rest. It doesn't matter if you use Apache, Express.js, Node.js, or IIS. Nginx can easily do the front-end job and route the traffic as per your requirements to the back end using its reverse proxy capabilities. With respect to comparing with Apache, let's wrap up with a famous quote from Chris Lea, "Apache is like Microsoft Word, it has a million options but you only need six. NGINX does those six things, and it does five of them 50 times faster than Apache."

CHAPTER 12

∎ ∎ ∎

Troubleshooting Tips and FAQ

Troubleshooting a web server is not fun, and this is mostly because of the pressure of the time ticking by while it's offline. The pressure mounts even further if the server remains down for a longer period. No business likes to suffer losses due to hardware or configuration issues. It is imperative that you baseline your servers and make yourself aware of the traffic when the going is good. That way, it makes it simpler to troubleshoot when the going gets tough. In this chapter, you will learn about the troubleshooting mindset and how isolation helps in troubleshooting.

First, What You Should Not Do

Often, when the server acts up, one of the common mistakes is to check the browser's (or client-side) error message. The errors that you see in a browser are usually generic messages sent by the server. It is considered good practice to hide detailed error messages from the public, and so those generic messages are not usually helpful for troubleshooting a server side issue. The server normally hides the details in logs, which should be your starting point.

Moreover, following a direction that you don't understand might *apparently* fix your problem but in most likelihood is not going to instill the confidence that you have taken the right steps.

First Commandment of Troubleshooting: Isolate the Issue

While troubleshooting, it is best to start by isolating the issue, identifying the root cause, and then fixing the problem by introducing changes. Depending on the situation this can be a very easy or a very difficult thing to do. A few scenarios should help in learning some basic troubleshooting skills.

Scenario 1: Page Cannot Be Displayed in the Browser

Let's set up a new server block and troubleshoot the issues one by one until the problem is fixed.
The server block in this case is not actually wrong. It is just that it needs additional actions on your side so that it starts working.

Start by logging on to WFE1 server (ssh -p 3026 user1@127.0.0.1) and change the main.conf (sudo vi /etc/nginx/conf.d/main.conf) file like this:

```
server {
    listen      90;
    server_name localhost;
```

© Rahul Soni 2016
R. Soni, *Nginx*, DOI 10.1007/978-1-4842-1656-9_12

```
    location / {
        root    /usr/share/nginx/html;
        index   index.html index.htm;
    }
}
```

Save the configuration and reload using `sudo nginx -s reload`. Ensure that you can browse the website locally after changes:

```
$ curl localhost:90
wfe1.localdomain
```

Now, try `http://127.0.0.1:8006/` using your host machine. Does it work? Ideally, it shouldn't. But why is that so, and how can you ascertain the root cause?

- You might notice that the request fails almost immediately and appears that the request is not even reaching the server. To ensure that is the case, check the access logs and you will find that the request is not even reaching the server. (You can tail the logs and make requests. If you don't see anything in the logs, it will give you a clue that the request is not really making it to the server.)

- So, if the request is not reaching, could it be that the port is not allowed (the server block is fairly simple and doesn't really have too many variables)? To test it, you can use telnet like this:

```
telnet 127.0.0.1 8006
Trying 127.0.0.1...
Connected to localhost.
Escape character is '^]'.
Connection closed by foreign host.
```

As you can see, the connection gets closed immediately. The conclusion is that there is something wrong with the connection, and your host is not even allowing the connection to the WFE1 server. A quick look at the network configuration and you can see that the guest port is 80 whereas the configuration says 90. Change the port as you can see in Figure 12-1 and try again.

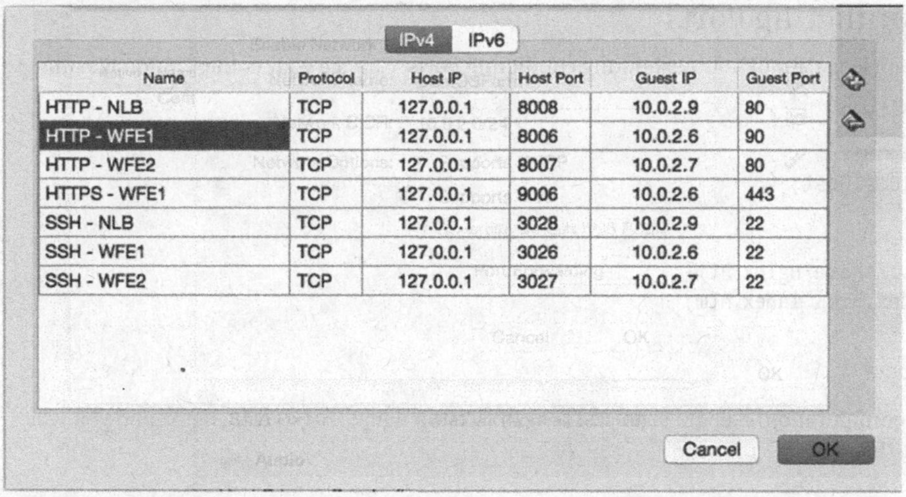

Name	Protocol	Host IP	Host Port	Guest IP	Guest Port
HTTP - NLB	TCP	127.0.0.1	8008	10.0.2.9	80
HTTP - WFE1	TCP	127.0.0.1	8006	10.0.2.6	90
HTTP - WFE2	TCP	127.0.0.1	8007	10.0.2.7	80
HTTPS - WFE1	TCP	127.0.0.1	9006	10.0.2.6	443
SSH - NLB	TCP	127.0.0.1	3028	10.0.2.9	22
SSH - WFE1	TCP	127.0.0.1	3026	10.0.2.6	22
SSH - WFE2	TCP	127.0.0.1	3027	10.0.2.7	22

Figure 12-1. Change the guest port to 90 for WFE1

- telnet will now work and the connection won't close automatically.

```
telnet 127.0.0.1 8006
Trying 127.0.0.1...
Connected to localhost.
Escape character is '^]'.
```

To get out of the `telnet` prompt, type ^] and hit enter.

Try browsing to `localhost:8006` from the host again. The behavior will now be different. The page will take a long time before it errors out. What does this imply? Telnet works on port 90 and you have checked it already. So, why does the page not render? If you make a quick educated guess about what all things can be in between, you will know that a proxy server or a firewall can make this happen. Since there is no proxy in this setup, let's check the firewall.

Just for testing (this is not recommended in production), let's disable the firewall by running `sudo systemctl stop firewalld`. Refresh `localhost:8006` and this time it should work. Great! So, you know it is because of firewall. Issue is isolated. Start the firewall service again by running `sudo systemctl start firewalld`. Now, instead of stopping the firewall, a better solution would be to create a firewall rule that allows port 90. Do that using `sudo firewall-cmd --zone=public --add-port=90/tcp --permanent` and your website will start working as expected.

Isolation, as you can see, has helped tremendously in giving a direction to this troubleshooting session. Not only that, you can remain confident of what you have done, since you have not shot an arrow in the dark after a random search.

Scenario 2: Conflicting Ports

In this scenario you will learn about troubleshooting conflicting ports. Change your configuration like this:

```
server {
    listen       3306;
    server_name  localhost;

    location / {
        root    /usr/share/nginx/html;
        index   index.html index.htm;
    }
}
```

After saving the configuration, execute sudo kill nginx to stop nginx. Try starting nginx and you will an error message like this:

```
$ sudo nginx
nginx: [emerg] bind() to 0.0.0.0:3306 failed (98: Address already in use)
nginx: [emerg] bind() to 0.0.0.0:3306 failed (98: Address already in use)
nginx: [emerg] bind() to 0.0.0.0:3306 failed (98: Address already in use)
nginx: [emerg] bind() to 0.0.0.0:3306 failed (98: Address already in use)
nginx: [emerg] bind() to 0.0.0.0:3306 failed (98: Address already in use)
nginx: [emerg] still could not bind()
```

The error message is evidently telling you that it doesn't like the port. To figure out which application has grabbed that port, you can run the netstat command:

```
$ sudo netstat -nlp | grep 3306
tcp6       0      0 :::3306                  :::*                        LISTEN      1264/mysqld
```

netstat is a built-in tool that can show you a lot of information about the network connections, routing tables, interface statistics, and more. The output reveals the application (mysqld) that has been listening on 3306. One way to resolve this issue is to change the port in your configuration. Another way would be to stop and remove mysqld from WFE1. Based on your requirement, you can decide which way is better.

A key lesson that needs to be highlighted in this scenario is that a good web administrator knows a lot about tools that are at his disposal. The more tools and utilities you know, the easier it would be for you to isolate the issue. Explore the tools in advance so that you can use it when needed.

Scenario 3: Bad Permissions

Bad permissions on the folder can lead to a variety of errors that are hard to troubleshoot. Typically, the end result would be 404 and it would mean that the file was not found. When you check out server, your file might already be existing. In these cases, it is recommended to check out your access logs (use nginx -V to find your access log path) and file permissions of the directory. The following command will give you permissions in a recursive fashion:

```
$ namei -om /etc/nginx/conf.d/main.conf
f: /etc/nginx/conf.d/main.conf
 dr-xr-xr-x root root /
 drwxr-xr-x root root etc
```

```
drwxr-xr-x root root nginx
drwxr-xr-x root root conf.d
-rw-r--r-- root root main.conf
```

In times of distress, logs are your best friends. Ensure that you are logging at the highest level during your troubleshooting session. Reproduce the error; read the logs; and more often than not, you will have decent pointers to act upon.

Scenario 4: Bad Configuration

Nginx command line has a switch -t that tests the configuration for any syntactical error. Keep in mind that this switch only takes care of syntax issues. There are a few things that it cannot test. For example, if you have a typo in your hostname, the switch will have no way to figure out if the name is correct or not.

nginx -t is one of the things that you take with a grain of salt. Run it to ensure that there are no syntactical and other common errors. But don't bet all you have on it. Certain settings related to configuration might not kick in when you say nginx -s reload. If you have any doubts, restart Nginx and test your expected output appropriately.

Scenario 5: Rewrite Rules

Rewrites happen all the time in Nginx and yet they are not logged by default. This can create a lot of confusion while troubleshooting. When you are seeing 404 or unexpected pages, ensure that the rewrite_ log directive is set to on.

```
server {
        #snipped
        error_log      /var/logs/nginx/site.com.error.log;
        rewrite_log on;
        #snipped
}
```

rewrite_log directive just sets a flag. When turned on, it will send rewrite related log messages with [notice] level and can help you tremendously in understanding what is going on within the hoods. Once you turn it on, look for messages in the configured log file.

Scenario 6: Log Only Your Requests

When you set the log level to debug, your error logs will log tremendous amounts of information and it might become overwhelming to troubleshoot if yours is a public facing website with a lot of traffic. To avoid it, you can set debug_connection directive to your public IP. This way, only your requests will be logged. The debug_connection directive is configured in your events block and looks like so:

```
events{
        debug_connection x.x.x.x;
}
```

Important Tools for Web Administrators

As mentioned earlier, a web administrator should explore and learn about as many tools as possible. The tools help in isolating the issues quicker. In this section you will find a list of tools that could prove useful in different scenarios.

ping

Send ICMP ECHO_REQUEST packets to network hosts. Useful to check if the host is reachable and which IP it is pointing to.

traceroute

It displays the route and measures the delay in packets across a network. To use it, simply type traceroute sitename.com

top

The top program provides a dynamic real-time view of a running system. It can display system summary information as well as a list of processes or threads currently being managed by the Linux kernel.

htop

It is a much more advanced version of top and a lot more configurable. It gives you an overall picture (Figure 12-2), and it is easily configurable. Use sudo yum install htop to install.

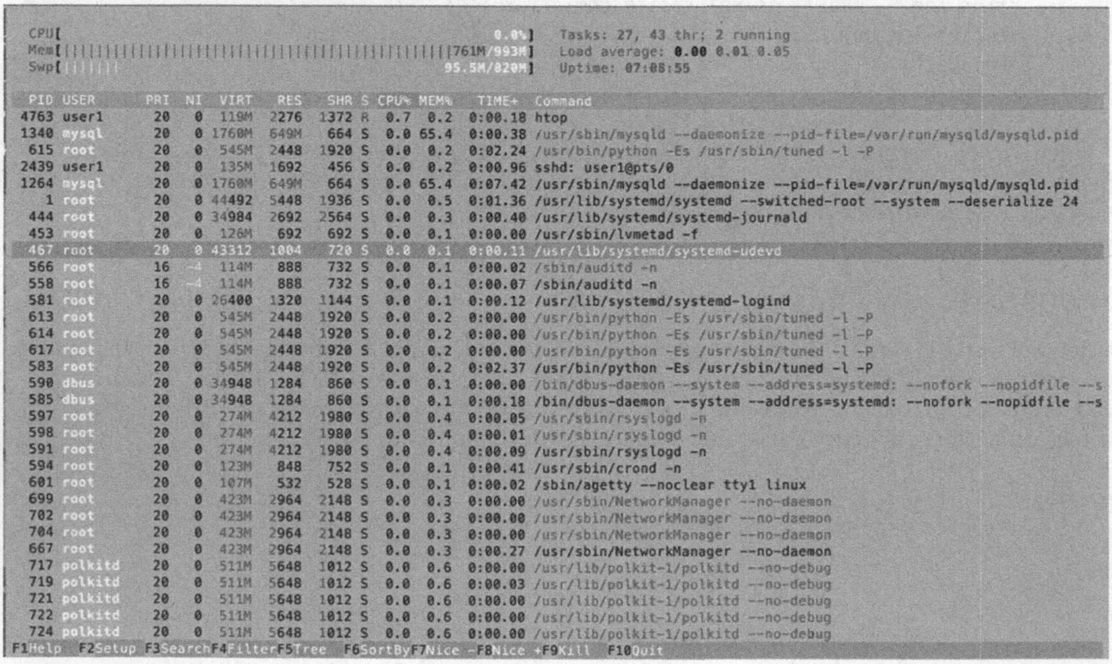

Figure 12-2. htop. Notice the function keys available in the bottom row

atop

Similar to top and htop, but has logging functionality for long-term evaluation and analysis. Use sudo yum install atop to install.

uptime

uptime gives a one-line display of the following information: the current time; how long the system has been running; how many users are currently logged on; and the system load averages for the past 1, 5, and 15 minutes.

free

This command displays the total amount of free and used physical and swap memory in the system, as well as the buffers and caches used by the kernel.

ifconfig or ip addr

This is used to get more details and configure the network interfaces.

```
$ ifconfig
enp0s3: flags=4163<UP,BROADCAST,RUNNING,MULTICAST>  mtu 1500
        inet 10.0.2.6  netmask 255.255.255.0  broadcast 10.0.2.255
        inet6 fe80::a00:27ff:fe90:7e9a  prefixlen 64  scopeid 0x20<link>
        ether 08:00:27:90:7e:9a  txqueuelen 1000  (Ethernet)
        RX packets 19143  bytes 13860101 (13.2 MiB)
        RX errors 0  dropped 0  overruns 0  frame 0
        TX packets 15411  bytes 3249752 (3.0 MiB)
        TX errors 0  dropped 0 overruns 0  carrier 0  collisions 0

lo: flags=73<UP,LOOPBACK,RUNNING>  mtu 65536
        inet 127.0.0.1  netmask 255.0.0.0
        inet6 ::1  prefixlen 128  scopeid 0x10<host>
        loop  txqueuelen 0  (Local Loopback)
        RX packets 128  bytes 10250 (10.0 KiB)
        RX errors 0  dropped 0  overruns 0  frame 0
        TX packets 128  bytes 10250 (10.0 KiB)
        TX errors 0  dropped 0 overruns 0  carrier 0  collisions 0
```

ulimit

It is not usual, but what if a single user starts too many processes so that the system becomes unusable for everyone else? The ulimit command can be helpful in getting and setting the limits of a system.

Use ulimit -a to know the current limits:

```
$ ulimit -a
core file size          (blocks, -c) 0
data seg size           (kbytes, -d) unlimited
scheduling priority             (-e) 0
```

```
file size               (blocks, -f) unlimited
pending signals                (-i) 3899
max locked memory       (kbytes, -l) 64
max memory size         (kbytes, -m) unlimited
open files                     (-n) 1024
pipe size            (512 bytes, -p) 8
POSIX message queues     (bytes, -q) 819200
real-time priority             (-r) 0
stack size              (kbytes, -s) 8192
cpu time              (seconds, -t) unlimited
max user processes             (-u) 3899
virtual memory          (kbytes, -v) unlimited
file locks                     (-x) unlimited
```

nslookup

Nslookup is a program to query Internet domain name servers. You can use it to get the IP address of the hostname:

```
$ nslookup google.in
Server:         192.168.1.1
Address:        192.168.1.1#53

Non-authoritative answer:
Name:   google.in
Address: 216.58.197.68
```

powertop

powertop (Figure 12-3) is a program that helps to diagnose various issues with power consumption and power management. It also has an interactive mode allowing one to experiment with various power management settings. Use sudo yum install powertop to install.

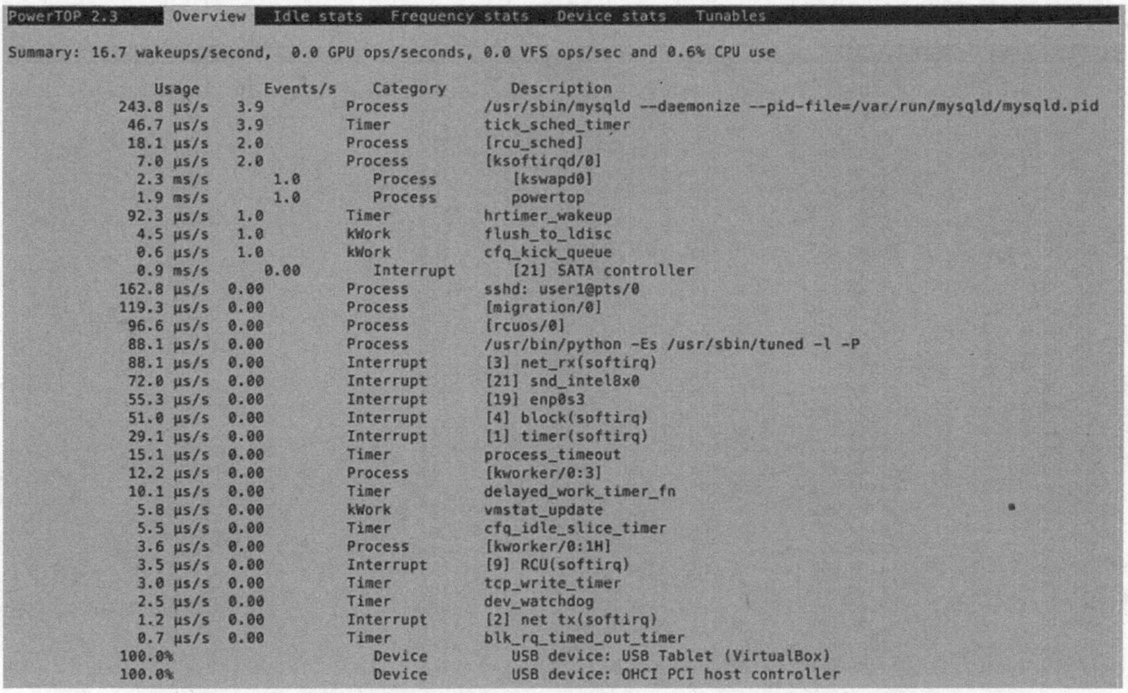

```
PowerTOP 2.3        Overview    Idle stats   Frequency stats   Device stats   Tunables

Summary: 16.7 wakeups/second,   0.0 GPU ops/seconds, 0.0 VFS ops/sec and 0.6% CPU use

          Usage         Events/s    Category       Description
        243.8 µs/s    3.9         Process        /usr/sbin/mysqld --daemonize --pid-file=/var/run/mysqld/mysqld.pid
         46.7 µs/s    3.9         Timer          tick_sched_timer
         18.1 µs/s    2.0         Process        [rcu_sched]
          7.0 µs/s    2.0         Process        [ksoftirqd/0]
          2.3 ms/s        1.0         Process        [kswapd0]
          1.9 ms/s        1.0         Process        powertop
         92.3 µs/s    1.0         Timer          hrtimer_wakeup
          4.5 µs/s    1.0         kWork          flush_to_ldisc
          0.6 µs/s    1.0         kWork          cfq_kick_queue
          0.9 ms/s        0.00        Interrupt       [21] SATA controller
        162.1 µs/s    0.00        Process        sshd: user1@pts/0
        119.3 µs/s    0.00        Process        [migration/0]
         96.6 µs/s    0.00        Process        [rcuos/0]
         88.1 µs/s    0.00        Process        /usr/bin/python -Es /usr/sbin/tuned -l -P
         88.1 µs/s    0.00        Interrupt      [3] net_rx(softirq)
         72.0 µs/s    0.00        Interrupt      [21] snd_intel8x0
         55.3 µs/s    0.00        Interrupt      [19] enp0s3
         51.0 µs/s    0.00        Interrupt      [4] block(softirq)
         29.1 µs/s    0.00        Interrupt      [1] timer(softirq)
         15.1 µs/s    0.00        Timer          process_timeout
         12.2 µs/s    0.00        Process        [kworker/0:3]
         10.1 µs/s    0.00        Timer          delayed_work_timer_fn
          5.8 µs/s    0.00        kWork          vmstat_update
          5.5 µs/s    0.00        Timer          cfq_idle_slice_timer
          3.6 µs/s    0.00        Process        [kworker/0:1H]
          3.5 µs/s    0.00        Interrupt      [9] RCU(softirq)
          3.0 µs/s    0.00        Timer          tcp_write_timer
          2.5 µs/s    0.00        Timer          dev_watchdog
          1.2 µs/s    0.00        Interrupt      [2] net_tx(softirq)
          0.7 µs/s    0.00        Timer          blk_rq_timed_out_timer
        100.0%                    Device          USB device: USB Tablet (VirtualBox)
        100.0%                    Device          USB device: OHCI PCI host controller
```

Figure 12-3. *powertop. Use tabs to switch between different screens*

iotop

iotop (Figure 12-4) is helps to diagnose issues with IO. Use sudo yum install iotop to install.

```
Total DISK READ :        0.00 B/s | Total DISK WRITE :      0.00 B/s
Actual DISK READ:        0.00 B/s | Actual DISK WRITE:      0.00 B/s
  TID  PRIO  USER     DISK READ  DISK WRITE  SWAPIN    IO>    COMMAND
 4785 be/4 root        0.00 B/s    0.00 B/s  0.00 %  0.01 % [kworker/0:3]
    1 be/4 root        0.00 B/s    0.00 B/s  0.00 %  0.00 % systemd --switched-root --system --deserialize 24
    2 be/4 root        0.00 B/s    0.00 B/s  0.00 %  0.00 % [kthreadd]
    3 be/4 root        0.00 B/s    0.00 B/s  0.00 %  0.00 % [ksoftirqd/0]
    5 be/0 root        0.00 B/s    0.00 B/s  0.00 %  0.00 % [kworker/0:0H]
    6 be/4 root        0.00 B/s    0.00 B/s  0.00 %  0.00 % [kworker/u2:0]
    7 rt/4 root        0.00 B/s    0.00 B/s  0.00 %  0.00 % [migration/0]
    8 be/4 root        0.00 B/s    0.00 B/s  0.00 %  0.00 % [rcu_bh]
    9 be/4 root        0.00 B/s    0.00 B/s  0.00 %  0.00 % [rcuob/0]
   10 be/4 root        0.00 B/s    0.00 B/s  0.00 %  0.00 % [rcu_sched]
   11 be/4 root        0.00 B/s    0.00 B/s  0.00 %  0.00 % [rcuos/0]
   12 rt/4 root        0.00 B/s    0.00 B/s  0.00 %  0.00 % [watchdog/0]
   13 be/0 root        0.00 B/s    0.00 B/s  0.00 %  0.00 % [khelper]
   14 be/4 root        0.00 B/s    0.00 B/s  0.00 %  0.00 % [kdevtmpfs]
   15 be/0 root        0.00 B/s    0.00 B/s  0.00 %  0.00 % [netns]
   16 be/0 root        0.00 B/s    0.00 B/s  0.00 %  0.00 % [writeback]
   17 be/0 root        0.00 B/s    0.00 B/s  0.00 %  0.00 % [kintegrityd]
   18 be/0 root        0.00 B/s    0.00 B/s  0.00 %  0.00 % [bioset]
   19 be/0 root        0.00 B/s    0.00 B/s  0.00 %  0.00 % [kblockd]
   20 be/4 root        0.00 B/s    0.00 B/s  0.00 %  0.00 % [khubd]
   21 be/0 root        0.00 B/s    0.00 B/s  0.00 %  0.00 % [md]
   24 be/4 root        0.00 B/s    0.00 B/s  0.00 %  0.00 % [khungtaskd]
   25 be/4 root        0.00 B/s    0.00 B/s  0.00 %  0.00 % [kswapd0]
   26 be/5 root        0.00 B/s    0.00 B/s  0.00 %  0.00 % [ksmd]
   27 be/7 root        0.00 B/s    0.00 B/s  0.00 %  0.00 % [khugepaged]
   28 be/4 root        0.00 B/s    0.00 B/s  0.00 %  0.00 % [fsnotify_mark]
   29 be/0 root        0.00 B/s    0.00 B/s  0.00 %  0.00 % [crypto]
  542 be/4 root        0.00 B/s    0.00 B/s  0.00 %  0.00 % [xfsaild/sda1]
   38 be/0 root        0.00 B/s    0.00 B/s  0.00 %  0.00 % [kthrotld]
   40 be/0 root        0.00 B/s    0.00 B/s  0.00 %  0.00 % [kmpath_rdacd]
   41 be/0 root        0.00 B/s    0.00 B/s  0.00 %  0.00 % [kpsmoused]
```

Figure 12-4. *iotop is useful in analyzing IO related issues*

iptraf

iptraf is an IP LAN monitor that generates various network statistics including TCP info, UDP counts, ICMP, and OSPF information, Ethernet load info, node stats, IP checksum errors, and others. You can install it using `sudo yum install iptraf`. To execute it, use `sudo iptraf-ng`

tcpdump

Tcpdump prints out a description of the contents of packets on a network interface. It can be run with the -w flag, which causes it to save the packet data to a file for later analysis. The following command, for instance, would print all passing packets:

`sudo tcpdump`

WireShark

WireShark is one of the most famous network protocol analyzers and has a GUI that makes visualizing network traffic a lot easier. It can be downloaded from `https://www.wireshark.org/`

Nagios

Nagios is monitoring software that helps you monitor many servers together. It can also alert you when things go wrong. It is one of the most famous monitoring solutions available, is open sourced, and has a plethora of plug-ins available.

zabbix

Zabbix is an open source infrastructure monitoring solution. It can use most databases out there to store the monitoring statistics. The Core is written in C and has a front end in PHP. If you don't like installing an agent, Zabbix might be an option for you.

w

A seemingly simple, but important command is w. It joins the output of uptime, along with the information about everyone logged on to the server.

```
16:33:16 up  8:03,  1 user,  load average: 0.00, 0.01, 0.05
USER     TTY      FROM             LOGIN@   IDLE   JCPU   PCPU WHAT
user1    pts/0    10.0.2.2         08:44    4.00s  0.19s  0.00s w
```

lsof

Another built-in super powerful tool is lsof. It is an acronym for List Open Files and as the name suggests, it gives you a list of all open files and network connections. One of the main reasons for using this command is when a disk cannot be unmounted and displays the error that files are being used or opened.

With this command you can easily identify which files are in use. You can use grep or other similar filters to narrow your list to show only files opened by any process or user. You can then kill the process if needed.

Common Pitfalls to Avoid

New and old users alike can run into pitfalls. Nginx administrators have been often found making some of the following mistakes. Read the following section carefully to avoid common configuration issues and mistakes.

Chmod 777

Don't use 777, ever. It has been mentioned earlier in the book as well, but it is worth cautioning you again. If you ever feel like using it, most likely you are not aware of what's going on. Try to isolate, identify, and fix the problem instead of doing chmod 777. You can use the following command to check the directory hierarchy for missing permissions:

```
namei -om /path/of/directory
```

Having Root Inside Location Block

If you have a configuration file that looks like the following, think again. Syntactically, there is nothing wrong here. But, having a root directive in each location block will imply that if there is a location block without root directive, there will be no root path for that location.

```
server {
    server_name www.site.com;
    location / {
        root /var/www/nginx-default/;
        # [...]
    }
```

```
    location /foo {
        root /var/www/nginx-default/;
        # [...]
    }
    location /bar {
        root /var/www/nginx-default/;
        # [...]
    }
}
```

Instead, have a common root directive and override where necessary, like so:

```
server {
    server_name www.site.com;
    root /var/www/nginx-default/;
    location / {
            # [...]
        }
    location /foo {
            # [...]
    }
    location /bar {
            # [...]
    }
}
```

This caution also applies to index directive.

Using if Blocks

It is one of those blocks in Nginx that are more frequently misused than used. An if block creates a block similar to location block, and if the condition matches, the inner block is executed. This execution helps in assigning the configuration inside the if configuration for the designated request. In general, it is better to avoid an if directive. That said, there are a couple of things that are 100 percent safe inside the if directive.

- return ...;

- rewrite... last;

A couple of problematic configurations to drive the point home:

```
# only second header will be present in response
# not really bug, just how it works
location /only-one-if {
    set $true 1;
    if ($true) {
        add_header X-First 1;
    }
    if ($true) {
        add_header X-Second 2;
    }
    return 204;
}
```

Consider the following configuration. In this configuration if is evaluated every time there is a request to site.com or *.site.com. This is inefficient since the evaluation will happen for each and every request:

```
server {
    server_name site.com *.site.com;
        if ($host ~* ^www\.(.+)) {
            set $raw_domain $1;
            rewrite ^/(.*)$ $raw_domain/$1 permanent;
        }
        # [...]
    }
}
```

To avoid evaluation on every request, you can split the configuration into two like so and get the same result:

```
server {
    server_name www.site.com;
    return 301 $scheme://site.com$request_uri;
}
server {
    server_name site.com;
    # [...]
}
```

You should also avoid using if to check the existence of files or directories. try_files directive is a more suitable choice in these cases. The following is an example of if block that you should avoid:

```
server {
    root /var/www/site.com;
    location / {
        if (!-f $request_filename) {
            break;
        }
    }
}
```

Replace such blocks with:

```
server {
    root /var/www/site.com;
    location / {
        try_files $uri $uri/ /index.html;
    }
}
```

Passing Uncontrolled Requests to PHP

If you pass all your PHP requests directly to the FastCGI back end, you are at risk. This is because the default PHP configuration tries to guess which file you want executed in case the actual file doesn't exist. For example, a request to /path/to/url/malicious.jpg/file.php might lead to execution of embedded code inside a malicious.jpg file. A lot of sites allow uploading pictures, so it is easy to upload a picture and get your own code to run on the server using this vulnerability. A typical configuration that leads to this looks as follows:

```
location ~* \.php$ {
    fastcgi_pass backend;
    # more config ...;
}
```

The preceding code block allows all requests ending with PHP to be sent directly to the FastCGI back end. To avoid this pitfall, you can do the following:

- Set cgi.fix_pathinfo=0 in php.ini (this will tell PHP to avoid processing the files if not found)

- Pass only the application's PHP file to Nginx like the following:

```
location ~* (file_a|file_b|file_c)\.php$ {
    fastcgi_pass backend;
    # [...]
}
```

- Disable execution of any code from the upload directories:

```
location /uploaddirectory {
    location ~ \.php$ {return 403;}
    # [...]
}
```

- Use try_files directives:

```
location ~* \.php$ {
    try_files $uri =404;
    fastcgi_pass backend;
    # [...]
}
```

Rewrite Issues

You should avoid writing complex regular expressions. Try to keep them as neat and clean as possible. Also be aware that rewrites are relative by default, so it becomes important to rewrite using an absolute path. Add http:// wherever necessary and intended.

Using Hostname in Configuration

Never use a hostname in a `listen` directive since it might not be able to resolve during boot time. It is preferable to use IP addresses that need to be bound. This will help Nginx even more since it will not have to look up the address.

Frequently Asked Questions

This section will answer some of the frequently asked questions across popular websites. Instead of replicating the entire content, you will be pointed to those links for further reading. A small summary will be presented with links wherever appropriate.

"Is there an option to compare Nginx and Nginx Plus?"

To summarize: You use Open Source Nginx for any site or service that is yearning for the best web server. Nginx Plus, in comparison, offers support and extra functionality that is often required by organizations.

You can find a feature matrix available at `https://www.nginx.com/products/feature-matrix/`

"Is there a location for sample configurations?"

Yes. In fact, Nginx has a wiki that contains a plethora of samples that might assist you with various common configurations. These include configuration samples for WordPress, FastCGI, Caching, Log Rotation, and more. Read about it here:

`https://www.nginx.com/resources/wiki/start/`

Scroll a bit to the Pre-canned Configurations section and you will find a huge list of configurations to get you up to speed instantly. See Figure 12-5.

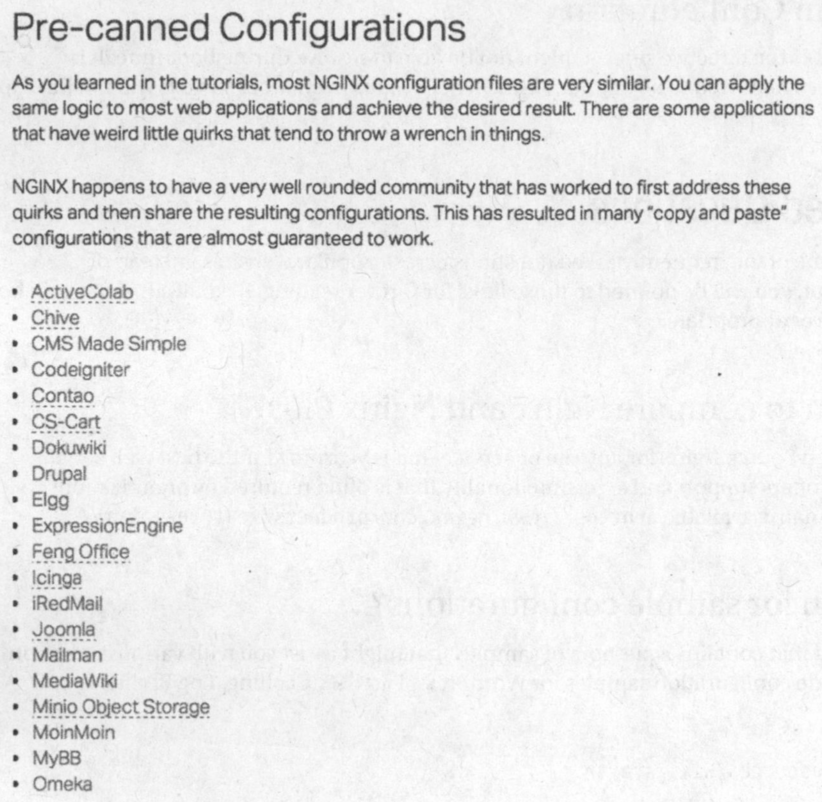

Pre-canned Configurations

As you learned in the tutorials, most NGINX configuration files are very similar. You can apply the same logic to most web applications and achieve the desired result. There are some applications that have weird little quirks that tend to throw a wrench in things.

NGINX happens to have a very well rounded community that has worked to first address these quirks and then share the resulting configurations. This has resulted in many "copy and paste" configurations that are almost guaranteed to work.

- ActiveColab
- Chive
- CMS Made Simple
- Codeigniter
- Contao
- CS-Cart
- Dokuwiki
- Drupal
- Elgg
- ExpressionEngine
- Feng Office
- Icinga
- iRedMail
- Joomla
- Mailman
- MediaWiki
- Minio Object Storage
- MoinMoin
- MyBB
- Omeka

Figure 12-5. A partial list of pre-canned configurations on Nginx website

"How can I redirect from www to no-www and vice versa?"

This is one of the most common requests and it is an important one. Your SEO depends on this and web administrators often like to stick with just one of the URLs. There is no right or wrong approach here, since a lot depends on various factors. There are famous examples like http://twitter.com where they don't use www prefix and others like http://www.facebook.com. To configure it, read the following discussion on StackOverflow:

http://stackoverflow.com/questions/7947030/nginx-no-www-to-www-and-www-to-no-www

"How can I write all http requests to https while maintaining a sub-domain?"

You can read more about this here:

http://serverfault.com/questions/67316/in-nginx-how-can-i-rewrite-all-http-requests-to-https-while-maintaining-sub-dom

"How can I find which flags Nginx was compiled with?"

This one is easy and has been discussed throughout the book. Simply execute nginx -V. There are other variations that will help you compare different configuration files:

```
http://serverfault.com/questions/223509/how-can-i-see-which-flags-nginx-was-compiled-with
```

"Is there any mechanism for detailed debugging?"

Yes. Nginx provides extensive debugging support. By default, it is turned off but it can be activated if you have compiled Nginx with --with-debug argument. Read more about detailed debugging at the following site:

```
https://www.nginx.com/resources/wiki/start/topics/tutorials/debugging/
```

"How many third-party modules does Nginx have?"

Plenty! There are a lot of third-party modules listed at the Nginx website, and new ones keep popping up. You can find the detailed list here:

```
https://www.nginx.com/resources/wiki/modules/
```

"What happens if I have Nginx Plus and the license expires?"

After your support contract expires, you are no longer licensed to use Nginx Plus or obtain support from Nginx, Inc. Access to Nginx Plus updates will be prohibited, and you must stop and delete your Nginx Plus instances. In short, you should contact them and renew in order to continue using Nginx Plus.

"Is there design or consulting help available?"

Yes. You can seek help in architecture, design or configuration using the Professional Services team at Nginx. Details can be found here:

```
https://www.nginx.com/services/
```

Summary

This chapter dealt with some troubleshooting scenarios and also a typical troubleshooting approach should you need help in case of desperate situations. You must keep adding various tools to your support toolbelt so that you can use them when the time is right. During pressure scenarios the thing that helps most is your knowledge about the infrastructure and how things are placed overall. The better you know your infrastructure, the better suited you will be to fix the issue. Keep baselining, learn new tools, engage with the community, and push the limits.

Happy learning!

Index

© Rahul Soni 2016
R. Soni, *Nginx*, DOI 10.1007/978-1-4842-1656-9

Get the eBook for only $5!

Why limit yourself?

Now you can take the weightless companion with you wherever you go and access your content on your PC, phone, tablet, or reader.

Since you've purchased this print book, we're happy to offer you the eBook in all 3 formats for just $5.

Convenient and fully searchable, the PDF version enables you to easily find and copy code—or perform examples by quickly toggling between instructions and applications. The MOBI format is ideal for your Kindle, while the ePUB can be utilized on a variety of mobile devices.

To learn more, go to www.apress.com/companion or contact support@apress.com.

Printed in the United States
By Bookmasters